"He who was seated on the throne said, behold, I am making everything new." revelation 21:5

as we start the new year together, I have such a sense of hope and possibility. I hope you do as well. I'm proud of you for wanting to spend time with Me, listening for what I have to tell you! this year will bring many challenges and opportunities. stay close to Me and I will find creative ways to let you know that I am there. it may be an innocuous remark someone makes, it may be an event that appears to be a coincidence, even though, as you know, there are no coincidences in life. you may have heard of the term "God-wink". I am the One who winks! I want your life to be full of fun surprises. I am the Exclamation Point of life!

I will also be there as your Comforter in hard times. you may feel alone sometimes, but feelings are not accurate reflections of truth. come sit with Me quietly. I will lead you and guide you into all Truth. then, speak that truth in your life today. faith works when you SPEAK out loud what you believe.

I don't want to be a Visitor in your life, nor an occasional Guest, even if you see Me as a Guest of Honor. I want to be your Friend. come and develop a Relationship with Me, where we love one another.

"there is so much more I want to tell you, but you can't bear it now. when the Spirit of Truth comes, He will guide you into all truth." john 16:12,13

"He prayed more fervently, and He was in such agony of spirit that His sweat fell to the ground like great drops of blood." luke 22:44

I know you start the new year out with strong intentions. that's good! that is why I want to bring this scene foremost to your awareness here today on this new day of the new year. Jesus, on the mount of olives in the garden of gethsemane, is giving us an example to follow. seek God the Father early each morning, especially when you are facing challenges or are under intense attack. your blessings manifest and multiply as you pray. talk with Jesus with the same focus and passion that He had when He poured out His heart for you! nothing else mattered in that moment.

then He sustained that one-pointed focus the entire day as He endured excruciating physical pain and deep mental anguish for you. it was a very personal act of sacrifice, so you would be forgiven, sanctified, and freed once and for all! there is no ambiguity here.

if you do anything out of sheer compassion, you will never be wrong. start your day and your year with thanks and gratitude.

"then Jesus shouted, Father, I entrust My Spirit into Your Hands! and with those words He breathed His last." luke 23:46

"My life is poured out like water, and all My bones are out of joint. My heart is like wax, melting within Me...they have pierced My hands and feet. I can count all My bones. My enemies stare at Me and gloat." psalm 22:14, 17

this is a Messianic psalm- a prophecy that was fulfilled to the very letter. I would like you to read the whole thing aloud to yourself right now. you can find psalms at the very center of the Bible. I placed them there at the center for many reasons, but one is that it makes it easier to find! just open to it now please- I will wait for you...

I love the partnership of psalms 22, 23, and 24. they are cohesive, each one complimenting the other.

after you have read all of psalm 22, preferably out loud, sit quietly and notice how you feel. it is the psalm of the Cross. aren't you grateful for Jesus' willingness to come at a time in history when He knew He would meet one of the most painful deaths possible- crucifixion? He wanted you to know that He was willing to give the utmost, everything He had, for you. the enormity of the full removal of all sin for eternity demanded a bold and powerful finality- that finality was at the Cross. feel it in the depths of your spirit.

"yes, it was the Lord's good will to crush Him and cause Him to suffer grief." isaiah 53:10

"when you believed in Christ, He identified you as His own by giving you the Holy Spirit, whom He promised long ago. the Spirit is God's guarantee (Seal) that He will give us the inheritance He promised." ephesians 1:13, 14

"He has commissioned us, and He has identified us as His own by placing the Holy Spirit in our hearts as the first installment that guarantees everything He has promised us." 2 corinthians 1:22

I am the Seal of the New Covenant! In these first few days of the new year, I am going to detail for you some of the aspects of My Name, for I want you to know Me.

God is a Covenant God and He always keeps His promises in the Covenant! as an envelope or package is sealed, so is your covenant with the Lord sealed by My Presence in you. your Relationship with Me, as part of the Triune Godhead, is just as important as your Relationship with God the Father and God the Son, Jesus. most of you don't take the time to get to know Me, or are afraid of Me. I want you to realize that you don't ever have to be afraid of Me or the way I operate. I am within you, leading you in the paths of righteousness and peace.

I am called the Comforter, the Advocate, the Teacher, and the Counselor, the One Who can soothe you when you are anxious or tired. come and be refreshed as you rest in My gentle Presence today.

"place me like a seal over your heart." song of solomon 8:6

"trust in the Lord with all your heart, and lean not on your own understanding. in all your ways acknowledge Him and He will direct your paths." proverbs 3:4, 5

each morning you cleanse your physical body in different ways. even so, each morning come to receive a fresh cleansing and infilling from Me! sit or recline in My Presence and I will come in like rushing Water to meet you there, smoothing all your rough and rocky places. think of how water makes you feel fresh and clean. you emerge from any body of water refreshed and rejuvenated.

water baptism is a large part of My spiritual renewing within you. I was there with john the baptist and I particularly showed the power of baptism when Jesus came to john for immersion. I descended as a Dove there by the jordan river and gave Jesus My complete validation to begin His ministry. along with water baptism often comes the Spirit baptism and the receiving of the gifts I disperse, although that can occur separately. I would actually like to baptize, renew, fill you each day, if you will only come to the River! I am the Water of Life!

"Jesus replied, I assure you, no one can enter the Kingdom of God without being born of water and the Spirit. humans can only give human life, but the Holy Spirit gives birth to spiritual life." john 3:5,6

"for the Scriptures declare, Rivers of Living Water will flow from his heart. when He said, Living Water, He was speaking of the Holy Spirit, Who would be given to everyone believing in Him. but the Spirit had not yet been given, because Jesus had not yet entered into His glory." john 7: 38, 39 "open up, heavens above, rain down righteousness." isaiah 5:8

this verse defines the meaning of "epic" that you use to describe worldly momentous times. I am continually raining down vast, epic-sized resources for you and for whosoever wants to avail themselves of them. there's nothing marginal about My power and Revelation! study your Word as if it were a map and you were lost in the desert. go BIG- and then come home!

are you a vessel for Me to fill? I am being poured out, even as the Lord was poured out! your sons and your daughters are prophesying, as foretold. do you see it? men of every age are having dreams and visions. this is the Latter Day Rain spoken of by joel- are you feeling it? can you look up and see the clouds heavy with the Rains that will bring so many blessings your heart will feel like it will explode with joy? step into the Puddles, dance in the Rain, I am here!

" for the rain He sends demonstrates His faithfulness. once more the autumn rains will come, as well as the rains of spring." joel 2:23

"suddenly, there was a sound from heaven like the roaring of a mighty windstorm, and it filled the house where they were sitting." acts 2:2

although wind can sometimes produce damage, more often it has a pruning or cleansing effect in nature. a soft wind brings relief from summer heat. I came as Wind to bring revival and power to the Body of Christ in the upper room. I am still fulfilling that same purpose today, even for mighty miracles. My intense power, "dunamis" in the greek, brings healing from physical illness, mental bondage, and spiritual strongholds. you are not meant to live in sickness or pain, nor mental bondage, where you continually return to unhealthy thoughts or actions. strongholds are a place you reside in for a longer period of time. you have access to power through Me to demolish and permanently destroy all these.

bring your need to Me right now. bring your burden for someone else. I am the Paraclete, the Helper. I will even give you the words if you don't know what to ask! I will also give you non-verbal sighs and sounds that will communicate effectively to Abba, Daddy, Father. come and talk with Me! let's sit together awhile right now, can we?

"the wind blows wherever it pleases. just as you can hear the wind but can't tell where it comes from or where it is going, so you can't explain how people are born of the Spirit." john 3:8

"and I will give you a new heart, and I will put a new spirit in you. I will take out your stony, stubborn heart and give you a tender responsive heart. and I will put My Spirit in you so that you will follow My decrees." ezekiel 36:26,27

" but I will send you the Advocate- the Spirit of Truth. He will come to you from the Father and will testify all about Me. and you must also testify about Me." john 15:26

on pentecost, I came as Fire, tongues of fire to be precise. I taught the people how to pray boldly and with confidence, and in other languages that they hadn't known. I gave them that authority and ability.

I am your Teacher and I will lead you and guide you into all Truth. My main purpose, though, is to point to Jesus. I inspired the Holy Bible's authors as they wrote and I will inspire you as you study the Scriptures. your heart will leap and burn as you read. don't read to find yourself- read the Bible to see Jesus fully revealed! read to experience My Presence deeper within your heart and mind.

since I am within you, My job and your job are the same, as it has been since that day in jerusalem! point people to Jesus! reflect His glory! shine brightly as a spotlight on Him- and even burn like fire!

"and when david prayed, the Lord answered him by sending fire from heaven to burn up the offering on the altar." 1chronicles 21:26

"He will baptize you with the Holy Spirit and with fire."luke 3:16

"the threshing floors will again be piled high with grain, and the presses will overflow with new wine and olive oil." joel 2:24

I am the Anointing Oil, with the heavenly scent of an expensive essential oil, that the Father Himself pours over your head. all you have to do is place yourself prostrate at His feet, in the Holy of Holies, and you will feel Me. think of all the time and effort you spend pursuing costly material things, some of them necessary but, if you are honest, most are just shiny distractions of this world.

come receive My oil of gladness, My Balm of gilead. remember as a child when you had a fever and your mother would put a cool cloth on your head? come, let Me place My Hand of healing upon you now. I am the Imprint of God's Hand, marked upon your forehead for all time. be made whole!

"how wonderful and pleasant it is when brothers dwell together in harmony. for harmony is as precious as the anointing oil that was poured over aaron's head, that ran down onto his beard, and onto the border of his robe." psalm 133: 1,2 "since you are eager to have spiritual gifts, try to excel in gifts that build up the church." 1 corinthians 14:12

I am the Excellent Disperser of gifts! as you cultivate your relationship with Me, I will enhance your gifts so that you stand out in an exceptional way. you are not average! the average person is self-absorbed, yet lacking in self-confidence. be honest, most people live average lives, whereas I want you to live a life of excellence! it takes tremendous courage to stand out and be different. come to Me for that which is unique. I am the Supplier of all kinds of gifts- faith, wisdom, prophecy, miracles, discernment, tongues, and limitless spiritual gifts. health, physical energy and strength, longevity of life, and peace in your mind and heart.

stay close to Me and I will liberally pour these gifts, and more, into you, so you can serve the Kingdom. we will talk more about gifts as you depend fully upon Me.

"it is the one and only Spirit who distributes all these gifts. He alone decides which gift each person should have." 1 corinthians 12:11

"so you should earnestly desire the most helpful gifts." 1 corinthians 12:31

"and God confirmed the message with the giving of signs and wonders and various miracles and gifts of the Holy Spirit whenever He chose." hebrews 2: 4

"but the fruit of the Spirit is love, joy, peace, patience, kindness, goodness, faithfulness, gentleness, and self-control and against such there is no law." galatians 5:22

a healthy tree produces much fruit- there is great abundance! when you are grafted into the Tree of Life and abiding in the Vine, fruits will effortlessly flow from your life. gifts are imparted, but fruits naturally emanate. you are empowered by the Living God, so this is not susceptible to your wavering emotions. He sent Me to live in you so that you would have the power to operate and live from a place of freedom and grace.

think of a tree in your yard or a plant on your porch. you water it, prune it, and place it near the sunlight. so, I am tending you- that these fruits, of which love is the highest, would be continually and generously flowing from your life. this process protects you and you are doing well with that- I see your generosity, your concern for others, your sensitivity- none of it escapes My Eyes!

"beware of false prophets who come disguised as harmless sheep yet really are vicious wolves. you can identify them by their fruit, that is, by the way they act...yes, just as you can identify a tree by its fruit, so you can identify people by their actions." matthew 7:16, 20

"the leaves of the trees were used as medicine for the healing of the nations." revelation 22:2

"greater is He that is in you, than he that is in the world."
1 john 4:4

I know it is hard to understand how I can be in you. how can you discern between My thoughts and your own thoughts? you will most often hear Me through Scripture, but as you spend time alone, as Jesus often did, you will start to hear and know My gentle whisper. I will not shout to drown out the many voices you are surrounded by. I will wait until I have your attention. ask Me specifically for this discernment gift.

as you focus on Jesus and His gentle Spirit, which is Me, My Voice will begin to become more recognizable. and then one beautiful day, it will become resonant within you. you will notice thoughts that seemingly come out of the blue. sometimes I will use circumstances and spontaneous events to speak, sometimes I speak through other people or even nature. I love spontaneity!

I want to alert you though, the enemy is also in the habit of trying to speak to you through people and events. he is devious. but once I indwell you, I will help to protect you by giving you wisdom about satan and his methods. I use "checks in your spirit", red flags you call them. listen and heed those carefully, My child!

"when the Spirit of truth comes, He will guide you into all truth. He will not speak on His own but will tell you all He has heard. He will tell you about the future." john 16:13
"then He breathed on them and said, receive the Holy Spirit." john 20:22

"by day the Lord went ahead of them in a pillar of cloud to guide them on their way, and by night in a pillar of fire to give them light." exodus 13:21

guidance from Me can come in varying ways. back then, the israelites needed concrete direction across the sinai desert. today My guidance and discipline are still an absolute necessity.

have you looked up at the sky lately? the large, puffy cumulus clouds make a grand display, especially when backlit by sunlight or pierced by My rainbow. look around you at nature. enjoy going to the beach, the mountains, the forests. listen to the bird call in the quiet of the morning. I was there when Father God, Elohim, spoke these into existence. I was hovering over the waters and this day I am still speaking through nature's stunning beauty. notice the clouds today! look up, especially at sunrise and sunset. make a divine appointment to be with Me as I paint the sky just for you! (maybe you can get out there even right now?) don't take a picture- just be with Me!

"and they will see the Son of Man coming on the clouds of heaven with power and great glory." matthew 24:30

"all this I have spoken while still with you. but the Counselor, the Holy Spirit, whom the Father will send in My Name, will teach you all things and will remind you of everything I have said to you." john 14:25,26

Jesus spoke these words in the upper room to the frightened disciples right before His crucifixion. then, He went on to say, "unless I go away, the Counselor will not come to you." I am the Spirit of Jesus Christ, not just a stand in for Jesus, because we are coequal members of the Godhead. therefore, you can totally and absolutely trust everything I speak to you. confirm what I speak to make sure it aligns with the Word, and then do as I say! I am your Great Counselor. a counselor is one who gives advice and guidance, leads you to make proper and healthy choices and decisions. ask Me for that Wisdom the same as you might ask any trusted friend to pray for you. Wisdom is the first and most important gift from Me in first corinthians chapter twelve.

I am your primary and main Source for guidance! as you rest in My Presence, the peace you feel about a decision will help you, the peace you feel will tell you that something is wisdom from Me. if there is no peace, don't go there.

"and I will ask the Father, and He will give you another Advocate, who will never leave you. He is the Holy Spirit, who leads into all truth. the world cannot receive Him, because it isn't looking for Him and doesn't recognize Him. but you know Him, because He lives with you now and later will be in you." john14:16.17

"in the same way, the Spirit helps us in our weakness. we do not know what we ought to pray for, but the Spirit Himself intercedes for us with groans that words cannot express." romans 8:26

I will intercede for you to the Father, according to His will, which is always for your highest good. I will intercede for those you love, as well. maybe today you are too upset, or sad, or afraid to even know <u>what</u> to pray for a situation or person. if that is the case, then just "sigh" in Me, especially when things pertain to illness or death; when you feel helpless and powerless. that's where I shine the brightest as your Comforter.

sometimes if you sit still and quiet enough, you may be able to feel My arms around you in a warm embrace. that's Me letting you know, I am there with you. it may not lessen the pain immediately, but it lets you know that you will never be alone as the pain ebbs. recognize your need for Me. receive My grace, I am here for you in the darkest night for I love you.

"but you, dear friends, must build each other up in your most holy faith, pray in the power of the Holy Spirit, and await the mercy of our Lord Jesus Christ, Who will bring you eternal life. in this way, you keep yourselves safe in God's love." jude 1:20,21 "the glory of the Lord shone around them." revelation 21:11

many people feel God is invisible. that is simply not true. I am the Shekinah Glory of God! now, that word is not in the Bible, but jewish rabbis coined the word from the hebrew "mishkan", meaning "He caused to dwell" or "tabernacle." the veil within the tabernacle separated the Holy of Holies from the outer courts.

sometimes My Presence seems veiled or shrouded, however, through Jesus and His victorious sacrifice, you may enter the Throne Room at any time! the veil has been removed, lifted. in fact, as the holy Bride of Christ, you have intimate standing with the Father and can see Him always. Abba Father says "you will be changed from glory to glory."

your mind in the natural will have a hard time understanding this. "now, you see in a mirror dimly, but then you will see face to Face." just as a mirror reflects an image, try your best to reflect God's actual love to others. you will never get it perfect, you will never fully understand this side of heaven, but you will shine with His glory and people will know there is something beautiful and different about you that they are attracted to!

"as the men watched, Jesus' appearance was transformed so that His face shone like the sun, and His clothes became white as light." matthew 17:2

"when the priests came out of the Holy Place, a thick cloud filled the Temple of the Lord." 1 kings 8:10

"this is how the birth of Jesus Christ came to be. His mother mary was pledged to be married to joseph, but before they came together, she was found to be with child through the Holy Spirit." matthew 1:18

this is too wonderful to try to explain in mere words- how the Incarnation occurred. you must just trust Me on this, just as you accept the miracle and wonder of how and when your own children are born. children are very very precious to Me. I am a Safe Haven for them and have taken many who have been mistreated into My bosom. I am there when children cry out. I give them continual hope and resilience in this dark and violent world. I cry also. I grieve for these events as I watch. I feel the emotions you feel very deeply, as I am embedded in your heart.

don't worry, as long as I am there on earth as the Restrainer, the evil one will never completely take over the world. My Permissive Will only allows so much. I grant only so much and no more. just as the Lord Jesus came through the wilderness temptation experience, trust that I am with you, will never leave you alone, and will carry you across the broad beach of this terrible time. your weakness is the fertile ground that brings complete dependence on Me. I will carry you through it all on wings like eagles, safely to the land of My Perfect Will.

"You made all the delicate, inner parts of my body and knit me together in my mother's womb. thank You for making me so wonderfully complex! Your workmanship is marvelous- and i know that full well. You watched me as i was being formed in utter seclusion, as i was woven together in the dark of the womb." psalm 139:13-15 (open your Bible now and read all of psalm 139 for deeper blessing and awareness of My love. it will take you one minute to read aloud, I timed it!)

"for though we live in the world, we don't wage war as the world does. the weapons we fight with are mighty for the tearing down of strongholds. we demolish arguments and every pretension (imagination) that sets itself up against the knowledge of God, taking every thought captive to make it obedient to Christ." 2 corinthians 10:4,5

stand in your authority and fight! I will give you that divine power. there's going to be many trials and tests in your lifetime. they aren't meant to tear you down, or I wouldn't allow them. they are meant to build you up in your faith. some of these trials are a result of your own choices, some are an attack from the adversary. be strong! I am with you!

let me validate- you ARE strong in Me! you are an overcomer! look how much you've already come through. you and I together can overcome anything. I'm right there in your corner. I'm the shade at your right hand. I gave you lots of protective equipment to wear- the helmet to cover your mind, the breastplate to cover your heart, the belt to hold it all together, the shoes of peace, the shield of faith. you don't have to run in fear from attacks. I am there, within you, united with the powerful Sword- the unerring Word of God. It will slice between bone and marrow, judiciously separating. pick it up now and fight!

"be strong in the Lord and in His mighty power. put on all of God's armor so that you will be able to stand firm against all the strategies of the devil. for we are not fighting against flesh and blood enemies, but against evil rulers and authorities of the unseen world, against mighty powers in the dark world, and against evil spirits in the heavenly realm. therefore, put on every piece of God's armor so that you will be able to resist." ephesians 6:10-13

" as Jesus was coming up out of the water, He saw heaven being torn open and the Spirit descending on Him like a dove." mark 1:10

what an awesome moment this was! all My plans were coming to fruition, beginning with Jesus' birth and then His baptism. it was such a pivotal moment in His life, as it will be, or was, in yours! I will be there at your baptism, imparting many gifts to you. I wanted to validate the beginning of Jesus' ministry, just as I want to validate and tangibly express My love to you. think of this baptism picture, the dove coming down, whenever you are in the vast body of the ocean, the great giant womb of God. think of your baptism whenever you immerse in any type of water. you will remember how I transformed you in that moment into a new creation! baptism is your free will choice to reach out to Me and in the process I anoint you with a holy joy that lasts forever. emotions are fickle, they come and go- but My joy is a deep well that never runs dry.

"make every effort to keep yourselves united in the Spirit, binding yourselves together with peace. for there is one Body and one Spirit, just as you have been called to one glorious hope for the future. there is one Lord, one faith, one baptism, and one God and Father, Who is over all and in all and living through all." ephesians 4:3-5

" not by might, not by power, but by My Spirit, says the Lord." zechariah 4:6

" for in Him we live, and move, and have our being." acts 17:28

this is the doorway that opens to My complete power- it is by God's grace and provision alone! if you had a natural father who was present in your life, he provided for you and loved you as best he knew how. if you didn't have the best father or didn't have a father present at all, I can still help you experience a dad's love. the hebrew word for Dad, or Daddy more accurately, is "Abba." I love when you call Me a special name, My child.

later on, I will reveal more through the story of the prodigal son- how Abba wants to run and throw His arms around you, a wide embracing love that welcomes you home. the Bible is faith pictures that can capture your attention. see yourself as that child coming home and Daddy God is running toward you, crying and celebrating you and telling you how totally awesome you are. you are My child, so very precious to Me! welcome home!

"then if My people who are called by My Name will humble themselves and pray and seek My Face and turn from their wicked ways, I will hear from heaven and will forgive their sins and restore their land. My eyes will be open and My ears attentive to every prayer made from this place." 2 chronicles 7:14,15

"all Scripture is God-breathed and is useful for teaching, rebuking, correcting, and training in righteousness, so that the man of God may be thoroughly equipped for every good work."
2 timothy 3:16

I have written you the greatest Love Letter you will ever receive! I was present as the forefathers and disciples were writing the sacred Scriptures and every single word is useful and meaningful, even the geneologies! open your Bible to any page and let Me speak exciting mysteries and promises to you. I will teach you how to understand, even if you find the Bible confusing or boring. I will bring it alive for you! the Bible will become "Rhema" or living Word to you. can you imagine and believe that it will become just as essential to you as air, water, and food? it will if you let Me show you how! take just a few minutes each day and when I say open any page, I mean that- I will confirm this by speaking to you through the verse or verses you turn to. it's fun!

the hebrew word for Spirit is "Ruach", which also denotes breath. "Ruach ha Kodesh" is Holy Spirit. I was there when you were formed in utero and breathed your spirit into you. I am living and sustaining you in each inhalation and exhalation you take. close your eyes right now and feel the spontaneous joy of paying attention to your breath as it enters and exits through your nostrils. then, notice your diaphragm moving up and down in your lower abdomen. relax and take a few of these longer breaths. feel how I am in each breath!

" He is the God who made the world and everything in it. since He is the Lord of heaven and earth, He doesn't live in man-made temples, and human hands can't serve His needs- for He has no needs." acts 17:24,25 "surely He took up our infirmities and carried our sorrows, yet we considered Him stricken by God, smitten by Him, and afflicted, but He was pierced for our transgressions, He was crushed for our iniquities; the punishment for our sins was upon Him and by His stripes we are healed." isaiah 53:4,5

Jesus and I work together when you are facing an illness or injury. He is the Great Intercessor, your eternal High Priest. He wears the priestly garment, the "tallit" in hebrew. I am the "tzitzit", the fringe or tassels, on His prayer shawl, His royal robe. remember the story of the woman who suffered with a hemorrhage for twelve years? she came up behind Jesus, most likely crawled, just to touch the hem, the blue tzitzit thread on Jesus' garment. and she was healed by her act of faith. in fact, Jesus turned to her and called her "daughter", the only recorded time He called someone by that name.

the blue dye "tekhelet" is also significant. if you are reading this outdoors, look up! what color is the sky? the sky is My blue dye- I created its beauty for you to enjoy and to help keep you healthy. go take a walk outside and talk with Me- tell Me everything that is going on in your life today!

"she touched the fringe of His robe for she thought, if i can just touch His robe, i will be healed. Jesus turned around and when He saw her He said, daughter, be encouraged! your faith has made you well. and the woman was healed at that moment." matthew 9:20-22 "open up ye gates and let the King of glory in!" psalm 24:7

once a gate or door is opened, you can enter. Jesus Himself holds the keys to every door and every place you want to go. I am the Key Itself! although possessing and holding the keys, Jesus gives you the choice, the free will, to move closer to Him through open doorways. I know your life is busy and you have many important things to do! just don't be too busy to come in through the open Gate, the unlocked Gate. there is a beautiful garden of a trusted Relationship beyond, a bright Oasis that will give an auspicious beginning to your day. there you will see and enjoy the glory of your Abba Father- He is waiting there in the Holy of Holies for you to arrive. know that at any moment you can be 100% aware of My Presence, noticing Me fully in the people, places, and events all around you- eyes open or closed, doesn't matter. anytime, anywhere, I am here! slow down, be still, and notice!

"God is our refuge and strength, a very present help in times of trouble. so we will not fear when earthquakes come and the mountains crumble into the sea. let the oceans roar and foam. let the mountains crumble as the waters surge! there is a River that flows through the city of our God, the sacred Home of the Most High (El Shaddai)." psalm 46:1-4

"be still and know that I am God! I will be honored by every nation. I will be honored throughout the world." psalm 46:10

"sing unto the Lord a new song, sing unto the Lord all the earth." psalm 96:1

I created music for you to enjoy, in fact your whole body is a wind instrument! and, just so you know, it doesn't really matter to Me if you have a technically beautiful voice or not. I love to hear you sing praises. even more, I love when worship pours out of your mouth. just start singing throughout the day, no matter where you are! will people look at you funny? you'd better believe it- but you know what? they will secretly be wishing that they had the freedom to be that joyous and free! I will make you so very joyful and happy (do you know the difference?) that when others look at you, they will become happy too!

matter of fact, just start humming or singing right now! if it's a classic hymn like "blessed assurance" that's great! if it's a more modern worship tune like "the Lion and the Lamb" that's wonderful also. worship is worship. I can also inhabit and use secular songs, turning their meaning into something beautiful and touching. think of the song "you light up my life" or "i want to know what love is." as you sing them, think of Me!

and then there is "singing in Me", called "singing in the Spirit." just hum and sing outside of the harmonies of the song in church worship, or on your cd or device. let your tongue be loose and don't censor yourself or try to control the experience from your head. I want you to enjoy like a little child who only knows the excitement of their parents' love and sings for the sheer joy of it! be a child again! sing and dance in My Presence.

"instead, be filled with the Holy Spirit, singing psalms and hymns and spiritual songs among yourselves, and making music to the Lord in your hearts." ephesians 5:19

"sing psalms and hymns and spiritual songs to God with thankful hearts." colossians 3:16

"to everyone who is victorious (overcomes), I will give to each one a white stone and on the stone will be engraved a new name." revelation 2:17

alright, you say, but You don't understand what I'm going through right now. ah, you forget, since I am within you, literally IN you, I can feel and sense what you feel. in essence, I am experiencing life with you. that's the miraculous thing, and the confusing thing about the baptism in Me. I am there all the time now!

in those days before, I only came upon people for a certain period of time, as I did gideon (judges 6:34) and david (1 samuel 16:13). today however, you are continually filled and refilled with My Presence and peace within you. that's why I came in the upper room, when the disciples felt the most alone and afraid. that's when I can come in the strongest for you also. "test Me and see!" when you feel alone, if you close your eyes and say My Name, I will come to you. I love you and I don't want you to ever feel alone.

this awareness is both liberating and somewhat challenging. you won't ever have to rely upon someone else to produce your happiness again! you will be free!

"after they prayed, the place where they were meeting shook. and they were all filled with the Holy Spirit and spoke the Word of God boldly." acts 4:31

"everything on earth will worship You; they will sing Your praises, shouting Your Name in glorious songs. selah." psalm 66:4

"selah" is found seventy one times in psalms and three times in the song of praise in habakkuk chapter 3. it is a musical term for an interlude and comes from the hebrew "salah", meaning to pause or to praise. most of the psalms were prayers set to music.

notice when you listen to a piece of music how the moments of silence enhance the composition. that is called a "rest". one great composer said that before he writes one note he always makes sure it is preferable to silence. selah is the rest in your life. you honor God when you trust completely in His will for your life. you honor Jesus when you rest at His feet, in utter surrender.

I am the Interlude! as you choose to shut off devices, I can whisper to you more clearly. I have a still, small Voice and I wont compete with the world for your attention. I am asking you to make silence a priority for a small portion of your day so that I can have your undivided attention.

"i have heard all about You, Lord. i am filled with awe by Your amazing works. in this time of our deep need, help us again as You did in years gone by. and in Your anger, remember mercy. i see God moving across the desert from edom, the Holy One coming from mount paran. selah." habakkuk 3:1-3 "they that wait upon the Lord will renew their strength; they will mount up with wings like eagles. they will run and not be weary, they will walk and not faint." isaiah 40:31

of the more than three thousand promises in the Bible, this is one of the most powerful. often a longer time of patience and acceptance is needed, just like the selah time. "but i want this resolved right now!" you cry to Me. yes, even so would I.

so…what can you do in that waiting period? praise will help pass the time. maybe you will even learn how to enter that timeless realm with Me or the joy of coming to Me daily. sometimes you will feel weary. I can give you a different perspective when you come quietly. we will "wind on down that road" together. that's a funny reference. I like to make you laugh and I have a good sense of humor, if you haven't noticed! I love surprises too! as you wait, I will bring fun into your life- lots of laughter and love to help you make it through graciously.

"we should live in this evil world with wisdom, righteousness, and devotion to God, while we wait for the blessed hope- the glorious appearing of our great God and Savior, Jesus Christ." titus 2:12,13

"Jesus spoke to the people once more and said, I am the Light of the world. if you follow Me, you won't have to walk in darkness, because you will have the Light that leads to life." john 8:12

a light shines. it obliterates dark places. you've seen how when you light even one small candle, it illuminates an entire room. Jesus' Face shone during the Transfiguration. moses' face shone after he had spoken with Father God. I am the Radiant Glory that is brighter than the sun! I am also the flicker of a Candle in a quiet room.

each Person of the Trinity is One and the Same, and yet each One relates and manifests uniquely to you. is the beach at noonday more beautiful than the waning light, the magic hour, at sunset? of course not, but it is experienced differently. I'm asking you to put in the effort to spend time with Me in worship of Jesus- holy, quiet moments where you may feel an urge to gently come to your knees, or even fall to your knees (don't hurt yourself!) maybe you can even lie fully prostrate, try it! Prostration and kneeling foster the humble spirit that is so important to Me.

I want all of your devotion, not just your mind. after you have been fully in My Presence, even for a brief time, undistracted, unrushed, you will visibly shine, your face, your smile, your eyes alive! shine on, My amazing child!

"i saw no temple in the city, for the Lord God Almighty and the Lamb are its Temple. and the city has no need of sun or moon, for the glory of God illuminates the city, and the Lamb is its Light." revelation 21:22

"i will see the goodness of the Lord in the land of the living. wait for the Lord. be strong and take heart, yes, wait patiently for the Lord." psalm 27:13,14

I can hear your questions already! "first, You say wait, but then You say take action. how do i know when to do what?" you see, that is where My ministry as Helper comes in. it is a daily, sometimes hourly, dependence on Me. then, too, I impart wisdom and discernment, as you need them, if you only ask Me to! the gifts and calling of God are irrefutable and they are always there at your disposal. read that again slowly.

I will tell you plainly, if you don't feel My peace about speaking something to someone or taking an action- and sometimes this happens really quickly, you have to be on your toes- then DON'T DO IT! just wait until I give you the go ahead. I will never lead you to do something that will contradict Scripture. hear My Voice to make the correct choice. a small event could change your entire life! choose rightly!

one more thing- discouragement is an emotion, but courage is a choice! choose joy! choose hope! choose to obey Me fully, as fully as you know how! I will give you rest in the Waiting Rooms of life.

"and now I will send the Holy Spirit, just as My Father promised. but stay here in the city until the Holy Spirit comes and fills you with power from heaven." luke 24:49

"now all of us can come to the Father through the same Holy Spirit because of what Christ has done for us." ephesians 2:18

you have <u>unlimited </u>access to the Throne Room through Me! meditate on that a moment! anytime, anyplace- you are free to come to Abba as His child, asking for whatever you need or just to be with Me! a wise prayer warrior will come and ask for My counsel and wisdom as to outcomes before going to a doctor or a human counselor, before you take medication or self-medicate. put the MBO acronym next to your prayer, asking for the "Most Benevolent Outcome"- meaning that which is most kind and that which will promote the benefit of others, as opposed to the "most beneficial outcome", which means receiving for your own benefit.

Jesus exhibited this as He went through the lashing and crucifixion which ultimately paved the way for your forgiveness and eternal life. in the garden, He cried out, with great drops of Blood from His brow, "Thy Will be done." I have a much much higher perspective. I am asking you to trust My Will and My Timing for your life as you bring your requests to the Throne. have tremendous courage and faith! I believe in you!

"for you have come to Mount Zion, to the city of the Living God, the heavenly Jerusalem, and to the countless thousands of angels in a joyful gathering. you have come to the assembly of God's firstborn children, whose names are written in heaven. you have come to God Himself, who is judge over all things. you have come to the spirits of the righteous ones in heaven who have now been made perfect. you have come to Jesus, the One who mediates the New Covenant between God and people, and to the sprinkled Blood, which speaks of forgiveness instead of crying out for revenge like the blood of abel." hebrews 12:22-25 "i am the Beloved's and He is mine." song of solomon 7:10

if you really understand how much I love you, it will transform your entire life! say it out loud right now wherever you are sitting, and I hope someone is near you that will hear you say this. say " i am the Beloved!" you broadcast to the world when you fall in love with someone or have something exciting happen in your life. this realization has <u>much</u> more meaning!!

my God supplies <u>ALL</u> my needs- say it! take the thought public! emotions will follow suit with your thoughts and words. speak My thoughts and truths and they will swallow up the negative thoughts. enlarge the area of your tent! this is faith in action! faith has an audacity to it! faith is everything to Me!

the enemy will try to tell you, "how can you be healed when you're still hurting?" respond with the Word, just as Jesus did. "my God calls things that are not as though they were." romans 4:17 (it's good to know the "address" of the verse, it gives authority). proverbs 4:23 says, "above all else, guard your heart" and one way to guard your heart is to quote a verse!

enlarge your vision and see things from the perspective of being the beloved. turn up the corners of your lips right now (that's a smile!) and have confidence in My love for you. I will never let you down!

"God showed us how much He loved us by sending His One and Only Son into the world so that we might have eternal life through Him. this is real love- not that we loved God, but that He loved us and sent His Son as a sacrifice to take away our sins."
1 john 4:9,10
"and God has given us His Spirit as proof that we live in Him and He in us." 1 john 4:13

"for all who have entered into God's rest have rested from their labors, just as God did after creating the world. so let us do our best to enter that rest." hebrews 4:10,11

the main fight you have is to remain in faith, in resting faith. let me remind you- the enemy, satan, seeks to wear out the saints. he wants to frighten and depress you. he wants your emotions to toss about like waves, carrying dirty seaweed in the sea.

365 times in the Bible I exhort you not to be afraid! it's a very dangerous place to allow yourself to get to. recognize the signs of fear <u>before</u> they get overwhelming, before you lose control of your mouth, your emotions, before you get feeling sorry for yourself. emotions are sometimes My stop sign to halt you! step away by yourself immediately and get your mind and eyes fixed back on Me. this will save you much grief.

this is the holy rest. it is the greatest honor you can give Me- trusting Me, as a child trusts, to protect you. flow with My grace- for true transformation exhibits an effortlessness. rest, knowing that you are loved!

"for He raised us from the dead along with Christ and seated us with Him in the heavenly realms because we are united with Christ Jesus, in order that in the coming ages He might show the incomparable riches of His grace, expressed in His kindness to us in Jesus. God saved you by His grace, through faith- and this not of yourselves, it is the gift of God- not by works, lest anyone should boast. for we are God's workmanship, created in Christ Jesus to do good works, which God prepared in advance for us to do." ephesians 2:6-10 "oh, that You would bless me indeed and enlarge my territory (expand my tent). keep Your Hand upon me, that i may not do evil. and the Lord granted his request." 1 chronicles 4:10

this is the prayer of a great man- jabez. I wish I had given him more recognition, but he understands!

I am the expanding Tentposts! I am always on the move, helping your circle of influence to increase like the widening ripples across a lake when a stone is thrown. just as I guided the israelites when to move their encampment, just as I answered jabez' prayer and gave him favor, and just as I shut the mouths of lions for daniel, so I am relevant for this time and will do the same today and forever.

I am in the business of increase- increased love, increased blessing, increased peace. I will never give up on you, or anyone you love for that matter. legacies are a big deal to Me. your children and grandchildren will all benefit from the seeds of faith and prayer you have sown in their lives. what a strong role model you are for the next generation! one day in heaven, your prayers and testimonies will be repeated and celebrated by many who chose salvation in Jesus Christ because of your faithful witness. that is My gift to you!

"enlarge the place of your tent, stretch your tent curtains wide, do not hold back; lengthen your cords, strengthen your stakes. for you will spread out to the right and to the left." isaiah 54:2,3 "then if My people who are called by My Name will humble themselves and pray and seek My face and turn from their wicked ways, I will hear from heaven and will forgive their sins and will heal their land." 2 chronicles 7:14

in these end times, signs have increased in scope and accelerated in speed and numerity. but don't worry or be afraid. all these things were predicted and must come to pass. chapters 24 and 25 that matthew wrote are definitive texts about the future and can give you hope in the midst. if you have time, read them now as these chapters give much awareness and urgency.

have you ever noticed that Jesus loved to be "in the midst" of things happening? so, too, you are "in the world but not of it." in fact, you can sense that the world is full of all sorts of foolishness and self-centeredness. in contrast, learn how and be willing to put your natural body, the earthen vessel, in a receptive state. you can choose what kind of tent you want to reside in- discontent or content. as you dwell in the tent of humility and gratitude, you will find peace. say thank you often, not just to Me, but to others who do things to bless you everyday. thank your spouse. thank your parents if you're blessed to still have them in your life. thank your coworkers for their diligent work. thank your children and grandchildren!

I thank you for taking the time today to listen to Me and to be interested in seeking My Face. I will heal your land!

"pray for each other so that you may be healed, for the prayer of a righteous man is powerful and effective." james 5:16

"fan into flames the gift that is in you through the laying on of hands. for God has not given us a spirit of fear, but of power, love, and a sound mind." 2 timothy 1:6,7

I am given as a gift when you, the Spirit-filled believer, lay hands on others. you can impart Me to them, if they are willing to receive. don't lay hands on someone lightly or in a rush, but discerning who needs that touch, that encouragement. in this way, through human touch, I impart the salvation, the healings, the miracles that people need. I do have other ways of working, but it is so thrilling to Me when you actually understand and enjoy flowing in participation with Me! don't be embarrassed! I am giving you the words you need. I will embody all the strength and beauty you feel you don't possess(although you actually do!)

touch someone today. ask them if they need prayer for anything and then ask them to pray for you as well. it will be a humble moment that will bring you a sense of connection and love with them. be patient with yourself! at first this will feel awkward, but the more you pray with others, the more natural and rewarding it will feel to you. look for opportunities and start today! this is a powerful mandate.

" then peter and john placed their hands on them, and they received the Holy Spirit. when simon saw that the Spirit was given with the laying on of hands, he offered them money… peter answered, may your money perish with you, because you thought you could buy the gift of God with money!" acts 8:17,18 "but He said to me, My grace is sufficient for you, for My power is made perfect in weakness. therefore, i will boast all the more gladly about my weaknesses so that Christ's power may rest on me. that is why i delight in weaknesses, in hardships, in persecutions, in difficulties. for when i am weak, then i am strong." 2 corinthians 12:9,10

so, right in the thick of it- that's where I am. I am also in every small detail. I know life seems like it is overwhelming- it was all so easy when you were young and innocent, just starting out in life. you hadn't yet been jaded by people and circumstances, some beyond your control or awareness.

it's alright- I know you are doing the best you can. don't feel guilty. that is the enemy's ploy to drag you down further. I am sufficient for all those little first-world problems. you have so much to be grateful for! lift up a sacrifice of praise to Me today. the birds are singing, the clouds are shining, the very rocks themselves are crying out to Me. notice the beautiful and excellent things in the world. I made them for you and then I wrote you the greatest Love Letter ever written, the Bible, to encourage you.

"for i resolved to know nothing except (to concentrate only on) Jesus Christ and Him crucified. i came to you in weakness and fear, with much trembling. my message and my preaching were not with wise and persuasive words, but with a demonstration of the Spirit's power, so that your faith might not rest on human wisdom, but on God's power." 1 corinthians 2:2-5 "they said to each other, were not our hearts burning within us while He talked with us on the road and opened the Scriptures to us?" luke 24:32

luke here is detailing the experience of his friend, cleopas and another disciple, as they walked the road to emmaus. they were walking the seven miles from jerusalem when Jesus appeared to them. at first I kept their eyes from recognizing Him, but eventually, through His revealing of Himself in the Word, in the breaking of the bread and in His giving of thanks, symbolic of communion, He was revealed to them. so too, in your life, sometimes Jesus seems hidden or far away. your body grows tired or your mind becomes anxious and frustrated.

if you have enough to eat and a comfortable home, be grateful! you are blessed! if you are struggling, realistically I know it is more challenging to pay attention to My Presence, or to even want to- try anyway! in the middle of the hunger or addiction or hopelessness, try to call out to Me, right in that moment of pain. I feel that pain and loneliness, as I am in you. I understand even your anger and I'm not upset when you express it, unless you blaspheme. death and disease are horrible. in those times, focus intently on the day when I will remove all the pain. there will be no more depression or heavy grief. I'm so sorry for your suffering, My child.

"He will wipe every tear from their eyes, and there will be no more death or sorrow or crying or pain. all these things are gone forever." revelation 21:4 (take this moment to read all of revelation chapter 21. it will give you the hope you need).

"write down the revelation and make it plain on tablets, so that a runner can carry the correct message to others. this vision is for a future time and it will be fulfilled." habakkuk 2:2

I want you to start a prayer and gratitude journal, if you don't have one already. you make your things-to-do lists and write down all your worldly plans and needs, your grocery lists even. how much more important are My eternal plans for you! write down what you hear from Me. write down your challenges and feelings also. I want to hear about your concerns, not judge you for them. I am here to help you, if you will only ask Me!

also, I'd love to share in the fun things in your life that you are grateful for. did you see something spectacular today? did someone bless or encourage you? write these down! if you feel like you don't have time, I will expand the time for you so that you will feel the increase of eternity. you have all the time you need- you have it all!

write down what you are thankful for, write down what you need Me for. I will respond to you, I will answer you!

"clearly, you are a letter from Christ showing the result of our ministry among you...He has enabled us to be ministers of His New Covenant. this is a Covenant not of written laws, but of the Spirit." 2 corinthians 3:3,6 "the Lord is in His holy Temple; let all the earth be silent before Him." habakkuk 2:20

this whole world is upside down and I know it confuses you sometimes. I am asking you to trust Me in these times. trust that, like a loving parent, I will respond to you. I am a very responsive God! as you come to Me with your undivided attention, I will give My undivided attention to you! how is that possible when there are over seven billion people on earth right now? well, your mind can't fully understand My Omniscience, My perfect ways, My timing and plans for each individual life.

that's one reason why I give you children, so you will feel a semblance of the depth of love I have for you personally. I was there when the egg was fertilized, the detectable heartbeat at six weeks. I heard your particular heartbeat even before that time. remember all that I have done for you.

in this topsy-turvy world, I am the Constant in your life. I love you, My little child.

"for I know the plans I have for you, says the Lord, plans to prosper you and not to harm you, plans to give you a future and a hope." jeremiah 29:11 (read all of psalm 139, especially if you have children, but even if not. it will bless you greatly.)

"and surely, I am with you always, even to the end of the age." matthew 28:20

I search all things and compare the spiritual with the spiritual, not the natural- as "deep calls to deep." when you become adept at swimming, you naturally head out to deeper waters. I want you to want a closer relationship with Me- that's why I was put _in_ you. can you see and understand that part of the Plan? you're meant to notice the cardinal at the window, the care I take returning lost things to you so you don't feel bereft, the spontaneous word that was just what you needed at the moment, the nourishing meal, the wedding song, the full moon, the Scripture verse in due season. I am with you in all these ways and more- any detail you can imagine- I planned it! I am your comfortable, safe, relaxing place- I am Home!!

but I want to make one thing crystal to you- I don't want to do this alone. I need you and your unique gifts and talents and personality. I need your sense of humor, your ferocity and boldness, your perseverance, your completely open and honest heart. are you in?!

"God has revealed it to us by the Spirit. the Spirit searches all things, even the deep things of God. for who among men knows the thoughts of a man except the man's spirit within him? in the same way no one knows the thoughts of God except the Spirit of God." 1 corinthians 2:10-12 "it was the Lord's Day and I was worshiping in the Spirit." revelation 1:10

usually when you hear the word 'worship' you probably think of singing, kneeling or lifting hands- which it is all that! however, worship can entail many things- serving, silence, walks, reading, conversations, the act of forgiveness, the generosity of tithing or the altruism of philanthropy.

I am the genesis of all these things as you and I partner together. notice in revelation 22, where Jesus says, "the Spirit and the bride say, come." when you come together with one or more other people, I fully arrive. it doesn't matter if it is one other person or a crowd, I show up to participate! hear Me on this! don't judge success with any kind of numbers. whenever you are engaging in worship, active participation in glorifying God, then you are a successful, wonderfully alive, complete, Jesus-focused being!

come on- let's dance together as if no one is looking! I want to show you how to go deeper in worship. put on some music, close your eyes, hum, whistle, clap, move freely! I inhabit the real and authentic praises of My people!

"God is Spirit, and His worshipers must worship Him in Spirit and in truth. the woman replied, i know that Messiah is coming. when He comes, He will explain everything to us. then Jesus declared, I Who speak to you am He." john 4:24-26

"I speak to him in dreams." number 12:6

throughout the Bible I spoke to people through dreams and visions, notably joseph, isaiah, daniel, solomon, and joseph, earthly father of Jesus, to name just a few. everything that is good and perfect, nurturing and excellent, in your life comes from Me! so, no I don't use nightmares to correct or rebuke you. I personally inspired the Word of God, which is the primary means to correct and guide you with great detail in all things. I will never give favor to something that doesn't align with the Word.

dreams are a useful way I can comfort and prepare you. psalm 127 says Father God "gives His beloved sleep." precious sleep- where the body is rejuvenated and the mind can heal and relax. if you awaken at night, simply whisper My Name, repeat a psalm you have memorized in part or full, or lie there and just abide in the Vine, of which I am the Lifeblood. that Blood has a voice and in the fourth watch of the night, just when it seems darkest, I will speak to you in a lucid way!

"all Scripture is God-breathed and is useful for teaching, rebuking, correcting, and training in righteousness, so that the man of God may be thoroughly equipped for every good work."
2 timothy 3:16,17

"all of these gifts must be done for the strengthening of the church." 1 corinthians 14:26

let's get into the spiritual gifts I give you, because they are very important to the health and efficacy of the Body of Christ, central to its influence. Jesus Christ is the Head of the church and you each are all separate parts of His Body, all equal to one another. you are called to build the Church of Christ and let Me tell you this plainly, the gifts are given to edify, to strengthen, to build up the Body and to spearhead its mission to the world- which is: to tell everyone in a non-judgemental and joyous way about the free gift of eternal salvation through Jesus' death and Resurrection, that He is the Source of all grace!

there are many spiritual gifts and you should flow freely in many or all of them! if you've spent any time in the Word with Me, you know how important Wisdom is. this is the first gift of the Spirit mentioned in 1 corinthians chapter twelve. it leads you to eagerly desire spiritual maturity. then, when I bring someone to ask for prayer or advice, you are ready, in season and out, to speak according to My leading. sometimes I may even have a Word of Knowledge for that person, which really requires that you listen carefully, speak sensitively, and only what I tell you. desire these higher gifts so that you can help many people in their time of need. edify someone and in the process you will be encouraged as well! this is how the Body, the Kingdom, and originally the world were meant to flow.

"He has made everything beautiful in its time. He has also set eternity in the hearts of men; yet they cannot fathom what God has done from beginning to end." ecclesiastes 3:11 (if you want to go deeper with the gifts, read 1 corinthians chapter 12 entirely. if you have time, do it now).

"let love be your highest goal! but you should also desire the spiritual abilities the Spirit gives- especially the ability to prophesy." 1 corinthians 14:1

I give My gift of prophecy so that you can encourage others and give them fresh Wind in their sails. I gave you your natural family to be in relationship with, so please stay close with them, with boundaries if necessary. prophesy good things to them!

prophecy should be used to edify the Body. your prophetic gift can and should uplift your spiritual family, brothers and sisters in Christ. it's a new day for the Body of Christ! in the Spirit of prophecy I tell you that the Body of Christ is arising in revival and will prevail against any and all evil! prophecy is a manifestation gift and is extremely important to the Church's health!

the earth is coming to a time of great turmoil, in fact, it is already there. people attack each other and the earth itself is groaning. yet, as you operate in the gift of prophecy, you will help people to focus on what I am doing in their lives and how I am working for them because I love them. they won't be able to deny that you are speaking from Me as I will give you the boldness and the correct divine words.

dispense hope, in the Name of Jesus. love outrageously and abundantly, as I do!

repossess and take authority over what is yours for good always overcomes evil. love has won through Jesus Christ!

"for prophecy never had its origin in the will of man, but men spoke from God as they were carried along by the Holy Spirit."
2 peter 1:21

"God loved the world so much that He gave His only Son, that whosoever believes in Him will not perish, but have eternal life." john 3:16

Jesus is the best Gift there is for you! eternal Life is the party Abba Father is having for you and I am God's divine Invitation! this was an exquisite offer of forgiveness that is unparalleled in history. you have heard of Jesus Christ- He is historically and scientifically validated to have been born, lived in nazareth, was crucified on a roman cross, and rose from the dead. "I and the Father are One," He says. looking at His life, He was either a madman or His claims are true.

through Jesus, God provides righteousness as a gift, a complete, compassionate, and finished Work. you don't have to do anything but say yes! I plead with you- He is the Bridge you have been looking for! say yes in this holy moment!

I want to bless you with all the blessings of abraham, isaac, and jacob. this Love is the highest spiritual gift, the mystery of the ages- agapeo in latin, ahava in hebrew- unconditional love- the love I Am.

filios is brotherly love- yet, even at that level I can and will still use you powerfully. feed My lambs!

"today is the day of salvation." 2 corinthians 6:2

"we walk (we live) by faith, not by sight."2 corinthians 5:7

the next spiritual gift, great faith, is faith that is a measure above and beyond salvation faith. this faith is essential to life! without it you will readily succumb to the constant barrage of the enemy and his cohorts. this gift enhances the other gifts, allowing you to operate in them with an authority that is far beyond just self-confidence or intelligence or charisma in the natural, fleshly realm. in fact, it is Jesus' gift to your spirit man from Me! faith is a power gift and is used for ministry in many ways. desire and ask for greater anointed faith daily!

for those who feel a Calling to step into one or many of the offices of the Fivefold Ministry- Apostle, Prophet, Evangelist, Pastor, and Teacher- extraordinary faith and diligence is required. these people are the forerunners who equip God's people to do His work here on earth.

yet, even those who aren't called to these areas of ministry should ask for the gift of increased faith. faith brings forth miracles, which spur salvation as people see the Hand of God moving in their lives. right this moment, ask out loud for more faith (did you do it?!) your Heavenly Father will not deny that child-like request- He is overjoyed, smiling at your sincere heart. now, watch how He will use you in a greater way today!

"it was He who gave some to be Apostles, some Prophets, some Evangelists, and some to be Pastors and Teachers, to prepare God's people for works of service, so that the Body of Christ may be built up until we all reach unity in the faith and knowledge of the Son of God and become mature, attaining to the whole measure of the fullness of Christ." ephesians 4:11-13 (hebrews chapter 11 is the "hall of faith." read it and let it inspire you today).

"then He sent them out to tell everyone about the Kingdom of God and to heal the sick." luke 9:2

if there is anything that will immediately get someone's attention, it is a physical healing. this was a huge part of Jesus' earthly ministry. yet, amazingly, even strong believers sometimes doubt that healings can spontaneously occur. I am the Guarantee of the miracles! step out in faith and boldly pray for someone. your faith and their faith will ignite into a miracle! if it doesn't happen immediately, please don't get cynical. just continue asking and praying with faith for correct timing.

I love to confirm myself- have you noticed? think back and perhaps you have already experienced a healing of this sort, or maybe it was a progressive healing that no doctor predicted. surely you have heard such testimonies or experienced God's mercy and grace, His lovingkindness, "hesed" in hebrew. healings are a power gift and should be evident in any Church, as many come for healing and prayer. it is an extremely important and touching gift that can pique someone's interest enough that their heart will be softened and opened to hear about Jesus. don't let this gift, or any gift I give, atrophy. if you don't use the gifts, I may remove them…step out boldly in faith- ask Me- I'm ready to respond!

"but for you who fear My Name, the Son of Righteousness will rise with healing in His wings. and you will go free, leaping with joy like calves let out to pasture." malachi 4:2

"but He was pierced for our transgressions, He was crushed for our iniquities; the punishment that brought us peace was upon Him, and by His wounds we are healed." isaiah 53:5 (trust Me, we will be coming back to this verse later!)

"You are the God Who performs miracles." psalm 77:14
"I have shown you many great miracles." john 10:32

let's go to a whole other level- let's go skydiving and kite sailing in the spiritual! agree with Me- miracles still occur, hundreds on a daily basis, but also extraordinary, supernatural miracles! your birth, at this time, this place in history, is a miracle. the very breath in your body is a miracle. do you believe a cancer can spontaneously or progressively disappear? do you believe in miraculous financial provision and favor? do you have faith that a resurrection could still occur today? what are the parameters of miracles, the limitations in your mind?

I am the hopeful Yea and Amen to all these questions and more. I am the Answer beyond the questions! I am the One who can and will show you that all things are possible in the Kingdom of Heaven right NOW- if you will only take My Hand and trust Me. if you or someone you love needs a miracle, ask and continue to ask Me.

miracles occur as you pray individually in the prayer language of tongues. your body is a Sanctuary, My Temple, where I reside while you are here on earth, and your tongue is an access point to the Holy of Holies. God's Presence is in your body. supernatural miracles occur as you pray personally and privately in tongues for protection, healing, or any need that you may not even know of.

"for Jesus Christ, the Son of God, does not waver between yes and no. He is the One whom silas, timothy, and i preached to you, and as God's ultimate "YES", He always does what He says. for all of God's promises have been fulfilled in Christ with a resounding Yea and Amen through Him." 2 corinthians 1:19, 20 "then choose this day whom you will serve, but as for me and my house, we will serve the Lord." joshua 24:15

in the fleshly realm, on this earth, you operate from the position of free will. I was part of the creative decision to extend that gift to you. the challenge to free will is that oftentimes as you are deciding which choices to make, outside forces, peer pressure, and subtle deceptive thoughts from the enemy try to influence you, and sometimes <u>do</u> influence you. your own flesh tries to have the upper hand and say so.

that is where discernment comes in. it puts up huge red flags that stop you from making a mistake- listen to these red flags! stop whatever you are doing and listen! discernment is a motivational, Wisdom gift and helps you with everyday situations, the little imperfect details in life. they can either drive you crazy, or you can enjoy the perfection in the imperfections. that's how I see you, My perfectly imperfect child!

as your Advocate, I will help you make the correct decisions and lead you to connect with the right people. I will give you favor to help you implement your dreams. ask Me for discernment daily so you won't be floundering around blindly. keep your mind clear- you don't want to numb your mind with drugs or alcohol, which are the devil's tools. stay vigilant and awake!

I'm your biggest cheerleader, your most ardent Friend! you've got this!

"then I will arrange to take you to another land like this one- a land of grain and new wine, bread and vineyards, olive groves and honey. choose life and not death!" 2 kings 18:32

"o jerusalem, jerusalem, how I longed to cover you with My feathers as a mother hen covers her chicks, but you were not willing." matthew 23:37

"and you will be My witnesses, telling people about Me- in jerusalem, throughout judea, in samaria, and to the the ends of the earth." acts 1:8

there's a lot going on at this time in history and I know you may be concerned and wondering what will come. three hundred and sixty five times I announce in the Bible "don't be afraid!" and even still today I say the same thing to you! don't be afraid! FEAR NOT! live with overwhelming faith in My plans for the earth, "for the plans I have for you are for good and not for evil, to prosper you and not to harm you, to give you a future and a hope." I'm repeating jeremiah 29:11- I hope you have that verse memorized!

jerusalem is My eternal City of Peace. it is the center of israel, the shining city on a hill. as you enter into her gates, you will see and know My glory. every prayer on every little piece of paper you folded up to put in My Western Wall, I will honor. mark the date down in your Bible or prayer journal- all that I have said, I <u>will</u> do. I will surely accomplish the Lord's will.

"but as He came closer to jerusalem and saw the city ahead, He began to cry." luke 19:41

"for what I want to do, I do not do." romans 7:17

in the ten verses here in romans chapter 7:14-22, the apostle paul writes "i" twenty eight times! i, i, i. me, me, me- as I look down upon earth, you are all so self-occupied and self-identified. because I created you, I know that this is the essential human condition, as survival is your number one biological priority. I understand why you are as you are.

I'm just reverentially exhorting you to turn your focus upon Jesus. as you do, He will become your priority! like a habit, it may not happen all at once, or it may! but each day I will transform your thoughts as you keep looking at Jesus and listening for Me. see more of Him and your topics of conversation will change- Scripture will naturally permeate your daily speech, things of earth will "grow strangely dim", as that worship song says.

speak about His miracles, His grace, His offices and Titles, His blessings to you as you walk your emmaus road, where He opens up Himself- and then run the seven miles back to jerusalem to tell everyone about Him! you're not living for yourself any longer- Christ Jesus is living in and through you!

"i live, but not i, for Christ lives in me." galatians 2:20
"since we live by the Spirit, let us keep in step with the Spirit." galatians 5:25

"the Spirit of the Lord is upon me, because He has anointed me to preach the gospel to the poor. He has sent me to heal the brokenhearted, to proclaim freedom to the captives and release from darkness the prisoners, to proclaim the acceptable year of the Lord's favor." isaiah 61:1

I asked you if you were all in with Me- because I am all in with you! I am in you, before you, and behind you, surrounding you completely with My grace and protection. I am the Lighthouse up ahead and the shade at your right hand. I gave everything I had for you.

how cool is it that in this Scripture from isaiah, you get to proclaim about yourself the exact same thing that Jesus proclaimed about Himself in the temple that day! and then you get to walk that talk each day!

I want to reduce you to love! today there are more hopeless people than ever before- teens being bullied and rejected, tempted by satan to take guns and act out, men and women addicted to opioids and relapsing over and over again until they overdose chasing the next high and die, rampant divorce, the very fabric of families being torn apart. I know you can't help the whole world- just help one person today. listen to their stories, empathize, pray with them. be My Hands and Feet today, will you?! speak My words. tomorrow details the manifestation gift of tongues and interpretation. I want to pray through you! pray in the Spirit, warrior!

"He must become greater, i must become less." john 3:30

"every knee shall bow and every tongue confess that Jesus Christ is Lord." isaiah 45:23 and phillipians 2:11

when I indwelt man in the upper room at pentecost, My manifestation came as the sound of rushing wind and as tongues of fire. the people began speaking in other languages, declaring the wonders and glory of God, and three thousand people were baptized that day! praising and praying in tongues isn't strange, although I'll admit it takes some getting used to! when you are alone in prayer, it is a mighty tool that I can use to specifically bring you peace. in corporate worship, singing or speaking in tongues can still be private, if spoken quietly, under the music.

in the Body, paul made clear that tongue interpretation will keep confusion from arising. in private prayer, you don't have to have that limit; you will be praying My express will for others as you intercede in prayer with tongues. so, if you want to go deeper in worship and prayer (and who wouldn't?) ask for this gift! while you're at it, ask for the interpretation gift as well. then, put on some worship music, close your eyes, and open your mouth during the singing. let yourself relax with Me. sing "holy, holy, holy" with the music, as the angels do. maybe lift your hands. with bold faith, you will start to praise. your free worship participation is a bold testimony, as surely as is using your tongue to testify daily in your known language of what the Lord is doing in your life. I equate your testimony with the holy Blood of Jesus!(revelation 12:11)

don't be embarrassed. speak boldly! the gift of tongues will bring you great joy and the joy of the Lord is your strength! it is also a help to the Kingdom causes, releasing angels.

"consider what a great forest is set on fire by a small spark. the tongue also is a fire." james 3:5

"you have forsaken your first love...he who has an ear to hear, let him hear what the Spirit is saying to the churches." revelation 2:4,7

of the seven churches mentioned in revelation chapters 2 and 3, only the church at philadelphia is called faithful. the church at smyrna is exhorted to be faithful. the others are described as loveless, compromising, corrupt, dead, and lukewarm. I'm sorry to tell you this because I know how hard you are trying and I don't want to discourage you, My little children.

try to remember back to when you first accepted My gift of eternal life by grace through faith. remember how excited and energized you were, everything was new and fresh? I understand how the accuser and the world have beaten you down since. you can't let that criticism and attack keep you from childlike devotion to Me. Jesus gave 100 per cent of Himself so that you could live as the Victorious Church! I promised you that the very gates of hell itself would not prevail against you!

come to Me in the ways that uplift you, in the ways I uniquely fashioned you- singing, gardening, cooking, reading, silence, preaching, fishing, raising children, ocean swimming, forest walking, dancing, scuba diving, traveling, playing instruments, sports, camping, painting, sewing, writing a book- all the variety of ways that make you smile! I am here waiting!

"Jesus replied, if you only knew the gift God has for you and Who you are speaking to, you would ask Me and I would give you Living Water." john 4:10

"He said to me, it is done. I am the Alpha and the Omega, the Beginning and the End. to him who is thirsty I will give to drink without cost from the spring of the Water of Life." revelation 21:6

maybe you've never even cracked open the book of revelation- too mysterious, too scary, too much! Abba Father specifically tells you in chapter one that He will bless you if you read and obey this book.

I'm telling you strongly, if you spend time reading the last thing I wrote down to you, revelation chapters 21 and 22- and try reading them out loud- your spirit man will rise up with such strength and freedom! there are so many beautiful images in these two chapters. it is My literary Masterpiece- a revealing of Jesus, as all of Scripture is. the description of the New Jerusalem, your Home, and all the gemstones it is constructed with, is powerful. the defeat of satan in chapter twenty is God's justice for you. the crystal sea and the Throne of God are described and revealed. then, Jesus speaks personally to you! (chapter 22:12,16) have I gotten your attention?

you and I are meant to call out together for Messiah's return. only Father God knows when that day will be. maybe He is waiting for the passion of your cry for His return to match the fervor of Mine. let's give it a try! right now, speak "come Lord Jesus" out loud over and over- again and again and again!

"Holy, Holy, Holy is the Lord God Almighty, Who was, and Is, and Is to Come! You are worthy, our Lord and God, to receive glory and honor and power, for You created all things. worthy is the Lamb Who was slain, to receive power and wisdom and strength and honor and glory and praise!" revelation 4:8,11 and 5:12

now is the time 2/24/21
Blessings wisdom and strength

"the field is white for harvest." john 4:35

I alluded to the Fivefold Ministries before. let Me explain those Offices further here. Apostle is the first Office mentioned, and the Apostles are very necessary to the life and health of the Body of Christ.

an Apostle feels a strong calling to travel and set up churches or build up churches in different locales. if you are strong in the administration gift, then you will excel and be a great blessing in this office. as well, you must have a blazing passion for the Church, not forsaking the gathering together, and willing to serve untiringly without complaint. the gift of great faith is essential in order to start and nurture a church.

Father God loves the Church and gave Jesus, His Only incarnated Son, as the Bridegroom for her. if you are married, remember your wedding day, the thrill, the excitement, the joy of the process of marrying your beloved. that's how Jesus feels about you! He is waiting at the altar for you to arrive!

"let us be glad and rejoice, and let us give honor to Him. for the time has come for the wedding feast of the Lamb, and His bride has prepared herself. she has been given the finest of pure white linen to wear." revelation 19:7,8 "worship God! for the testimony of Jesus is the spirit of prophecy." revelation 19:10

there is a difference in the gift of prophecy and the Position. one who functions in the Office or Position of Prophet, must devote much more time to prayer and "soaking", meaning remaining, in My Presence. I am the One who gives you the words to speak. often those Words seem to come very spontaneously, but they are a by-product of remaining tight with Me. you must trust Me and not try to edit yourself or qualify things in your mind. "My thoughts are higher than your thoughts and My Ways are higher than your ways," says isaiah. the Prophetic Office is one of the most important for the church, for the Bride needs to change with the times and grow, staying relevant and powerful throughout life.

your Words of prophecy should, and will, exhort, encourage, and enlighten others! speak a Word with love, in season, to uplift someone. try to be very kind and humble as you prophesy, just as Jesus was. Jesus is your great High Priest and Prophet, so emulate Him in everything you do! I know- it's not easy! just do the best you can and I will help you with all the rest.

"consequently, you are no longer foreigners and aliens, but fellow citizens with God's people and members of God's household, built on the foundation of the apostles and prophets, with Christ Jesus Himself as the Chief Cornerstone. in Him the whole building is joined together and rises to become a holy temple in the Lord. and in Him you too are being built together to become a dwelling in which God lives by His Spirit." ephesians 2:19-22 "except a man be born again, he cannot see the Kingdom of God." john 3:3

God equips Evangelists with great boldness, for His greatest desire is for <u>ALL</u> men to come to know His love and to love Him in an intimate Relationship. this is what salvation, or being born anew, means. Father God's heart is passionately focused on those who haven't yet heard or fully understood His gift of grace through Jesus' sacrificial death and Resurrection. this is not dogmatic or judgemental in any way, as I love everyone! I am always on the side of the underdog, cheering you on. I go looking for the lost sheep, the one who has wandered away, and the rebellious son, for he didn't know the consequences of his actions.

I inspired the greatest Evangelists of all time- peter, paul, billy graham, who preached personally to over 200 million people, and many millions more he touched via television. I may not use you in such a vast way (or maybe I will!) but if there is even one person (and there are more than one!) that you can touch with the gospel of peace through Jesus Christ, I will be well pleased! I'm not really into numbers, I'm into loving people!

"I will make you fishers of men." 1 timothy 2:4

"the Lord spoke to me with His strong Hand upon me, warning me not to think the way everyone else does. He said, do not call conspiracy everything that these people call conspiracy; do not fear what they fear and do not dread it. the Lord Almighty is the one you are to regard as holy, He is the one you are to fear, He is the one Who should make you tremble. He will keep you safe, He will be to you a sanctuary." isaiah 8:11-14

I am there to protect you. I know that today there are many storms, many controversies, many things that seem fear-worthy. I am asking you to call upon the Blood, the Blood that was sprinkled on the Mercy Seat. It cries out "hands off" to the adversary and his peons. satan knows that you are covered and protected under the sacred Blood of Jesus and so he will do anything he can to get you distracted or entertained away from that focus. he knows. you should know as well.

even as you minister in these offices, and I desire that for you, or even as you receive from those who walk in these offices, pray for them. pray to sit under a ministry that reveals Jesus, for His Name is above any other Name.

"it will be just like this on the day the Son of Man is revealed. on that day no one who is on the roof of his house, with his goods inside, should go down to get them. likewise, no one in the field should go back for anything. remember lot's wife! whoever tries to keep his life will lose it, and whoever loses his life will preserve it." luke 17:30-33

"His anointing teaches you about all things, as that anointing is real, not counterfeit- just as it has taught you, remain in Him."   1 john 2:27

Pastors and Teachers I group together, as those two functions do tend to work better together under the anointing. a Pastor has a compassionate heart for the flock, the group of people under His authority. he is interested in them individually as he shares messages from his and God's heart. think back on your school days- the teachers you learned the most from had a deep interest in the subject they were teaching and also in the people (you!) they were conveying it to.

Pastors, feed your people. give them meat, mature spiritual food, to grow on and give them much encouragement. train them how to focus on Jesus.

Teachers, "study to show yourself approved." be interested in the things of God and expound on Jesus, who "called us out of darkness and into His marvelous Light!"

people, encourage your leaders. help your pastors preach by paying attention and responding to Me as they flow in the anointing. continue to meet with your spiritual community with glad hearts and a song and much true affection and love to share! aspire to be an acts chapter 2 church- alive and loving, a light to the world! I love you!

"keep watch over yourselves and all the flock of which the Holy Spirit has made you overseers. be shepherds of the church, which He bought with His own Blood." acts 20:28

"do you not know that your body is a temple of the Holy Spirit, Who is in you, Whom you have received from God? you are not your own, you were bought at a price. therefore, honor God with your body." 1 corinthians 6:19,20

I am with you at all times! the mystery of My Omnipresence is difficult for your natural mind to totally fathom, so just trust Me on this one! once infilled with Me, it is not possible for you to leave My Omnipresence, since I am in you eternally. nevertheless, it is possible for you to leave My manifest Presence. that occurs mostly when you're not following what I directly told you to do. there is still grace for the pit or the pigpen that you are in, even if they are of your own fashioning. I'd much rather that you live in higher altitudes! the flesh is the world of self-effort, the golden calf.

Father God does not recognize the flesh. He doesn't see you as your flesh. He sees you as perfect because He sees Jesus when He looks at you.

don't worry, one day soon your mortal flesh will be glorified-it will become incorruptible, as your spirit man is. it won't be long now, so keep very close to Me. learn how to stoke the anointing Fire through silence, worship, study, and prayer. walk hard after this vertical Relationship we have, your most important Relationship ever!

"absent from the body, present with the Lord." 2 corinthians 5:8

"i can do all things through Christ Who strengthens me."
phillipians 4:13

what are the purposes and dreams you want to accomplish
with your life? what are the Lord's purposes and ideas for your
life, as you know them to be thus far? how do these two
juxtapose with one another?

in light of the reality of spiritual warfare (don't worry I've
given you tools and serious skills we will get to), what are
satan's designs for your life? the enemy doesn't really mess
too much with people who are ineffectual for the Kingdom. he
always attacks those who are threats to his purposes. also, he is
a coward, so he continually attacks children, the elderly, and
the more vulnerable ones. satan's purposes are "to steal, kill,
and destroy" by any means necessary. he respects no one and
nothing is sacred to him. do not give him even one millimeter
of a toehold in your life and keep your family covered by the
Blood in prayer.

God's purposes are for mankind's highest good and "for all
to come to a saving knowledge of Jesus Christ as Savior",
respecting your free will. God loves you unconditionally and
will always do what is best for you in every situation. He
wants you to have "good days" and He blesses and provides
for you constantly in many ways you wont know until you
reach here.

I am the Plumbline! align your purposes with Mine- and
through spiritual addition and multiplication, you will receive
the things that you desire, I promise you!

"seek ye first the Kingdom of God and His Righteousness
and all these things shall be added unto you as well." matthew
6:33

"he that dwells in the secret place of the Most High shall abide under the shadow of the Almighty." psalm 91:1

this is My 911 verse for you for when you have an emergency. if you're anxious about something and can't get to sleep, say this verse, or all of psalm 91, out loud- several times if you need to (this is easier if you have it memorized!)

the Secret Place is the place where you and I are alone together- the Secret Place is Jesus. it is a personal time and Relationship apart from and above all others in the world.

I want you to know that no matter what you have done, or haven't done, "I am your Refuge", your place of safety. you can tell Me anything. even if you are mad at Me, I will listen. I get angry sometimes, too!

surely, "the same Power that raised Christ from the dead dwells in you." access it through close intimacy with Me. I don't want fake words or false promises, empty rituals. I desire mercy and not dead, burnt offerings (works). Jesus paid once for all time, for all sins, if you will just receive!

"don't be afraid, the prophet answered. those who are with us are more than those who are with them. and elisha prayed, O Lord, open his eyes so he may see. then the Lord opened the servant's eyes, and he looked and saw the hills full of horses and chariots of fire all around elisha." 2 kings 6:16,17 "for God did not give us a spirit of fear, but of power, love, and a sound mind (self-control)." 2 timothy 1:7

if I didn't give you a spirit of fear, guess who it came from? I give only good and perfect gifts and because you are My child you have the right, the birthright, to reject out of hand, out of your life, those thoughts and emotions that are destructive and contrary to My will for you.

even beyond that, know that fear cannot exist where I am, for "perfect love casts out fear." your body is My Temple! I am living and breathing and moving through you and I am an unabashed Optimist! you should be also, as you radiate from Me!

so while the enemy may try his best to bring you down with fear, know that he is already defeated. he was defeated two thousand years ago. proclaim that victory- actually take that victory march each day in your walk with Me.

"i sought the Lord and He answered me and delivered me from all my fears. those who look to Him are radiant; their faces are never covered with shame. in my desperation i prayed, and the Lord listened. He saved me from all my troubles. for the angel of the Lord encamps around (is a guard around) those who fear Him; He surrounds and defends you." psalm 34:4-7

"though a thousand may fall at your side, ten thousand at your right hand, it will not come near you." psalm 91:7

"this is love, not that we loved God, but that He loved us and sent His Son as an atoning sacrifice for our sins." 1 john 4:10

love is the greatest fruit you can exhibit in your life. whoever doesn't love can't truly know God, because God is love! He generously created the entire world and all that is in it, all of its beauty. He "fearfully and wonderfully" made you. He crafted a beautiful, all-encompassing path for us to be in eternal peace forever. how great is the love He is lavishing upon us- He calls us His very own sons and daughters!

notice how you protect and care for your own children and grandchildren. even when they make mistakes, sometimes costly mistakes, you are always willing and able to forgive them. you see the good in them. in fact, pause for a moment and meditate on the fact that you would give your life for your child or children. I gave you the ability to procreate and feel this depth of love so that you would have an inkling of how much I love you. I know that you would lay your life down for someone you love- and that's what I did for you, My son, My daughter!

live in that love as much as you can- there is no plan B.

"O Lord, You have examined my heart and know everything about me. You know when i sit down or stand up. You know my thoughts even when i am far away. You see me when i travel and when i rest at home. You know everything i do. You know what i am going to say before i even say it, Lord. You go before me and follow me. You place Your Hand of blessing upon my head. such knowledge is too wonderful for me to understand! i can never escape from Your Spirit! i can never get away from Your Presence!" psalm 139:1-7 "count it all joy when you fall into various trials, knowing that the testing of your faith produces patience." james 1:2

I don't expect you to feel happy all the time, however, recognize the deep wellspring of joy that is within you because of My residence there. it is also a fruit of the lifestyle of living in union with Me! tap into that "river of Living Water" more and more. it increases in flow when it is moving through you to others- have you noticed this yet?

when you need a healing- pray for someone else to be healed. whenever there is a lack, focus on the supply- better yet, focus on the Supplier! I am Jehovah-jireh, your Provider! haven't I always come through for you, maybe not always in the way you expected, perhaps not in the way you felt to be the best timing. I have honored you with the gift of joy in your life. this inner joy means you have a confident expectation of good in your life because you know that I love you.

in the garden of eden, after the fall from grace, I asked "who told you that you were naked?" genesis 3:11 they felt ashamed of what they had done and needed redemption. I came to remove any shame, curse, or fear from your life, My child. receive that gift.

"Jesus replied, if you only knew the gift God has for you and Who you are speaking to, you would ask Me and I would give you living water." john 4:10

"and the peace of God, which transcends all understanding, will guard your hearts and minds in Christ Jesus." philippians 4:7

shadows fall gracefully in the evening. I knew evenings would be nostalgic in life, so I paint stunning sunsets, offer quiet, reflective moments as birds fly overhead. some of you have a loving spouse to cling to, but some of you are alone and the body feels worn, like the days clothing that is cast off. I understand these things- I, also, laid My head on a rock and walked until My feet and legs ached- I know how especially the legs get really tired at night. you see, I understand how it is at different stages of life. I understand pain and loneliness. I experienced it also.

no matter where you are right now, close your eyes. like every one of the seven billion people on your small, blue marble, breathe in, then slowly breathe out. humor Me. do that again. My peace is in you. I drop it in as casually as a soft rain. no challenge in this earthly tent of yours can remove that gift once you've received and opened it. and there is no greater witness to the world of your Relationship with Me than the fruit of peace- in all situations. I never would make light of what you are going through, but there is enough peace in just this moment.

"for He Himself is our Peace." ephesians 2:14
"when i am afraid, i put my trust in You." psalm 56:3

"we also pray that you will be strengthened with all His glorious power so you will have all the endurance and patience you need. may you be filled with joy." colossians 1:11

patience is a by-product when you take the time to wait on Me. what does that look like specifically in your life, in the details? well, it isn't something you can read about or learn from a book; it is experiential. several times here I have asked you to close your eyes, or listen to your breath. so, right now, read the Scripture above once more, slowly, and then close this book or your device over on your lap and just sit with Me for a minute…

what happened? what peripheral sounds did you hear? what internal feelings registered? impatience, boredom, confusion maybe? don't worry, these are all common to man. your brain jumps around to different subjects all the time- but with submission to My request, and practice, you will begin to look forward to the few brief moments of quiet with Me. then, surprisingly, you will also begin to become more patient and forgiving with other people.

life is training for the eternal, as well as a part of the eternal. bear the fruit of patience with others today.

"since God chose you to be the holy people He loves, you must clothe yourselves with tender-hearted mercy, kindness, humility, gentleness, and patience. make allowance for each others faults, and forgive anyone who offends you. remember, the Lord forgave you, so you must forgive others." colossians 3:12,13 "we prove ourselves by our purity, our understanding, our patience, our kindness, by the Holy Spirit within us and by our sincere love." 2 corinthians 6:6

twenty six times in psalm 136 My lovingkindness is proclaimed by king david. paul was able to embody kindness even in a jail cell. ask Me for kindness when someone says or does something that you don't like. I will give you the self-restraint not to react.

kindness is Who I am! My mercies are new and fresh every morning. since it is an essential part of My nature, I want you to exhibit kindness as well. show it not just in your public persona, but also in your most private moments, with those you love the most. I realize sometimes you get tired or frustrated. you won't get it right 100% of the time. sometimes you don't have to respond at all, you can just let something go completely, as if it never happened. I do that a lot- it's called forgiveness! it is an especially mature and challenging character trait to master. stay close to Me and I will help you to be like Me.

"give thanks to the Lord for He is good, His unfailing love endures forever." psalm 136:1

"do not quench the Holy Spirit. do not scoff at prophecies, but test everything that is said. hold on to what is good."
1 thessalonians 5:19-21

goodness is the train of My Robe! I delight in helping people, holding an umbrella over you when it is raining! I am there in your altruistic endeavors, in fact, I even spark the imagination to think of new cures for diseases or new programs to relieve poverty and help addiction. every generosity flows from the goodness that mimics Mine, since God created you in His image.

stay near Me through worship, communion, listening to the Word being preached, reading My personal Word to you daily. that's how I can immerse you in My goodness.

My mercy will follow you, but also precede you. it will surround you entirely and you will have a tangible radiance better than any beauty treatment. your smile will be real and genuine, and you will smile almost all the time! everyone will know that you are filled with My goodness!

"surely goodness and mercy will follow me all the days of my life." psalm 23:6

"if you plan to do evil, you will be lost; if you plan to do good, you will receive unfailing love and faithfulness." proverbs 14:22

are you noticing a pattern here? each fruit builds upon your character and leads to the next fruit manifesting. love begets joy, joy begets peace, peace begets patience, and so on.

without faith is is impossible to please Me. I prefer to say it in the positive- with faith, I can draw you into ever closer relationship with Me.

every marriage reflects My faithfulness as you trust one another through the good and the bad. it's a picture of our Relationship- the bride and the Bridegroom Jesus. think about this- when you are physically separated from your spouse (although I don't suggest that for long periods of time) you still feel and know their love. you and I are never separated, I am in you. I know it is hard to understand when you aren't able to see Jesus with your natural eye. you will understand with complete clarity soon.

"faith is the confidence that what we hope for will actually happen; the evidence (assurance) of things not seen." hebrews 11:1

"now i, paul, appeal to you with the gentleness and kindness of Christ." 2 corinthians 10:1

gentleness is perceived by the world as a weakness, just as humility is, except in spiritual leaders. humility is actually a strength, as long as your boundaries preclude abuse or codependency. there are times for spiritual warfare- even gentle Jesus turned the tables in the temple and stood up to satan in the desert. we will get into spiritual warfare next. use the wisdom gift to complement the fruit of gentleness. "be gentle as doves, but shrewd as serpents", matthew exhorts.

I've often been described as a gentleman, and that is true. I will never force you to do anything and I don't regard shouting as consistently useful, nor do I enjoy it. elijah found this out at the mouth of the cave. I also don't like to repeat Myself- ask jonah when you see him!

I am authoritative in My gentleness. I want you to be the same way in your character so that you will command the respect that a child of Mine deserves from the world. your life is not about you- it's about the people around you and how you relate with them and love them. be gentle with others today- look at their interior, their souls, not their exterior!

"let your gentleness be evident to all." philippians 4:5

"and after the earthquake there was a fire, but the Lord was not in the fire. and after the fire came a gentle whisper." 1 kings 19:12

"so be on your guard, not asleep like the others. stay alert and be self controlled." 1 thessalonians 5:6

because life consists of many imperfect relationships, there will be times when those closest to you will either knowingly or inadvertently hurt you. there will also be times in your worldly jobs, or even ministries, when people will reject you outright or persecute because you carry My Name.

I'm going to rush in to help you there- please trust that! what I don't want is for you to lash out in anger or bitterness. don't hit send on that negative email. ask Me first if there should even be a response at all, and if so, what response. your witness is more important than making a point. don't text something better off said voice to voice in a call, or face to face even better. this is wisdom and will save you many embarrassments. get self control from Me and impart it to others by your example.

self control also concerns fleshly appetites. live simply and do things with moderation. notice what time period I chose to come in and to inhabit the earth? it was a simple and ordinary time and place. emulate Jesus in His lifestyle and in everything, child. (no, you don't have to wear sandals and grow your hair long unless you want to!)

"so humble yourselves under the mighty hand of God, and at the right time He will lift you up in honor. give all your worries and cares to God, for He cares for you. stay alert! watch out for your great enemy, the devil. he prowls around like a roaring lion looking for someone to devour. stand firm against him and be strong in your faith." 1 peter 5:8,9 "finally, stand your ground, putting on the belt of truth and the breastplate of righteousness in place, with your feet shod with the readiness that comes from the gospel of peace. in addition, take up the shield of faith, with which you can extinguish all the flaming arrows of the evil one. put on salvation as your helmet, and take the sword of the Spirit, which is the Word of God." ephesians 6: 10-17

you can rest assured that I will always represent God's heart when I speak. He wants to protect you and let you know that you are the safest when you are surrounded by His Presence. His triune Presence includes Me. the three of Us function as One- co-equal and co-eternal. I know this is intricate for you to understand. "Adonai ehud" translates "the Lord our God is One God." that is still true within the Trinity.

let's delve into deeper aspects of spiritual warfare now. are you aware that you possess spiritual armor? I not only equip you with gifts and produce fruits from your growth, but I also help you stand your ground in defending the Kingdom. you may feel pressed down but you aren't crushed. you may feel persecuted, but you are never abandoned. you may feel struck down, but you are not destroyed. I will help you break down strongholds, areas of bondage in the mind, changing habits and releasing memories.

"i press on to possess that perfection for which Christ Jesus first possessed me. no, i have not achieved it, but i focus on this one thing: forgetting the past and looking forward to what lies ahead, i press on to reach the end of the race and receive the heavenly prize for which God, through Christ Jesus, is calling us." philippians 4: 12-14 "when the Spirit of truth comes, He will guide you into all truth." john 16:13

the belt of truth is the first spiritual weapon mentioned in ephesians chapter 6. a belt holds everything up. it also keeps things held in. I want you to have the confidence to know that even though things may appear shaky in the natural, I am holding it all together. I am the God of order, not chaos. when it appears the most chaotic on the outside, like shadrach, mesach, and abednego going into the fire (daniel 3:26), that is precisely the moment when I am most powerfully moving. I am the Fourth Man in the furnace with you!

don't depend on your flesh to see the truth- that will only camouflage your favor. depend on Me to hold everything in your life together. don't worry- you don't have to get it perfect- I'm looking for faith and I will use even your mistakes for your highest good. My peace will guide you through seasons of green lights, you will know when something is My Will. I will guide you with checks in your spirit, red flags, to keep you from trials. you will have instincts and conscience for the times to wait.

learn how to discern and listen for My Voice. how? notice your own thoughts and notice if you sense a thought that seems different from anything you would normally think. you will learn that My thoughts are usually totally different from your usual thoughts. as you listen and follow the things I say to you, you will hear Me clearer each time.

"in the last times there will be scoffers. these people are the ones who are creating divisions among you. they follow their natural instincts because they do not have God's Spirit in them. but, you, dear friend must build each other up in your most holy faith, praying in the power of the Holy Spirit." jude 1:18-20 "i am the Righteousness of God in Christ Jesus." 1 corinthians 5:21

the breastplate of Righteousness is your body armor, protecting your spiritual heart and vital organs. as often as you feel caught in guilt or despair, confess that you are now made <u>entirely</u> righteous, once and for all, by the precious and powerful Blood of Jesus! His grace is free, but it isn't cheap (one of you came up with that saying and I think it's awesome!). your righteousness cost Me everything and I willingly did that for you!

let me explain- cause this is so cool. I no longer see you as sinful or defective in any way. I see you as perfect, without spot or blemish, because of what Jesus accomplished. His sacrifice bought your complete redemption and sanctification. confess this and it releases My favor to you! see yourself as worthy and perfect, even though you are still walking that out as long as you are on the earth. don't talk down about yourself (or others!) keep your heart transparently pure!

you will still make mistakes, maybe big ones, but I can and will use your mistakes to catapult you to a higher level of faith and blessing! furthermore, when you are under attack from the devil, My Righteousness will protect you, as you confess it out loud. you can't trust anything the enemy says. he is a liar and the father of all lies. don't trust him for a second, nor lower your guard. stand firm and resist him at every turn. keep your breastplate over your heart!

"righteousness and peace kiss each other." psalm 85:10
"in the same way, abraham believed God, and God counted him righteous because of his faith." galatians 3:6

"it is for freedom that Christ has set us free. stand firm then." galatians 5:1

as you stand, it is necessary to have your feet firmly planted on the solid Rock. footwear is extremely important- supporting the twenty seven bones and the arches in each foot, but if you've ever walked on wet or sinking sand, you know it doesn't matter what shoes you have on, it will be challenging. the gospel (good news) of the peace we have through Jesus Christ's crucifixion and Resurrection is part of the firm Rock we stand on- Jesus Himself!

I'm asking you to be ready to share that news, making the most of every opportunity that I present to you. that is how you carry peace to others, by sharing Jesus with them. practice your testimonies, write them down. have them at the ready! maybe you've never heard of Divine Appointments, or God Opportunities. they are real! I am working behind the scenes constantly because I know that sharing your testimony with others is a little bit out of your comfort zone. I applaud every risk you take and I soften the hearts of those whom you open up to! tell them what I have done in your life- the door is open!

"but you will not even need to fight. take your positions then stand still and watch the Lord's victory (see the deliverance of the Lord)." 2 chronicles 20:17

"I looked for someone who might rebuild the wall of righteousness that guards the land. I searched for someone to stand in the gap in the wall, so I wouldn't destroy the land." ezekiel 22:30

"without faith it is impossible to please God."hebrews 11:6

hebrews chapter 11 is called the "hall of faith." the word faith is used twenty eight times in this chapter. it is used 430 times in the entire Bible, one of the most oft used words. the most often used Word in the Bible is "Jesus" and "Lord"- 7,484 times! the word "God" is used 3,970 times.

the more you're doing for the Kingdom, the more you will be attacked by the enemy and the world. as you hold up the shield of faith, the heaviness, the weight of it will strengthen you in your inner man. hold your faith high by speaking only God's thoughts and promises about your life. change topics of conversation to Him, to His grace and mercy in situations in your life that you are sharing about. hold your shield high by spending time proclaiming Jesus to the world. as you do so, you will effectively extinguish (quench) all the fiery darts that the enemy hurls. I said quench in this verse because I surround you with an ocean of protection, a shield of water not wood or metal.

satan doesn't like his devices exposed- they include fear, guilt, addiction, violence, depression, and more. the devil is a pusher and he pushes these. in contrast, I lead with peace. don't make impulsive decisions! seek godly counsel, study the Word and align your choices with the Bible, pray, sing praises, worship in silence, and use strong discernment.

these are the pillars of faith. have faith in Me. I will show you "How to Spend the Night in the Lion's Den"!! (hint: you need a lot of faith!!)

"faith comes by hearing and hearing by the Word of God." romans 10:17

"set your mind on things above, not on earthly things. for you have died, and your life is now hidden with Christ in God." colossians 3:2,3

the helmet of salvation covers your head and protects your mind. a "covering" protects from evil or danger; it is a refuge, a shelter, which envelops you. I am your Covenant, a covering for you, a sacred trust, and solemn agreement backed by My full and complete investment in you.

you've heard before that the battlefield is in your mind and that is the truth. I created your brain to solve problems, to ensure survival, and to bring you happiness. your brain stores memories and emotions even from childhood. because of its survival instinct, the mind tends to fluctuate and focus on problems, unless it is trained to do otherwise. just as an athlete trains their body, you must train your mind to turn from worldly, temporal concerns. as you focus on Jesus, and remember all He has done for you, your mind will settle.

first thing in the morning, before you even get out of bed, whisper His wonderful Name as the first word out of your mouth. thank Him for a new day of life. then, throughout the day, close your eyes and draw your attention over and over to the eternal Presence of God. keep your awareness fixed on your Savior. this will cleanse your mind as you meditate on the eternal realm and not on the problems or pleasures of this life.

"therefore, i urge you brothers, in view of God's mercy, to offer your bodies as living sacrifices, holy and pleasing to God- this is your spiritual act of worship. do not conform any longer to the pattern of the world, but be transformed by the renewing of your mind." romans 12:1,2 "in the beginning was the Word, and the Word was with God, and the Word was God." john 1:1

the final spiritual weapon paul lists is the only offensive weapon, the sword of the Spirit, which is the "Rhema" or living Word of God. to some the Bible seems dry or lifeless, but once it is infused in your mind with My understanding, every page shimmers with life- even those geneologies I had you look at! they show patterns and history. they show Jesus' connection through time.

the Word is able to "rightly divide between soul and spirit," joint and marrow, meaning it can guide you and show you deeper truths. at different times in your life, the same passage you've read many times will come alive with fresh awareness. study and memorize the passages I lead you to! Know My promises! carry your Bible with you! keep it open around your home so it is available. as your sword, the Bible is a powerful weapon to come against the enemy with, as Jesus did in the wilderness. He rebuked and silenced satan very easily with the quoting of Scripture. you have that same authority as you wield the Bible as the weapon it is. rebuke him and he flees quickly.

remember, joseph was thrown in a well by his brothers, but I used it to catapult him to the king's palace! the brothers came and begged forgiveness and joseph replied, "don't be afraid of me. am i God that i can punish you? what you intended for evil (to harm me), God used for good. He brought me to this position." genesis 50:20 I would love if you were able to call these verses up verbatim, as a walking concordance, but keep in mind that a heart for Jesus is as important as Bible knowledge.

"Thy Word is a lamp unto my feet and a light unto my path." psalm 119:105

"pray in the Spirit on all occasions with all kinds of prayers and requests." ephesians 6:18

I called it the sword of the Spirit so that it would give a reference to using My power within the context of Scripture. some of the best worship is Bible verses set to music. I already touched on the gift of tongues in prayer. here, I want to go further on that as spiritual warfare. some of you may feel too inhibited to pray in tongues, even privately. that's okay. it doesn't make Me love you any less, just so you know!

still, you will be more effective in outreach to others, especially for miracles, if you use My gift of tongues to pray to Abba. I want to call you to a deeper communication in and with Me. go to a quiet place. have your Bible there and maybe a pen and paper or a journal. spend a little time in a comfortable position in silence. notice any sounds near you-nature, soft worship music if you desire, your breathing, maybe a pet nearby if you have one.

then, begin to thank Me for your blessings in this moment. move to continued praise and then humbly come with any thoughts or concerns. many people just pray in their mind, but I love the sound of your voice and the sound of your laughter; even your tears, which I will catch in My jar. I am honored when you share things with Me. during these times, occupy yourself solely with remaining in My Presence.

"the Spirit alone gives eternal life. human effort accomplishes nothing. and the very words I have spoken to you are spirit and life." john 6:63

"Jesus then took the loaves, gave thanks, and distributed them to those who were seated, as much as they wanted, and likewise of the fish, and when they were filled, He said, gather up what remains so nothing is lost." john 6:11,12

everything multiplies in Jesus' Hands! this miracle of the five loaves and two fish, the feeding of the five thousand, is the only miracle repeated in all four gospels. notice there were were twelve baskets <u>full</u> left over here! God is a God of abundance!

He is pouring Me out even more so in these end times, as He knows you have need of more Spirit. the Lord doesn't function like the economy of the world, so don't try to figure it out in your head, My child. the more you need Him, the more He will supply. this is called the "Hundredfold Principle", and there is even the Thousandfold and more for those who believe! God is seeking addition and multiplication for you!

enlarge your capacity to receive from Me- how much of Me can you contain? as much as you want, that I will impart!

"where, o death, is your victory? where, o death, is your sting? for the sting of death is sin, and the power of sin is the law. but thanks be to God! He gives us the victory through our Lord Jesus Christ!" 1 corinthians 15:55-57 "during the fourth watch of the night, Jesus went out to them, walking on the lake. when the disciples saw Him, they were terrified. it's a ghost, they said and cried out in fear. but Jesus immediately said to them, don't be afraid! it is I! peter replied, Lord, if it's You, tell me to come to you on the water." john 14:25-28

Jesus says, come, take the step of faith and walk on the water. He is calling you to a higher place of faith, a deeper relationship with Him. "think of what you were when you were called," paul says. "not many of you were wise by human standards; not many were influential. but God chose the foolish things of the world to shame the wise. God chose the weak things of the world to shame the strong." 1 corinthians 1:26,27

I want you to be confident in My power in you. don't worry if you need to speak at a presentation or event. I give you leadership roles in the world and I will give you the words at the exact moment you need them. that power is biblical- read the verse below and believe it! I love you more than you love your own children. I will certainly provide all you need.

"I don't speak by My own authority. the Father who sent Me has commanded Me what to say and how to say it." john 12:49

"don't worry about how to respond or what to say. God will give you the right words at the right time, for it is not you who will be speaking- it is the Spirit of the Father speaking through you." matthew 10:19,20 (read this in full context, it will bless you!)

"the Spirit searches all things, even the deep things of God. for who among men knows the thoughts of a man except the man's spirit within him? in the same way, no one knows the thoughts of God except the Spirit of God. we have not received the spirit of the world, but the Spirit Who is from God, that we may understand what God has freely given us." 1 corinthians 2:10-12

this is deeper truth here, identifying Who I am and how God the Father reveals through Me. read it once again very slowly. your natural eye cannot see, your natural ear cannot hear, your natural mind cannot conceive what God is doing- only I can uncover the mysteries for you.

the Mystery is Jesus, freely given, for all men, for all time. think of how many people have lived on earth down through history. there are over seven billion now, so calculate, if you can, how many there have been throughout all time- trillions! that is the Father's vast heart for each of you!

He made a way so there would be no chasm to cross anymore and He foreordained this before He even created the world.

"oh, the love that the Father has lavished on us! that we should be called children of God!" 1 john 3:1

"give, and it will be given to you; a good measure, pressed down, shaken together, and running over, will be poured into your lap." luke 6:38

I am generous! I own the cattle on a thousand hills, and I enjoy giving you beautiful things and experiences to enjoy in life! just remember, ultimately you are only stewards, even of your earthly body, so don't put too much time into accumulating things. however, I do want you to deeply regard and appreciate the blessings I have given you without feeling guilty. enjoy your family in your home. enjoy your comfortable, reliable vehicle. enjoy nice clothing, healthy food, and vacations. just please don't base your identity or value on these things. you are worth so much more to Me than any object you possess.

I want you to live an abundant life, in all aspects. in fact, that is one of the main reasons I came down to the earth in manifested form. be the kind of person I was, who shares with others and loves to bless people! part of your witness is a healthy, peaceful, generous life!

"call on Me and I will show you great and mighty things which thou knowest not." jeremiah 33:3

"then eli realized it was the Lord who was calling the boy. so he said to samuel, go and lie down again and if someone calls again say, speak Lord, your servant is listening. so samuel went back to bed. and the Lord came and called as before, samuel, samuel! and samuel replied, here i am, speak, your servant is listening." 1 samuel 3:8-10

sometimes I will come and speak to you while you are sleeping or in your dreams. can I get a witness to that, meaning have you ever experienced that? the more you notice the variety of ways I speak to you, the more I will be able to impart to you! I call to you daily, many times a day. the heavens themselves- sky, clouds, sunrise, sunset, storms, full moon, stars- speak and declare My glory. psalm 19:1

I communicate through the Word primarily, but I also speak through you. people may not even be aware that you are saying exactly what they need to hear from Me, but you should be aware of My speaking through you. as you walk close to Me, I will instruct you when and what to speak to people as they need. it will be an unmistakable nudge from Me. sometimes your heart will start to pound or you will receive other physiological promptings. more often, you will just know in your heart.

I also regularly use the witness, or testimony, in your spirit to convey something to you. pause and listen for Me often throughout the day so that you will know what My thoughts sound like! I will make it as clear as I can for you and confirm Myself constantly to you.

"whom should I send as a messenger to this people? who will go? and i said, here i am, send me!" isaiah 6:8

"then He said to His disciples, the harvest is plentiful but the workers are few. ask the Lord of the harvest, therefore, to send out workers into the harvest field." matthew 9: 37,39

when there is some wonderful news, the birth of a child, a wedding, important health news, it is usually shared rather quickly. the dominance of the internet makes this even more common.

I am asking you to be a bold witness to the greatest news ever given! use words if necessary! you've heard that expression and it is very clever. I agree this is an important directive, especially for introverts or those who are naturally shy. just submit to the fact that I can overcome inherent personality traits and use you in different ways than how you may feel comfortable being used! introduce people to Jesus Christ!

the time is growing short- I want to instill in you a sense of urgency for these days. Jesus Himself exhorted you to proclaim the Kingdom. you will face ridicule and persecution for your testimony, but take a stand anyway! never let anyone tell you what you can't do! and "after you've done everything you can, just keep standing." it is enough.

"what I tell you in the dark, speak in the daylight. what is whispered in your ear, proclaim from the rooftops." matthew 10:27

"Jesus replied, you do not realize now what I am doing, but later you will understand." john 13:7

when you are close to Me, no one needs to force you to do anything- it is our close Relationship that brings revelation and willingness to serve from the inside of your spirit. here, Jesus wanted to wash peter's feet, but peter didn't comprehend the significance of it. how often we turn from what Jesus has for us because we don't recognize what He is doing at that moment.

you can learn the most about Me and My power by interaction with Me! you can't just read about Jesus or Myself- a relationship is experiential, a day by day walk together, a day to day conversation with Me, even a moment by moment reality!

you will not fully understand My workings in this earthly dispensation, so don't obsess about that. what Jesus says above is still true- "later you will understand."

"when i was a child, i talked like a child, i thought like a child, i reasoned like a child. when i became a man, i put childish ways behind me. now we see as in a mirror dimly, but then face to Face. now i know in part; then i shall know fully, even as i am fully known." 1 corinthians 13:11,12 "be completely humble and gentle; be patient, bearing with one another in love. make every effort to keep the unity of Spirit through the bond of peace. there is just one Body and One Spirit, One Lord, one faith, one baptism, One God and Father of us all, Who is over all and through all and in all." ephesians 4:2-6

in My complete humility I present this passage to you- it was spoken by paul, with chains on his hands and feet, in prison.

the sound of the trains off in the distance makes Me feel at home. it is a nostalgic sound that reminds me of when the final trumpet call will come; like resting on a level place with nowhere else to go. that's how it was for paul at that time in his life, he was resting with Me there.

that's how it is for you sometimes. you can feel the thing that is afar off as if it is already forming, changing, and becoming, because it is!

"day and night they never stop saying,
   Holy Holy Holy
   is the Lord God Almighty
   Who Was, and Is, and Is to Come." revelation 4:8

"I am the True Vine and My Father is the Gardener. He cuts off every branch in Me that bears no fruit, while every branch that does bear fruit, He prunes so that it will be even more fruitful." john 15:1,2

you are a living branch, abiding in Me, extending out from Me, offering fruits to the world. to abide is "to remain stable or fixed, to bear patiently, to wait for expectantly." I know there are some in the world who test your patience. these irritants produce the Pearl of Great Price, as the pearl comes from the oyster I created. when you feel tired at the end of the day, come and refresh by My side. there's no better testimony to My invigorating power than when you are really tired, fed-up even, and you come to absorb from Me anyway.

the nature of the Vine is that the branches must be lifted up by a trellis to bear fruit. I will honor that authentic need. speak with Me all day long, especially when you are frustrated or angry.

another resource is family- I gave you family and friends to share with. sometimes a brother or sister may get caught up in their own life trials. they forget to call or they say the wrong thing. just forgive them. I will draw closer at those times of your need and affirm you completely.

remember I told you I am with you always! you are never alone, My child.

"a man of many companions may come to ruin, but there is a Friend who sticks closer than a brother." proverbs 18:24

"much is required from those to whom much is given, for their responsibility is greater." luke 12:48

if this is touching your heart and making it burn, then most likely you were given a greater measure of faith, in accordance with God the Father's awareness of your heart's state and condition. you are blessed! not everyone is interested in the deeper things of God. I call theirs a bandaid faith, but that's okay- I still love them just as much!

however, if you feel a more passionate calling or urgency, don't feel like you are strange or weird. I love people who are sold out for Jesus! He was and is sold out for you!! He is the highest of the High Priests, the Savior of the world, so make Him preeminent in your life, lifting Him high above ALL other names!

I will honor you for that as you find creative ways to praise, discuss, and poin to Jesus each day. thank you, beloved one- you are the one I love!

"david, wearing a linen ephod, danced before the Lord with all his might, while he and the entire house of israel brought up the ark with shouts and the sound of trumpets. as the ark was entering the city of david (jerusalem), michal, daughter of saul, watched from a window. and when she saw king david leaping and dancing before the Lord, she despised him in her heart… david said to michal, i will celebrate before the Lord. i will become even more undignified than this, and i will be humiliated in my own eyes. and michal daughter of saul had no children to the day of her death." 2 samuel 6:14,21-23 "now that I, your Lord and Teacher, have washed your feet, you also should wash one another's feet. I have set an example for you." john 13:13

I have called you to a servant lifestyle, even as Jesus was the Servant Master. this is not a false humility. I have called you to be poured out, even as He was. this servanthood doesn't connote weakness, but exhibits great strength. I have called you to receive the abundant overflow- so much overflow that you might even have to build an ark! no, not similar to noah's directive, totally different! Abba is pouring Me out upon the earth- there is Revival coming! there are floods of mercy being poured out even right this moment! your sons and daughters are prophesying, do you hear them as they sing? mature men are dreaming new dreams, young men are receiving new visions from Me and writing them down to send out to the world. men and women are being poured into and then pouring out to the entire world.

"give and it will be given to you, pressed down, shaken together and overflowing." luke 6:38

"surely He has borne our infirmities and carried our sorrows." isaiah 53:4

borne literally means "to be lifted up or off." carried means "removed at a great distance." your sorrows denotes any of your pain, in the hebrew "makob." our infirmities is the hebrew word "kohle", which means sicknesses of any kind-physical, mental, emotional. He lifted them off of you forever.

as you speak this most powerful promise out loud, all sickness and pain will be removed. you may say, well, why does my hip or shoulder still hurt? stay with this promise longer, let the verses penetrate and jump out at you. what does that mean, to penetrate? as you meditate on the promise, the Word and My working within you come alive and impart fresh enthusiasm and hope. that eventually, or immediately (always believe for a miracle), manifests as healing and removal of suffering.

this verse in particular brings a heavy anointing and the anointing breaks and destroys the yoke, the burden. I want to be emphatic here-persevere with this verse- days, weeks, months, years if need be. never give up, never give in- I am your Healer!

"Jesus turned and saw her. take heart, daughter, He said, your faith has healed you. and the woman was healed from that moment." matthew 9:22

"wisdom is the principle thing; therefore, get wisdom though it cost you all you have, get understanding. esteem her, and she will exalt you; embrace her and she will honor you." proverbs 4:7,8

sit at His feet. spend time with Him. there is excellence there. that time is pure and full of peace. it will nourish you and give you fresh anointing for each day. what does that mean? maybe you haven't experienced My anointing yet- the flow of God's power. time with Me will be a beautiful embrace where I have the leeway to allow you to hear and feel Father God's heart. lay your head on His chest, on His shoulder. hear His heartbeat. shema! listen! he who has an ear to hear, let him listen to what I am saying. to you that overcome "I will give a white stone with a new name written on it." revelation 2:17

God gave solomon riches, honor, and wisdom, yet he turned from the daily, sanctified connection with the Lord and allowed the worship of false idols, negating his gift. he died at sixty years old, reigning for only forty years because of this. LISTEN!

"as the rain and snow come down from heaven, so is My Word that goes out from My Mouth: it will not return to Me empty, but will accomplish all that I desire and achieve the purpose for which I sent it." isaiah 55:11

"as soon as simon peter heard him say, it is the Lord, he wrapped his outer garment around him, and jumped into the water." john 21:7

peter was disillusioned after the crucifixion. he was angry and discouraged. the enemy tried to tell him, and us, that it was all worthless. Jesus comes to the lake, sees peter, prepares a meal for him, and then begins to restore him.

God finds you when you are at the bottom of yourself and your

self-sufficiency, when you think you have failed and will never be of any use to the Kingdom.

Jesus restores you carefully, just in the way you need. He isn't surprised by anything you will do. He doesn't reject you in those moments.

do you love Him?

not, have you made a mistake.

do you love Him?

not, have you gone back on your word.

do you love Him?

not, are you perfect.

say yes to the inquiry, do you love Him? no other inquiry is as important.

"peace I leave with you; My peace I give you. I do not give to you as the world gives. do not let your heart be troubled and don't be afraid." john 14:27

"for You created My inmost being; You knit me together in my mother's womb. i praise You because it am fearfully and wonderfully made." psalm 139:13,14

God hasn't put you on earth to live an ordinary life. He has given you unique abilities and ideas. you were created for amazing things in life- think of this, you are fashioned in His very image.

think of all the thousands of different types of animals in the world. think of all the millions of stars and planets, innumerable by scientific standards. think of the very dna that makes up your own body- look at the organs, the neural pathways of the brain, the immense capacity of the heart to love- all endless and limitless!

ordinary is now extraordinary! I am the One whose Name is so prominently connected to you that as you are forming and birthing, I see and participate with you there. I have been putting in the work since day one of your creation in the womb. can you see that, can you understand?

"when we tell you these things, we do not use words that come from human wisdom. instead, we speak words given to us by the Spirit, using the Spirit's words to explain spiritual truths...for who can know the Lord's thoughts? who knows enough to teach Him? but we understand these things, for we have the mind of Christ." 1 corinthians 2:13,17 "then He returned to His disciples and found them sleeping. simon, He said to peter, are you asleep? could you not keep watch with Me for one hour? watch and pray so that you will not fall into temptation, for the spirit is willing but the flesh is weak." mark 14:37,38

not only has peter let the Lord down by not staying awake when He asked him to, but peter goes on to betray Him, disavowing knowing Him at the worst possible time- when Jesus was most alone. yet, peter's weakness was what made him qualified for forgiveness and honor; he is even chosen to head the Church!

you may not feel qualified. you may even feel broken and useless. but don't worry- I am in the Restoration business- I am the Repairer of Walls and the Mender of Breaches. I can replace, retrieve, reinstate, re-establish and rejuvenate you. if you fail or fall, you don't have to hide or pretend with Me because I already know all about it! just come and tell Me what you're feeling. I am actively redeeming you, actively rescuing you, and on your side at all times.

"so you, too, must keep watch! for you don't know what day your Lord is coming. understand this: if a homeowner knew exactly when a burglar was coming, he would keep watch. you also must be ready all the time, for the Son of Man will come when least expected." matthew 24:42-44 "commit to the Lord whatever you do and your plans will succeed." proverbs16:3

commit.

what does that word mean to you? commit means to keep going, no turning back, to dedicate yourself.

are there things you don't feel so excited about, but you are committed so you persevere? nobody said you have to always like it, but are you getting better at it? do you complain less? do you look for the blessing more? do you see the successes despite the minor setbacks? you may have heard, "your setbacks are a set-up" for My grace to reign completely in you. repeat that out loud right now. "my seeming setbacks are a set-up for Your grace to reign completely in me. amen." keep following the dream I gave you--a dream written down becomes a goal, a goal with steps to it becomes a plan, and a plan with action becomes reality!

now go and get excited about My purpose in you! fear is excitement in need of an attitude adjustment and I am the Adjuster!

"we can rejoice when we run into problems and trials, for we know that they help us develop endurance, that perseverance develops strength of character, and character, the confident hope of salvation. and this hope will not lead to disappointment, because God has poured out His love into our hearts by the Holy Spirit, Whom He has given us." romans 5:3-5 "as iron sharpens iron, so a friend sharpens a friend." proverbs 27:17

God the Father knew you and chose you, according to His foreknowledge, through the sanctifying work of the Spirit, sanctifying meaning that I have made you holy! 1 peter 1:2

even though you may know that in your head, sometimes I see you get mad, overly sad in extended depression, disappointed, discouraged, and just overwhelmed by life. I want to tell you firmly that although I created you to be an emotive being, these dark emotions are not from Me and do not serve you. they are a normal part of human experience though. when you feel them, it doesn't mean you are defective, just the opposite! it means you are real- really human! a good cry can be cathartic. Jesus Himself was "a Man of Sorrows." yet, He allowed the emotions to flow through, not becoming stuck in the darkness, moving through toward God's redeeming light and love.

I am grieved a lot! throughout history I have watched you torture and kill each other, lie and hurt each other. I've also watched you encourage, exhort, and self-sacrificially give to one another. when you begin to feel negative emotions like fear, desire for revenge, extreme grief or pain- immediately come and cast them on Me through worship, prayers of thanks in the midst, and meditating on My Promises.

"in a wealthy home, some utensils are made of gold and silver, and some are made of wood and clay. the expensive utensils are used for special occasions, and the cheap ones are for everyday use. keep yourself pure and you will be a special utensil for honorable use. your life will be clean, ready for the Master to use you for every good work." 2 timothy 2:20,21 "the Spirit clearly says that in the latter times some will turn away from (abandon) the true faith; they will follow deceptive teachings and spirits." 1 timothy 4:1

yes, I am clearly stating this. I want you to be very aware, so that you are not participating in or condoning any open, expressed sin. okay, here we go, putting down the Plumbline, the high standard of holiness that no person has ever been able to keep. the letter of romans correctly says that all men sin and fall short of the glory of God. I am asking you, pleading with you, don't be judgemental as you hold this standard out or you will drive away the very people I am sending to you. like the samaritan woman at the well, prod gently with My love, while also correcting as you feel My discerning direction.

iron not only sharpens iron but purifies it, refines it, brings out its luster and beauty. it is often not pleasant when it is occurring, the pruning, the refining. feed your soul with silence and some solitude in those times and I will help you through. you will feel alone, but not lonely- that's when I can reveal Myself more clearly to you.

"but who will be able to endure the day of His coming? who will be able to stand and face Him when He appears? for He will be like a blazing fire that refines metal, or like a strong soap that bleaches clothes. He will sit as a Refiner and Purifier of silver, burning away the dross." malachi 3:2,3 "who are you? they demanded. Jesus replied, the One I always claimed to be. I have much to say about you and much to condemn, but I won't. for I say only what I have heard from the One Who sent Me, and He is completely truthful. but they still didn't understand that He was talking about His Father. so Jesus said, when you have lifted up the Son of Man on the cross, then you will understand that I am He." john 8:25-28

I want to go a little deeper with you. in john 16:13, Jesus reveals "when the Spirit of truth comes, He will guide you into all truth. He will not speak on His own, but will tell you what He has heard. He will tell you about the future. He will bring Me glory by telling you whatever He receives from Me."

God the Father, God the Son, God the Holy Spirit.

We are co-equal, co-eternal, cooperating always together as We Create(d), Redeem(ed), and Comfort(ed) you.

as such, the Trinity co-exists together as One. I am active in you now. Jesus has finished His redemptive work and sits at the Father's right hand, yet still interceding as your High Priest. Father God decides when and how things progress from here.

God is the Great I AM.

I am eternal within you.

Jesus is before time began- the Word.

the First, the Last.

the Alpha, the Omega.

the Aleph, the Tov.

Start to Finish complete.

the Beginning and the End.

"I and the Father are One." john 10:10

"for the Lord Himself will come down from heaven with a commanding shout, with the voice of the archangel, and with the trumpet (shofar) call of God." 1 thessalonians 4:16-18

"blow the trumpet in zion." joel 2:15

"on the day of atonement, sound the shofar." leviticus 25:9

I have purposely left My "catching up" mystery ambiguous to you, so that you would be ready at any moment. if you knew exactly when Messiah would come, some of you would delay your urgency and passion until that time.

instead, like a child, full of expectancy for the next exciting thing, stand ready for My arrival! you can speculate if that heightens your sense of immediacy, but don't argue over when it will be. spend your time living humbly, simply, with as much grace and gratitude as you can in the midst of the thrills and challenges of life.

I am coming soon!

"but you aren't in the dark about these things, dear brothers and sisters, and you won't be surprised when the day of the Lord comes like a thief. so be on your guard, not asleep like the others...Christ died for us so that, whether we are dead or alive when He returns we can live with Him forever. so encourage one another with these words." 1 thessalonians 5:4,6, &10

"come let us return to the Lord. He has torn us to pieces; now He will heal us. He has injured us, now He will bandage our wounds." hosea 6:1

returning, in hebrew "teshuvah", is a common theme throughout the Bible. if you will notice though, it was suggested mostly before Jesus came as He IS your Return! it is still important that you recognize where you have gone astray, made a mistake, or deliberately sinned. You will often need to repent, just know that it all is fully covered by your innate awareness of redemption and full forgiveness.

"and we know that God causes everything to work together for the good of those who love God and are called according to His purpose for them." romans 8:28

once in relationship with Jesus, past, present, and future sins are covered by grace for all time! catch that! catch the fire of gratitude and wonder in your heart. catch the cool rain of forgiveness as it drops on your hand and tongue. shema! hear the clarion call of the shofar telling you the Day of Atonement is here now and forever! this is the Jubilee year!

"for if you return to the Lord, your relatives and your children will be treated mercifully by their captors, and they will be able to return to this land. for the Lord your God is gracious and merciful. if you return to Him, He will not continue to turn His Face from you." 2 chronicles 30:9

"then God created man in His own image, in the image of God He created them; male and female He created them." genesis 1:27

I created all human life- the merging of the ovum and the sperm, the zygot. the instant they merged, that instant, you were alive and had an imbued spirit from Me. at six weeks, you had a measurable heartbeat, although I heard it beat before then.

I am the Advocate for the unborn who cannot cry out from the womb. children are a beautiful part of My Holy Covenant. until the age of reason, each precious child that dies is immediately in My Presence. they are innocent and pure, yet helpless. many say that their souls are not relevant, collateral tissue. I say that they are the most treasured members of My Kingdom.

"one day some parents brought their children to Jesus so He could touch them and bless them; but the disciples scolded the parents for bothering Him. when Jesus saw what was happening, He said to them, let the children come to Me and forbid them not, for the Kingdom of God belongs to those who are like these children. I tell you the truth, anyone who doesn't receive the Kingdom of God like a child will never enter it. then He took the children in His arms and placed His hands on their heads and blessed them." mark 10:13-16 "in Him we have redemption through His Blood, the forgiveness of sins in accordance with the riches of God's grace that He laid on us with all wisdom and grace." ephesians 1:7

Father God is so rich in kindness and love that He didn't give you what you deserved. He purchased your freedom with His own Blood. now you are totally under that Blood, cleansed and transformed.

this Blood is always and eternally sufficient and powerful, although applying the Blood increases its efficacy. what does that mean, to apply the Blood? pray and intercede for yourself and others saying, "cover them, protect them from any injury, illness, danger, or accident in the Name of Jesus and by Your Blood. amen." this is an extremely effective warfare prayer and brings angels, thousands, to your aid! also, speak about Jesus' sacrifice with a thankful heart and share with others what He has personally done for you. this honors His Blood sacrifice and gives protection.

"remember that the heavenly Father to Whom you pray has no favorites...for you know that He paid a ransom to save you from the empty life you inherited from your ancestors. and the ransom He paid was not mere gold or silver. it was the precious Blood of Christ, the sinless, spotless Lamb of God." 1 peter 1:17-19

"I know your deeds, that you are neither cold nor hot. I wish you were one or the other! so, because you are lukewarm-neither hot nor cold- I will spit you out of My Mouth." revelation 3:15,16

one of Jesus' titles is "the Lion of the tribe of judah." revelation 5:5 He will return with great power and ferocity.

the Church, at its best self, is the lioness, the Bride of Christ, "ariel" in the hebrew. I want you to understand this analogy. in the natural, the lioness is the main hunter in the pride. I give you this example so that you will remain very brave and bold as people or events come against you. there will always be push back against the heavenly agenda, always those who will take offense. in fact, if you aren't experiencing attack, you may be too complacent in your walk.

I urge you to stand firm and not compromise. trust Me to keep you from any imminent danger or attack and to tell you when to fight and when to wait. an adult male lion's roar can be heard up to five miles away and can warn off intruders or reunite scattered members of the tribe. listen for My Voice above all others! I will make it commandingly loud for you!

"trust in the Lord with all your heart and lean not on your own understanding. in all your ways acknowledge Him and He will direct your paths." proverbs 3:5,6

"i will meditate on all Your works." psalm 77:12
"i will meditate on Your wonders." psalm 119:27
"i will meditate on Your promises." psalm 119:148

perhaps you have sought out meditation instruction- oh, and the enemy was really quick in copycatting that! "think about a mantra", he says. "empty your mind" is another directive, or worst of all, don't have any parameters at all, just allow your mind to go wherever it wants to. can you see the subtle fallacies in these deceptive teachings?

I call you to meditate on and memorize the accurate and powerful Word of God, My promises, and all the wonderful blessings I have given you and the ways I have protected and guided you. the Word of God has many layers, layer upon layer upon layer.

you can read the Word superficially or you can go deeper. which do you want? I call on you to meditate on the perfection of My love, My holiness, My Name. this is a life-changing practice. begin today to memorize one verse that is meaningful to you (maybe you already have memorized many verses, I hope!). take the verse and break it down. break it down word by word and meditate on it. I will bless that obedience.

"and now, brothers and sisters, one final thing. fix your thoughts on what is true, honorable, and right, pure, lovely, and admirable. meditate on things that are excellent and praiseworthy." phillipians 4:8

"be prepared in season and out of season; correct, rebuke, and encourage- with great patience and careful instruction." 2 timothy 4:2

here, paul wrote from prison and knew his time on earth was coming to a close. he had fought hard, endured much persecution, finished his race, and kept his faith. what a great testimony! I was there with him, inspiring him as he wrote this, one of his last letters to his protege timothy. I want you to have the same strong life of integrity and honor.

when Father God decides to bring this world to a close, all the effort and sacrifice you have made will be worthwhile! I can tell how much faith you have because of the thankfulness and gratitude you exhibit in your life. there are days when you feel you are in a storm and there are halcyon days, peaceful and calm, as when the waves lap quietly to shore.

stay the course, eagerly awaiting My return and the climax of history. I'm trying to inspire you to be hungry for Christ! are you overly involved with the world or are you longing for My arrival there?

"now there is in store for me the crown of righteousness, which the Lord, the Righteous Judge will award to me on that day- and not only to me, but to all who have longed for His appearing." 2 timothy 4:8

"shadrach, meshach, and abednego (their hebrew names are hananiah, mishael, and azariah- the first three names were babylonian names) replied, o nebuchadnezzar, we do not need to defend ourselves before you. if we are thrown into the blazing furnace, the God whom we serve is able to save us. but even if He doesn't, we want to make it clear to you, your majesty, that we will never serve your gods or worship the gold statue you have set up." daniel 3:16-18

nebuchadnezzar- a strange name, right? he was given great power and influence as the anointed king after the reign of king cyrus, but he succumbed to ego and pride, building a large golden statue that he ordered people to bow down and worship. this is the way the world operates, subtly infecting our thoughts and actions, little by little, until we start to do things we would never imagine ourselves doing. instead, I want to ignite you with My Fire- within the fiery furnace is your victory!

I have given you infinite potential and will orchestrate immense opportunities for you today! how will you use them? use them to further the Kingdom and I will give you favor in all aspects.

that's not to say you won't have times when things don't go your way. in fact, I told you before, the more you are seeking to advance the Kingdom purposes, the more the enemy will come against you. I don't think you will be literally thrown into a furnace or lion's den anytime soon though! however, figuratively, you are in the same circumstances as that great man of faith, daniel. be very bold and courageous, as he was!

"this is the message that was written- "mene,mene (numbered), tekel (weighed), parsin (divided)." daniel 5:25

"one man of you shall chase a thousand, for the Lord your God is He Who fights for you." joshua 23:10

one hundred and ninety times in the Bible the Lord uses the word "fight" and says He will fight for you. do you believe Him and His Word of Promise?

it doesn't seem that there is any solution possible in the natural for the situation you are in sometimes- good! that's where I do My best work! I am not making light of the battle you are in, not at all, in fact, just the opposite. this day to day struggle is a serious thing and has immeasurable consequences, especially in the spiritual realms.

the passage above was in the final words of joshua to the people he had lead the many years. here, joshua was of an advanced age, one hundred and ten years old! he exhorts the israelites to be very courageous- the same words God spoke to him many years earlier. he repeated those words incessantly to himself in private many times throughout his life (I heard him) as he encouraged and built himself up in the Lord.

edify yourself today! speak My promises frequently out loud to yourself, and to others. real spiritual power can whisper and still get its point across. speak Scripture to a situation!

be very strong and courageous as you go out to battle!

"the battle belongs to the Lord, and He will fight for us." 1samuel 17:47

"but ruth replied, do not entreat me to leave you nor forsake you. whither thou goest, i shall go and whither thou stayest i shall stay. thy people shall be my people, and thy God shall be my God." ruth 1:16

naomi had lost everything- her husband and both sons, her home. there was a severe famine and so she had to leave her home to travel to moab. in this story, ruth is the faithful daughter-in-law. she was dedicated and loyal to naomi, and in response God provided boaz, her Kinsman Redeemer, a shadow and type of Christ. boaz marries her and provides all she needs.

are you lost? feeling hopeless and bereft?

stay dedicated. persevere! the Lord will bring you through- and give you the hundredfold blessing as reward besides. this Mystery gives peace to your longing, for the Kingdom is outside of time's boundaries. God knows everything you have ever done or will do. the Cross, where all your sins were purged, is truly outside the dimension of time. Jesus saw it all!

nothing shocks Me for I am beyond time.

"there is no one like the God of israel. He rides across the heavens to help you, across the skies in majestic splendor. the eternal God is your Refuge, and underneath are the Everlasting Arms." deuteronomy 33:26,27 "yet jerusalem says, the Lord has forgotten us. never! can a mother forget her nursing child? can she feel no love for the child she has borne? but even if that were possible, I would not forget you! see, I have engraved your name on the palms of My Hand." isaiah 49:14-16

this means YOU- personally and individually important to Me, as each of your children and grand-children are important to you.

real and lasting self-worth comes from your loving Relationship with Me and from consciously creating a life that is authentically yours. answer these questions- maybe write down the answers and then ask Me about the timing. I will help. it is worthwhile to reflect on what brings you purpose and equanimity.

what is unique about you?
what brings you joy when you spend time doing it?
what steps do you need to take to achieve these goals?
what can you contribute to the world?

"but now, thus says the Lord, Who created you, o jacob, and He Who formed you, o israel, fear not, for I have redeemed you, I have called you by name, you are Mine. when you pass through the waters, I will be with you and through the rivers, they shall not overflow you. when you walk through the fire, you shall not be burned, nor shall the flame scorch you." isaiah 43:1,2

"O God, we thank You and praise Your glorious Name! but who am i, and who are my people, that we could give anything to you? everything we have has come from You, and we give You only what You first gave us! we are here for only a moment, visitors and strangers in the land. our days on earth are like a passing shadow, gone so soon without a trace." 2 chronicles 29:13-15

I draw to your awareness many remembrances, memories, of God the Father's goodness and provision to you. rehearse His deeds of grace- speak of them when you get up in the morning. if you are blessed with a spouse, talk together at night as you lay on the bed about how the Lord blessed you that day. did He keep you from a near accident at an intersection or a tire blowing out beside you? did He give favor at your workplace? did your children do well and come home safely from school?

the human tendency is to grumble or murmur, as the israelites did. but negative words delay and sometimes stop My blessing in your life. notice all the thousands of small, ordinary moments each day. each of them have eternal significance. give thanks out loud and often! you could fill a book with hundreds of things to be grateful for each day! why don't you? write them down!

"we love because He first loved us." 1 john 4:19

"this i recall to my mind, therefore i have hope. the Lord's lovingkindnesses indeed never cease, for His compassion never fails. His mercies are new every morning. great is Thy faithfulness." lamentations 3:21-23

good morning, My child! how are you today? I hope you slept well. whether you wake up feeling good or feeling pain in your body or mind- to awaken is a blessing! do you have a beloved one next to you, a warm, comfortable bed and home, family, friends, health, enough food? you are blessed!

grace upon grace is upon you today. every time you use up the grace you need, more comes! grace and truth came to you through Jesus Christ. you cannot separate grace and truth. what God has joined together let no man put asunder.

if you earn it- it's not grace. grace is a free gift.

if you work for it- it's not mercy. mercy is undeserved.

grace and mercy produce power and strength, and they are given as a gift, new every morning like the manna in the wilderness. unmerited favor- you get what you don't deserve. what a magnificent plan- all is forgiven!

"God saved you by His grace when you believed. and you can't take credit for this; it is a gift from God. salvation is not a reward for the good things we have done, so none of us can boast about it. for we are God's masterpiece. He has created us anew in Christ Jesus, so we can do the good things He planned for us long ago." ephesians 2:8-10

"lift up your hands in the sanctuary and bless the Lord."
psalm 134:2

"joshua commanded the people, shout! for the Lord has given you the city." joshua 6:16

let's meditate on the purpose and function of praise and worship. when joshua conquered jericho, guess who marched around the walls in the forefront? the worshipers! those blowing the shofar, musicians. worshipers, and singers, preceded the return of the Ark of the Covenant to jerusalem. worshipers are the forerunners, the watchmen on the wall. they are always on the forefront of the battle, along with pastors. pray for them diligently!

so, praise comes first- exuberant singing, dancing, and lifting of the hands are all appropriate. in corporate gatherings, praise stimulates and exhorts, meaning builds up, the Body of Christ. then, praise will shift into a more quiet, deeper communion with God. here, with others who are worshiping in Spirit and truth, you bless the Lord. angels continually surround the Lord's Throne and you can join them in adoration and honor at any time in your daily life. worship flows energetically from the communion in the Holy of Holies. deepen your relationship with Me through worship. it takes time- wait in silence and allow My Presence to rest with you.

"enter His gates with thanksgiving and into His courts with praise." psalm 100:4

"after the death of joshua, the israelites asked the Lord, which tribe should go first to attack the canaanites? the Lord answered, judah, for I have given them victory over the land." judges 1:1,2 "in addition, you must count off seven sabbath years, seven sets of seven years, adding up to forty nine years in all. then on the Day of Atonement in the fiftieth year, blow the ram's horn long and loud throughout the land. set this year apart as holy, a time to proclaim freedom for all who live there. it will be a Jubilee Year for you!" leviticus 25:8-10

I am Suddenly!

I sometimes act quickly, using that suddenly for many purposes. things are increasingly speeding up in the natural realm now, as are events in the spiritual realm. do you notice this? the present dispensation is called the Church Age and it is the end times of the Church Age. soon, I will be removed from the world and every believer whom I indwell will also be removed. the antichrist will then come to power. this is not a fantasy or a delusion. things are setting up for it right now, in fact, everything is in its place. I know when enough is enough.

be ready! for it will come as a "suddenly." keep a strong focus on Jesus in your daily walk and life's endeavors. also, keep an eagle's eye on occurrences in israel, and jerusalem in particular. I have reestablished jerusalem as the capital of israel, in a major prophetic fulfillment. I don't want you to act with alarm; but be vigilant and keep watch! alert others in discerning ways so that it is palatable for each as they need. Jesus is close at hand, even at the door.

"don't you remember what i told you about all this when i was with you? and you know what is holding him back, for he can be revealed only when his time comes. for this lawlessness is already at work secretly, and it will remain secret until the One holding it back steps out of the way." 2 thessalonians 2:5-7 "the Lord Jesus, on the night in which He was betrayed, took bread, and when He had given thanks, He broke it and said, take, eat, this is My Body given for you." 1 corinthians 11:23-25

I hope you participate in taking communion regularly and often! it is a celebration remembrance and gives you great strength and healing. you can do this even in your own home, particularly if you have a spouse who will agree with you on the blessing and participate with you. this way, you can take communion on a daily basis, after thanks as Jesus did, and before your regular meal. this will edify you and help to break any illness or injury off your body. communion opens your eyes to see Jesus! (luke 24: 35)

when you gather together for worship and the Word, the effect of communion becomes more pronounced. everyone is in agreement and that unity brings power. by the way, it doesn't matter the size of the Body, in fact, I only had twelve disciples at first. sometimes smaller is more powerful, like a family. don't despise the small things of Mine.

try your best to be, and stay, rooted into a local Body. attend faithfully! pray for your pastors. tithe. speak well of everyone God brings together. encourage one another! I founded the Body, through Jesus, peter, paul, lydia, timothy, and others. she is important- the beautiful Bride of Christ!

"for where two or three are gathered together in My Name, there am I in the midst of them." matthew 18:20

"then make the Ark's cover- the Mercy Seat, the Place of Atonement- from pure gold. it must be 45 inches long and 27 inches wide. then make two cherubim from hammered gold and place them on the two ends of the Atonement Cover. mold the cherubim, making it all of one piece of gold. the cherubim will face each other and look down on the Atonement Cover, with their wings spread above it. they will protect it." exodus 25:17-20

God the Father says to moses, "I will meet you here and talk with you." how incredible it seems that God would deign to talk face to Face with moses. and yet, that is your priceless opportunity every single moment of every single day as long as you are alive! and then into eternity! God wants to talk with you! Jesus wants to reminisce with you! I want to laugh happy tears with you!

through the Word you have hidden (memorized, meditated on) in your heart, through praise and singing, within the utter silence of worship, come to the Holy of Holies, where I am. the veil is torn for you to enter!

"then Jesus said, let's go off by ourselves to a quiet place and rest." mark 6:31

"darkness fell across the land until three o'clock and suddenly the curtain of the Temple was torn in two. then, Jesus shouted, Father, I entrust My Spirit into Your Hands." luke 23:45, matthew 27:51, and mark 15:38

"job stood up and tore his robe in grief. then he shaved his head and fell to the ground to worship saying, i came naked from my mother's womb and i will be naked when i leave. the Lord gave what i had, and the Lord has taken it away. praise the Name of the Lord. in all this, job did not sin by blaming God." job 1:20, 21

job had lost children, health, home, livestock, career- everything except his wife. a final encounter with the Lord afterward draws him to a more profound faith and a restoration.

no matter how bad things look, no matter how awful things may be at this time for you, no matter what you've been through- there will come a time when you will be able to use this experience for something positive.

I am more than willing to show you how much I love you and to confirm exactly how I want to use this situation and you- will you allow Me to?

notice the fear, identify it, call it out or get quiet with it (satan doesn't like to be called out) and then release it to Me.

"we overcome by the Blood of the Lamb and the word of our testimony." revelation 12:11

"i baptize you with water, but He will baptize you with the Holy Spirit." mark 1:8

baptism is a public declaration of faith, a commitment- there's that word again. I make a Covenant, holy and irrevocable, with you when I enter into your spirit. I give you complete and unconditional acceptance. your part is just to say yes and then rest in that love!

your baptism will be a thrilling and joyful moment for you! if there's an ocean or lake near you, be baptized there- the vast sky above, maybe even a rainbow will appear! then, when you come up out of the water you will feel and BE cleansed, renewed, and on fire! My Presence usually always contains a spark of enthusiasm and excitement.

no matter what age you are, if you haven't been baptized yet, do it- you won't regret it.

"for you were buried with Christ when you were baptized. and with Him you were raised to new life because you trusted the mighty power of God, Who raised Christ from the dead." colossians 2:12

"instead, let the Spirit renew your thoughts and attitudes. put on your new nature, created to be like God- truly righteous and holy." ephesians 4:23,24

you won't get this perfect all the time with all the pressures around and within. I'm so proud of you and the standards you do your best to uphold! yes, I get disappointed at your choices and even sad sometimes- it's just because I see your full potential and I want you to fulfill that here on earth. lashing out at people only brings you down, making a terrible situation worse.

remember when you were a child and didn't have to worry or even think about paying bills, making doctors or dentists appointments, servicing the car, getting directions, or driving. if you were blessed, your parents took care of all that. in the same way, come to Me, ask Me for what you need, trust My wisdom and timing. then, let go and go be a child- enjoy the life you have been given. I want that for you because I love you and I want you to be blessed! I want to kiss you, My child!

"unfailing love and truth have met together. Righteousness and peace have kissed!" psalm 85:10

"do not bring sorrow to (grieve) God's Holy Spirit by the way you live." ephesians 4:30

"if anyone is in Christ, he is a new creation." 2 corinthians 5:17

the butterfly goes through a long process of metamorphosis to transform from caterpillar to larvae to butterfly. it takes a long time to spin the chrysalis and then the waiting period as the change occurs. if someone were to interrupt the process and strip the silky threads off too soon, the caterpillar would die.

if baby sea turtles were plucked from the nest after hatching and carried to the water's edge, their legs would not be prepared for the swimming ahead of them.

life is a process of growth and preparation. you will understand when we are reunited. just linger in My Presence.

My Heart is a Nautilus shell, ever spiraling with grace.

My Heart is a Hidden Bird, that rejoices at morning.

My Heart is a Poinciana Tree in full bloom, the boughs bent with a profusion of flowers.

just keep being a divine sponge- absorbing as much of Me as you can daily!

"now we see in a mirror dimly, then we shall see face to Face." 1 corinthians 13:12

"but while he was still a long way off, his father saw him and was filled with compassion for him. he ran to his son, threw his arms around him, and kissed him." luke 15:20

the Father has such a tender and loving heart toward you. do you see that? He loves you and I love you, not in spite of your faults or mistakes, but because of them. your flaws, supposed flaws, make Me love you more! here in this story of the prodigal son, see how I <u>RUN</u> toward you! I have a love relationship with you that nothing you do can change. come back home- please don't put up barriers between you and I.

revelation says "God will wipe all tears from their faces." that means there are tears to wipe. I tell you, when you see Me, tears of joy will leap from your eyes! and then I, with My tender Hand, will wipe them away and look into your eyes- oh, those eyes I put the golden flecks in, those crystal blue eyes, those deep brown eyes. I can't wait for that day when I have those moments with you, looking into your eyes. see and know that this is reality, even though it seems to be "invisible" right now. there is no substitute joy on earth.

"his father said, look, dear son, you have always stayed with me and all I have is yours. we had to celebrate this day! your brother was dead and he's come back to life. he was lost but now is found." luke 15:31,32 "at that time, the Kingdom of heaven will be like ten bridesmaids, who took their lamps and went out to meet the bridegroom. five were foolish and five were wise. the foolish took their lamps but didn't take any oil with them." matthew 25:1-3

I love to give you foretastes of the radiance and perfection of heaven!

close your eyes and think back to that moment when the bride (maybe you) was walking down the aisle toward her groom. maybe you remember walking, maybe you were the one standing at the altar and waiting. have you ever noticed how the bride's eyes shine with the complete joy and confidence in her beloved's love?

every time you attend a wedding or see a video of that moment, you can feel the feeling being recaptured. there is a principle in the spiritual realm called the Replacement Principle. God has a replacement of joy and grace for whatever has come against you to kill, steal, or destroy. He will give beauty for ashes, the oil of gladness for your mourning. He will give back all the years the locust have eaten!

if you are divorced, or your spouse has "graduated", that love is not lost or worthless. if single, keep praying for God's best spouse for you or dedicate yourself to service. the joy of the Lord is your strength and I will dance with you at that wedding celebration!

"let us rejoice and be glad, giving the glory to Him, for the time has come for the wedding feast of the Lamb and His Bride has prepared herself...and the angel said to me, write this: blessed are those who are invited to the marriage feast of the Lamb." revelation 19:7,9 "therefore, this generation will be held responsible." luke 11:50

in the verse above, Jesus speaks to those who are in the End Age. you are in training for ruling and reigning! if you are young, below twenty years old, recognize that you are in the Benjamin Generation. don't let anyone look down on you or negate your influence- see how the youth are rising up in the world for their particular secular causes- your voice should be just as effective for the Lord! I have given this generation great favor, just as jacob gave benjamin. act boldly!

if you are in the mid-life season, put more energy and focus into the Kingdom than your career, or even your family. be My ambassador. God is First, family second, work third. take a stand and hold to that firmly amid the many distractions!

if you are mature, wisely use your time as a prayer warrior and astute Watchman on the wall. don't let your passion or vigor dim! you are the generation that holds the office to inspire the youth and move the Hand of God. persevere in prayer!

your legacy is every life you've touched.

"take note of the fortified walls and tour all the citadels, that you may describe them to future generations." psalm 48:13

"the seed fell among the thorns, which grew up and choked the plants. still other seed fell on fertile ground where it produced a crop- a thousand, sixty, or thirty times what was sown. he who has ears, let him hear." matthew 13:7-9

Jesus gave seven Kingdom parables in matthew chapter 13. the number seven is the number of completion and perfection in the spiritual. I highly suggest you study all seven parables, but let's focus here on the parable of the sower. as you speak with others in your day-to-day life, you are scattering seed. there will be hard, rocky people, disinterested ones, as well as those who are oppressed in various ways. keep speaking to them anyway, as you discern they can receive.

then, there will be good soil, just ready to soak up all the love and wisdom that you have. those people will benefit greatly, even miraculously, from your ministry as you interact with them. first of all, be a compassionate listener, as Jesus was. then, as you sow, focus on spiritual subjects- testimony is important and life changing! skillfully weave in what Jesus has done for you, and draw out what He has done for them.

that is how good soil will be fertilized, watered, and then grow to a great harvest! judge each day not by the harvest, that is My part, but by the seeds you plant and water!

"for God desires for all men to be saved and to come to the full knowledge of Christ Jesus." 1 timothy 2:4

"there is a time for everything, and a season for every activity under heaven." ecclesiastes 3:1

I am Timeless Eternity!

in "chronos", or natural time, you are in the twenty first century. in the spiritual realm, you are living in "cairos" time- waiting on God's timing for the seasons of your life. maybe in your life you feel like at this time you are stuck in the waiting mode, but My time is much different from yours. to Me, "a day is as a thousand years and a thousand years as a day." psalm 90:4 this is your "appointed time" in God, the right time for you.

I wait to see you and be with you with baited breath- I wait for you to want to come and see Me! time collapses in the eternal present- but I still miss you when you're busy with other things! linger with Me here in this moment. it's more important than the relationship you are praying to come. it's more important than the job or career you seek- your meaningful purpose is already working itself out in cairos time. you are both "in the world and not of it."

I know, I know, you cant see it yet! it is just up ahead a little bit- snap your fingers, it is here!

"for God saved us and called us to live a holy life. He did this not because we deserved it, but because this was His plan from before the beginning of time- to show us His grace through Christ Jesus." 2 timothy 1:9

"the Lord your God is with you, He is mighty to save. He will take great delight in you, He will quiet you with His love, He will rejoice over you with singing." zephaniah 3:17

I am the Gatherer and you are part of My Remnant, the Disapora! you were meant to be born in this era, at this exact time in history. I sent your particular spirit into your jar of clay, your body, and although I have this foreknowledge, you constantly amaze Me each day! you yourself realize that your own child will walk and speak one day; even so when the moment actually arrives, aren't you still proud and overjoyed for them? that's a tad of how I feel about you as I closely observe and applaud your accomplishments!

I want to sing to you. I want to let you hear My Voice-listen! be really still and I promise you I will make Myself known to you. it may be a natural event that symbolizes My Presence- such as thunder in the distance, a wind in the trees or wind chimes ringing, a cat's purring, the ocean's roar, a ukelele. these are foreshadows and slight imitations. let them carry you deep within. My greatest blessing to you is intimacy and relationship with Me- silence is the luxury I give for you to experience that closeness. close your eyes for just a moment here and tell Me what you hear. I am singing with utter abandon!!

"the third I will bring into the fire, I will refine them like silver and test them like gold. they will call on My Name and I will answer them." zechariah 13:9

"there is therefore now no condemnation for those who are in Christ Jesus." romans 8:1

I am Unconditional Love!

Father God loves all people, even those caught in deception, even those who don't love Him yet. that doesn't mean that He loves the rebellion or sin, not at all. it certainly doesn't mean that He sweeps your sin under the rug, not at all. He brings it right out into the Light and transforms it through Jesus' sacrifice. He is compassionate enough to know that You need His love to be restored. so don't feel guilty! I can use conviction to turn you away from a bad choice, but on the whole, guilt and shame are from the enemy. if you are hurting and feeling hopeless, caught in addiction or blatant sin that you know is not right, please let Me help you. I "am for you, not against you." My grace is always abounding toward you- you are swimming in My grace. there is a flood of Grace!

I AM!

I AM able

I AM able to do

I AM able to do what you ask

I AM able to do Above what you ask

I AM able to do Exceedingly Above what you ask

I AM able to do Exceedingly Abundantly Above what you ask.

I AM able to do Exceedingly Abundantly Above ALL that you ask or imagine! ephesians 3:20

beyond your wildest dreams! yet, it's not a matter of your feelings! you need to believe it even when you don't feel it or see it YET!

"we walk by faith, not by sight." 2 corinthians 5:7

"indeed, the very hairs on your head are numbered."
matthew 10:30

I am (often) Spontaneous!

follow My instructions immediately if you know that it is Me! when I ask you to delve deeply into the Word, just know that I will help you turn to the right book, chapter, and even the specific verse that you need. get your Bible please- hopefully it is right near you as you read this each day.

right now, open it to any area. as the Book falls open, spontaneously take your finger and place it on either page that the Bible falls open to. now read that section!

this is just one method I use. I will also bring to your mind passages, stories, or even topics, like patience or healing, that you can then research in the concordance in the back of your Bible or in a more detailed concordance. soon, the outlines and stories will become familiar and you will find yourself becoming intensely interested as you see Me confirm Myself in where I lead you to read. be an astute scholar of the Word.

"taste and see that the Lord is good." psalm 34:8

"but let me say this, dear brothers and sisters, the time that remains is very short. so from now on, those with wives should not focus only on their marriage. those who weep or rejoice or buy things should not be absorbed by their weeping or their joy or their possessions. for this world as we know it will soon pass away. I want you to be free from the concerns of this life." 1 corinthians 7:29-32

is it possible to be both present in the world and not present at the same time?

can you literally be in the world and not of it?

when you hold a newborn child in your arms, time suddenly suspends itself. you experience the fullness of time and eternity in those few precious moments. take a second here- I will leave some space, some silence, some space for silence. write what immediately captures you and draws and aligns you with Me into eternity.

what do you sense is My purpose for sending you to earth? go and pursue these purposes- and use the joy you find there to show others how!

"i was blind but now i see!" john 9:25

"instead, you must worship Christ as Lord of your life. and if someone asks you about your hope, always be ready to explain it. do this in a gentle and respectful way." 1 peter 3:15,16

draw closer to Me. I can mostly speak to you when there is complete silence, no distractions, although once I have Lordship of your life, you will know My Voice even in a crowd, even in a hurricane!

as your walk with Me progresses, our time together will become the center of your life, our Relationship the center of your being. it was that way at first, remember? remember the excitement when you said "yes" and stepped into that holy, set apart moment with Me? it was an exquisite time!

but over the years, the cares of the world hardened your heart a bit. open up to Me fully again! stay open in your heart each moment. I have so much in store for you- above all you can ask for from Me. wait until you see what I have prepared! keep hope- innocent, child-like hope- alive in you!

"therefore, we who have fled to Him for refuge can have great confidence as we hold to the hope that lies before us. this hope is a strong and trustworthy anchor for our souls. it leads us through the curtain into God's inner sanctuary." hebrews 6:18,19

"and this hope will not lead to disappointment. for we know how dearly God loves us, because He has given us the Holy Spirit to fill our hearts with love." romans 5:5

"I tell you the truth, if you have faith and don't doubt, you can do things like this and much more." matthew 21:21

why is it that weddings, your birthday, Christmas, and other special events bring such expectation and joy? isn't it because it is a time that makes you feel completely loved for a little while? at these times, others give you presents, hug you, pay attention to you with love- you feel special.

the majority of life is seemingly mundane, ordinary moments- walking, driving, preparing meals, cleaning and arranging- organizing a life. and that's okay- that's necessary. Jesus spent much of His time walking many miles. celebrate the day-to-day moments when faith is steady and no trial or attack is at hand. pause. breathe it in! it's not boring- it is priceless, just as you are to me! there is no one exactly like you in the whole world- you are My Christmas! You are My perfect, unique, one of a kind, son, daughter, child.

"Jesus turned around and when He saw her, He said, "daughter, be encouraged. your faith has made you well. and she was healed from that moment." matthew 9:12

"then john (the baptist) testified, i saw the Holy Spirit descending like a dove from heaven and resting on Him… so i testify that He is the Son of God." john 1:32

I point to You, Jesus.   what a beautiful Name- Jesus!

all the details of Scripture point to the excellence and loveliness of His character and His compassionate love. I devote much of My ministry to teaching and encouraging you, but I would be remiss if I didn't spend the majority of My time exalting and focusing on Jesus Christ- His offices, His Titles, His miracles, His very character.

let's start with one of the most often recorded Title, second only to Son of Man, which is how He referred to Himself primarily. Jesus, You are the Son of God. You were incarnated, through Me, began Your ministry, healed all who came to You, and never wavered from fulfilling the purpose for which You came- the redemption and sanctification of mankind as You conquered sin, satan, and death.

blessing and honor, wisdom and thanksgiving, all worship and power are due to You- the Only Incarnate Son of God!!!

"God showed us how much He loved us by sending His One and Only Son into the world so that we might have eternal life through Him." 1 john 4:9

"Jesus Christ is the same yesterday, today, and forever."
hebrews 13:8

Jesus Christ is Pre-existent, Pre-eminent, and Eternal! read
and meditate on john 1:1-3 again- "in the beginning, the Word
already existed. the Word was with God and the Word was
God. He existed in the beginning with God. God created
everything through Him and nothing was created except
through Him. the Word gave life to everything that was created
and His life brought Light to everyone. the Light shines in the
darkness and the darkness can never extinguish it." every time
you open the Bible, ask to see more of Jesus revealed.

Jesus Was, Is, and Is to Come.

Jesus is Pre-eminent, Above everyone and everything.

Jesus is All in All, the Lamb that was slain before the
foundation of the world.

amen.

there is nothing I can add that will state it any clearer.

"so the Word became human and made His home among
us." john 1:14

"behold, the Lamb of God, Who takes away the sins of the world." john 1:36

"but one of the twenty four elders said to me, stop crying! look, the Lion of the tribe of judah, the Heir to david's throne, has won the victory." revelation 5:5

these two titles work so effectively together that they complete each other. Jesus is the Lion and the Lamb! the lamb was the traditional sacrifice, unblemished and innocent, given as a substitution to remove all guilt and penalty, particularly on yom kippur. Jesus fulfilled this necessary function entirely. He was without sin and willingly gave Himself in your place. He was not murdered. He laid down His life for you of His own accord.

when He returns to earth for the second time in history, Jesus will come as a Lion to greet His people. nations that oppose israel and the Body will fall away like chaff. He will stand upon mount zion and roar His disapproval at all evil entities. He will also manifest full Deliverance and your complete freedom at that time.

"every knee shall bow, every tongue confess that Jesus Christ is Lord to the glory of God the Father." isaiah 45:23, romans 14:11, and philippians 2:10

"Jesus answered, I tell you the truth, before abraham was even born, I AM!" john 8:58

you probably know the story- when moses asked God the Father whom he should say sent him to pharoah, Father God replied, "tell them I AM sent you." exodus 3:14

the passage above leaves no doubt- Jesus Christ is not only the Son of God, He is God, co-equal and co-eternal. when He made this statement to the pharisees, He was accused of blasphemy and sentenced to die, and yet He didn't back down from the truth.

many other Titles, with great Authority, come from this Most Holy Place of I AM.

" I am the Bread of Life." john 6:35

" I am the Light of the world." john 8:12

" I am the Gate (the Door)." john 10:9

" I am the Resurrection and the Life." john 11:25

" I am the Way, the Truth, and the Life." john 14:6

an entire book could be written on each one of these Titles. they are full of such important revelation. know that you can never ever overestimate Jesus' influence and power!

"I and the Father are One." john 8:58

"martha said to Jesus, Lord, if only You had been here, my brother would not have died...Jesus said to her, I am the Resurrection and the Life. whosoever believes in Me will live, even after dying. everyone who lives and believes in Me will never die." john 11:25,26

I just couldn't skip past this Title- this story of lazarus' resurrection is a pivotal moment in history. Jesus had previously resurrected others- jairus' daughter, the widow's son, and probably others not recorded- but lazarus was His close friend and, significantly, this miracle occurred right before His own death and Resurrection. He gives life and " life more abundant!" see what perspectives He can change for you- believe, hope, receive- this is your God!

delving into this story offers so much comfort and hope, especially if you are temporarily separated from someone, as martha and mary were. but even more so it reveals the Omnipotence of Jesus as One with God. lazarus had been dead for four days, however Jesus transcended the bounds of time and flesh. at His friend's grave, the Word says, "He wept" but the weeping didn't raise lazarus. Jesus didn't just point His finger, mutely. He called out, "lazarus, come forth!" He spoke out loud and He got specific with who He wanted to raise from the dead. you do the same as you speak out your faith today.

"since we have been united with Him in His death, so shall we be resurrected as He was. we know that our old sinful selves were crucified with Christ so that sin might lose its power in our lives. we are no longer slaves to sin. for when we died with Christ we were set free from sin, and since we died with Christ, we know we will also live with Him." romans 6:5-8 "and God has given His Spirit as proof that we live in Him and He in us. furthermore, we have seen with our own eyes and now testify that the Father sent His Son to be the Savior of the world." 1 john 4:13, 14

I know you have heard this before, but it bears repeating- if you are drowning in an ocean, you don't need someone to teach you how to swim, you don't need to read about swimming- you need someone to rescue you!

once rescued, don't drift away! stay close to your Savior, your royal Lifeguard!

you were separated from God because of His Holiness and your sin. you were drowning. now, that chasm has been closed forever. I'm surprised it was never recorded that Jesus said He was the Bridge. as the Bridge, He made the Way for you to cross over and come at any time into the Holy of Holies, where God and Jesus sit on the Throne. so He took your place, giving you His Righteous, sinless character, and He continues each day to save you from your mistakes, bad choices, and satan's attacks.

Jesus saved you at the Cross.

He is saving you each moment that you need Him NOW.

He will save you and bring you into eternal, manifested communion with God.

"He generously poured out the Spirit upon us through Jesus Christ our Savior." titus 3:4

"for Christ did not enter into a holy place made with human hands, which was only a copy of the true one in heaven. He entered into heaven itself to appear now before God on your behalf. and He did not enter in again and again, like the high priest here on earth who enters the Most Holy Place year after year with the blood of an animal." hebrews 9:24,25

if you are spiritually mature, and hunger and thirst after a faith that's more than superficial, plunge into the book of hebrews chapters six through ten. yes, the whole five chapters! they detail Jesus' consummate work as our High Priest. He was the Sacrifice and is also the Priest Who offers the sacrifice. He is even now the Mediator for you! do you need anything today? ask Jesus to intercede for you!

although His propitiary (substitutional) work was finished at the Cross, afterward He was resurrected, walked the emmaus road, redeemed peter, exhorted thomas, and performed many other miracles in the forty days He was on earth in His glorified body.

Scripture says He is seated at God's right Hand. in His Timeless Identity. He is standing at the Altar, awaiting His Bride to revive and walk down the Aisle toward Him.

He is rising and coming in the clouds. He is riding the White Horse as King of Kings and Lord of Lords!

"it was necessary for Him to be made in every respect like us, His brothers and sisters, so He could be our merciful and faithful High Priest before God. since He Himself has gone through suffering and testing, He is able to hep us when we are being tested." hebrews 2:17,18

"I am the Alpha and the Omega- the Beginning and the End. to all who are thirsty I will give freely from the springs of the waters of life." revelation 21:6

four times in revelation I revealed this Title of Jesus to the apostle john. Jesus is the Aleph and the Tov, the hebrew letters for A and Z. He was there before genesis. He is present all through Scripture, every book revealing Him in different ways. He is coming back exactly as it is prophesied in revelation.

a further Word of Knowledge I want to show you- Jesus has no end. He is Eternal with God the Father and God the Holy Spirit. He completed the redemptive work for which He was sent, but He lives forever to reign in heaven.

you will reign with Him, each of you with diverse capacities according to your gifts and created abilities. I am preparing you for a fantastic heavenly reign! it begins here on earth as you stand, speak, and act with authority. reign in life! walk like the royalty you are, the son and daughter you are. hold you head up high! you are Mine!

"look! I stand at the door and knock. if anyone hears My Voice and opens the door, I will come in, and we will share a meal together as friends. those who are victorious will sit with Me on My Throne, just as I was victorious and sat with My Father on His Throne." revelation 3: 20,21

"there is a Friend Who sticks closer than a brother."
proverbs 18:24

think about your very very close friends, maybe the three people closest to you. Jesus had the devoted friends peter, james, and john. who are your closest friends? what sort of dynamic is involved in those intimate relationships of yours? do you interact with them daily? how?

I hope I am at the top of that list! I want to be your Friend and have time to talk directly with you! I am closer than a brother or sister, closer than a child of yours, closer than a spouse.

most people in the world, in fact the majority, shift and change according to how other people respond or react. not many have the courage to remain transparent and authentic in all times and places, as I do. I never change!

those people who are closest to you- reach out to them today- let them see your fears and worries- and then give those fears and worries to Me as you pray together, laugh, and cry together. I have made the bonds of human family and friends to be very strong for this exact purpose. as you bind together in love, you help one another make it through.

"greater love has no man than this, that he lay down his life for his friends." john 15:13

"inside the Tent of Meeting, the Lord would speak to moses face to face, as one speaks to a friend." exodus 33:11

"God has put all things under the authority of Christ and has made Him Head over all things for the benefit of the church. and the church is His Body, it is made full and complete through Christ, Who fills all things everywhere with Himself." ephesians 1:22

Jesus established the church through peter and the other apostles. they received ambassadorship through Him, as the Head of the church. I've told you how important it is to be in consistent and dedicated fellowship in the Body. don't give up meeting together and encouraging one another. it is your earthly form of covering and protection.

in just a little while, you will see how it was all necessary to the smooth transition to your Home here with Me. you're going to be such an effective leader, guide, worshiper, artist, chef, animal lover, writer, musician- fill in your desire and gift to serve! you already are walking in these areas now, in this prelude to eternity! enjoy your life in the world- I made it all for you!

"all the believers devoted themselves to the apostle's teaching, and to fellowship, and to sharing in meals, including the Lord's Supper, and to prayer. a deep sense of awe came over them all, and the apostles performed many miraculous signs and wonders. and all the believers met together in one place and shared everything they had." acts 2:42-44 "therefore, since we are surrounded by such a huge crowd of witnesses to the life of faith, let us strip off every weight that slows us down, especially the sin that so easily trips us up (ensnares us). and let us run with endurance the race God has set before us. we do this by keeping our eyes on Jesus, the Author and Finisher of our faith (the Champion Who Initiates and Perfects our faith)." hebrews 12:1,2

although you make, or hopefully have made, the free will choice of accepting salvation, Father God, in His Omnipotence, knows whose heart is open and willing. in that respect, God is the Initiator, giving you even the beginnings of your faith walk. oh, what grace!

then, as you walk the journey of faith, "He is faithful to complete that work" He began in you. philippians 1:6

your humble response to this is such a blessing to Me! I see how grateful you are, I see how sincere your faith is, and you bring Me tremendous joy! keep digging deep wells- people are thirsty to hear your powerful testimonies as they search for hope in this fallen world. that is a part of the reason why social media is so powerful and alluring today- people are looking for that connection. come primarily to Me for validation and you will have plenty of confidence and assurance as you move through life.

"justice will dwell in the wilderness and righteousness live in the fertile field. and this righteousness will bring peace, yes, quietness and confidence forever." isaiah 32:16,17 "for unto us a Child is born, unto us a Son is given. the government will be upon His shoulders and He will be called Wonderful." isaiah 9:6

you know how you feel when you listen to that louis armstrong song "what a wonderful world"? that's how I want you to feel when you are relating with Me. I want to help you to see and realize that your life is spectacular- there are people who don't even have the ability to buy food or have access to clean water. you have the luxury of silence, to come and hear My Voice. you have been given so many riches and blessings.

step back a moment. you are running at full speed- and all with good intentions, I see that! I just want you to come away for awhile. "arise, My darling, My beloved and come away! look, the winter is past; the rains are over and gone...catch all the foxes, those little foxes, before they ruin the vineyard of love, for the grapevines are blossoming!" song of solomon 2:10,11,15

too many distractions, too much busyness, and you miss the most precious moments I have prepared for you. children grow up in the blink of an eye. sunsets fade into evening. the years come and go, time moving quicker as you mature. cherish every second! see the wonderful in each moment. I provide just small glimpses, enough for you to step back and open your mouth in awe.

"in quietness and confidence is your strength." isaiah 30:15

"Counselor." isaiah 9:6

look unto Me for counseling, not worldly psychologists who spin things in unhealthy self-focus. look unto Jesus for your confidence. "for God has chosen the things the world considers foolish, things counted as nothing at all." 1 corinthians 1:27

can you look at the Word and its Promises? spend your time studying its precepts, instead of focusing on your circumstances.

God the Father chose the Servant place for Jesus. in that humble place is the protection from every attack. I use small things, seemingly weak things, the most powerfully- it doesn't make sense to your mind, I know. I'm asking you to let go of your natural deduction of this. get close with Jesus is what "look unto" means- for you are positionally powerful there. I see potential in you, so much potential! depend on Me to reveal those opportunities as you rest at My Feet.

when paul and the believers were having a disagreement, they met together and prayed. I revealed areas of agreement to them- read acts 15:22-35. here's a portion- "so we decided, having come to agreement, to send you official representatives, along with our beloved barnabas and paul, who have risked their lives for the name of our Lord Jesus Christ. we are also sending judas and silas to confirm what we have decided. for it seemed good and right to the Holy Spirit and to us to lay no greater burden." see how they deferred to Me in their discernment and decisions? do the same, child. seek wise counsel, pray, wait for agreement.

"martha, martha, the Lord replied, you are worried and upset about many things, but only one thing is needed. mary has chosen the better part and it will not be taken from her." luke 10:41,42 "the Mighty God" isaiah 9:6

I am interested in the details of your life! I am very focused on all the details of your life! I am mighty to save you from any danger or attack! each of these five names here reflect a different quality of My Godhead Nature. five reflects My grace- the five smooth stones from the river, the five loaves, the five talents given- and grace is the centerpiece of the mysterious Plan that Mighty God knew would cover the multitude of sins, the wrong choices, all the suffering.

the entire world is a platform to show forth God's might and glory and His grace will eventually bring everything into the state of perfection that will be eternal.

"may God give you more and more grace and peace as you grow in the knowledge of Him and our Lord Jesus... make every effort to respond to God's promises." 2 peter 1:2,5

"His Mighty Arm has done tremendous things." luke 1:51

"the Everlasting Father." isaiah 9:6

right relationship requires the right posture.
reread that a moment please.

today I want you to know, understand, and function in right Relationship with Me. you are My child and you are My friend. the Everlasting Father created you, crafted the plan of redemption, and inhabits you eternally by faith!

you are Righteous positionally as you accept this by faith. so don't take on the world's judgement or the enemy's fear! I am not frowning upon you, I am never disappointed in you. I promise that I will always be on your side! be confident in that.

once you have accepted My Highest Love, exhibited by Jesus, there is no more guilt or condemnation. it is handled! Jesus nailed it to the Cross- PAID FOR!

"because you are sons, God sent the Spirit of His Son into our hearts, the Spirit Who calls out, Abba, Father." galatians 4:6

"the Prince of Peace. His government and its peace will never end. He will rule with fairness and justice from the Throne of His ancestor david for all eternity. the passionate commitment of the Lord of heaven's armies will make this happen." isaiah 9:7

I want to open the Floodgates of peace for the world! there are governmental strongholds that I am working to dismantle, but I'm also interested in just individual hearts- in your heart specifically! I want you to know and feel My Peace deeply, even in the midst of painful emotions that wash over you like waves. settle underneath the turmoil at the surface and feel My calm.

I am your Threshold! I am the Plank that lies under the sill of the door. I am the Point at which a physiological effect begins to be produced, as the degree of stimulation of a nerve center produces a response. I am ABOVE the threshold of consciousness.

I am that Peace!

"this is what we speak, not in words taught us by human wisdom but in words taught by the Spirit, expressing spiritual truths in spiritual words...but we understand these things, for we have the mind of Christ." 1 corinthians 2:13,16

"God sent His Son into the world not to judge (condemn) the world, but to save the world through Him." john 3:17

you have been thoughtful and generous.

you have clothed yourself with humility, quickly offering love and forgiveness to others.

you have worshiped Me with energy, not caring who is watching.

you have lived, and are living even now, this moment, an amazing life, shining out to the world My love for them.

I am so proud of you! I want to brag on you and show the angels and the elders the faith testimony of your life! Well Done!

keep going! don't give up ever!

you are a radiant star in My Heaven!

"finally, all of you should be of one mind. sympathize with each other. love each other as brothers. be tenderhearted and keep a humble attitude." 1 peter 3:8

"there is no fear in love, for perfect love casts out fear." 1 john 4:18

fear is one of the devil's most powerful weapons. it keeps you down, afraid to step out in faith. it also keeps you from stepping out in the gifts I have imparted to you. fear keeps you isolated from others, making you feel powerless and worthless.

concentrate instead on My perfect love for you. tell other people about what I've done in your life, where I've brought you from, what I've brought you to!

in john chapter five, that paralytic man could not get to the water for healing; for thirty eight years he laid there. Jesus had compassion on him and gave him the healing he wanted! I don't want you to live in pain or physical suffering. come to Me. I distribute liberally, even to all generations. don't look in the natural- see clearly in the spiritual.hear My heart for you beyond the lapse of time.

"for the Spirit God gave us does not make us timid (I have not given you a spirit of fear), but gives us power, love, and a sound mind (self-discipline)." 2 timothy 1:7

"the Lord will cause your enemies who rise against you to be defeated before your face; they will come at you one way and flee before you seven ways." deuteronomy 28:7

I am the Boomerang!

people will say, what just happened? what's happening is that the plans of the enemy, all the evil, are all backfiring. it's all turning in on itself. the victory was already accomplished at the Cross and the Resurrection tomb, but it's all coming around to full manifestation in the natural. you see, the enemy can never resist trying to take things to the next more despicable level, therefore, that is his undoing. you must be as clever as the serpent, children. notice how he targets children, the elderly, even animals are not beneath his schemes, as he is a bully. when you resist the devil, he will flee, like the coward he is. his time and influence in the world is coming to an end quickly.

stand against him with the Power and Authority of Jesus Christ and His Blood, Who defeats him in every way, shape, and form. I am there giving you the direction, for I love you and don't want you to suffer.

"five of you will chase a hundred, and a hundred of you will chase ten thousand, and your enemies will fall by the sword before you." leviticus 26:8

"the eternal God is your Refuge, and underneath are the Everlasting Arms." deuteronomy 33:27

isn't it comforting and wonderful to have someone patiently listen to you, embrace you, and just say "everything is going to be alright"? even if they aren't entirely sure of that, or can't see what will happen up ahead, it still calms and relaxes you to hear it.

how much more so if Someone actually knew how and when everything was going to be alright? I am that Someone! My Everlasting Arms wrap around the world offering forgiveness and grace. I'm the Silver Lining to all the dark clouds.

if there is even the slightest chance that you feel in your spirit that the things I speak here are true, won't you give the benefit of the doubt and the benefit of faith? I decree that all these Promises will come to pass very soon and that everything will be made New!

"if only there were someone to arbitrate between us, to lay His hand upon us both, someone to remove God's rod from me, so that His terror would frighten me no more." job 9:33,34 "then a fire burns deep in my heart, it rages in my bones (it feels like fire shut up in my bones)." jeremiah 20:9

I'm sorry to have to reveal the depth of the evil of the enemy to you. I don't want it to taint your child-like faith or make you cynical, the world does enough of that to you. however, you must know- your adversary, the devil, prowls around like a roaring lion seeking whom he may devour (1 peter 5:8). he is vicious. he never has a second of leeway or mercy toward anyone. he doesn't care if children, even infants, suffer and die, in fact, he seeks the total destruction of the human race by any means necessary.

likewise, demons seek to torment you and bring you into bondage, even though you are filled with Me. they can't possess or enter your body once you believe, but they can try to plant thoughts, like suicide or addictive behaviors. they can wake you in the middle of the night, have you noticed?

during seasons of attack, especially in the night, grab your Bible immediately- even holding it is powerful! pray, stay near the Shepherd and in the middle of the flock (satan attacks at weak times when you are out on the periphery alone).

hey, My child, hey, son, hey, daughter- stay <u>right next to Me</u>. I will protect you!

"I am the Good Shepherd, Who lays down his life for His sheep. the hired hand is not the shepherd who owns the sheep. he cares nothing for them. so when he sees the wolf coming, he runs away." john 10:11,12 "blessed shall you be in the city, and blessed shall you be in the country. blessed shall be the fruit of your body, the produce of your ground, and the increase of your hands. blessed shall be your basket and your kneading bowl. blessed shall you be when you come in and blessed shall you be when you go out." deuteronomy 28:3-6

I command the blessings upon you! I impart the increase and favor- it flows from the Father toward Jesus and then through Me to you- this is the sacred Trinity in action. this is the Anointing that I bestowed on the high priest aaron, on king david, on many of the people I used throughout time.

this deuteronomic blessing has stood through time as My Covenant with the nation of israel and with any who come to defend her as her sister nations. it extends to the Body of Christ, My Emissary in the world. it also extends to you and your family individually. I will bless you from generation to generation as you stand in My love with faithfulness.

"the Lord will open to you His good treasure, the heavens to give the rain to your land in its season, and to bless all the work of your hand. you shall lend to many nations, but you shall not borrow. and the Lord will make you the head and not the tail; you shall be above only and not beneath." deuteronomy 28:12,13 "to comfort all who mourn, and provide for those who grieve in zion- to bestow on them a crown of beauty instead of ashes, the oil of gladness instead of mourning, and a garment of praise instead of the spirit of despair. they will be called oaks of Righteousness, a planting of the Lord for the display of His splendor." isaiah 61:3

you're not alone, you're not forgotten. you don't have to be strong all the time. even Jesus fell when He was carrying the Cross. even Jesus suffered anxiety on the Cross and cried out in despair. if something doesn't seem to turn out your way in the natural, trust Me, God will make it up to you and give you the hundred and thousand fold blessing for your trouble and pain!

look beyond this world and its problems and sorrows, its joys and appetites- lay your head on His chest, dwell within His very heart...

"instead of their shame, My people will receive a double portion, and instead of disgrace they will rejoice in their inheritance, and so they will inherit a double portion in their land, and everlasting joy will be theirs." isaiah 61:7

"the fundamental fact of existence is that this trust in God, this faith, is the firm foundation under everything that makes life worth living. it's our handle on what we can't see. the act of faith is what distinguished our ancestors, what set them above the crowd." hebrews 11:1

the foundation of God's throne is righteousness and truth. the foundation of your life is faith in that righteousness and truth. when things begin to shake in the natural, when your constructs fall away, that is the time to turn to Me. allow your faith to kick in, and stand up for what you believe! be on the "sunrise side of the mountain." trust that no matter how dark things appear, or how alone you may feel, it will all be worth it! the debris from the storm will clear and you will be standing authoritatively with Me.

faith comprehends as fact what cannot be seen or heard by the senses. I am a rewarder of faith- you can count on that promise!

"after job had prayed for his friends, the Lord made him prosperous again and gave him twice as much as he had before." job 42:10

"that same day two of Jesus' followers were walking to the village of emmaus, seven miles from jerusalem. as they walked along, they were deep in conversation, talking about everything that had happened. in the middle of their talk and questions, Jesus HIMSELF (emphasis Mine!) suddenly came and began walking with them. but God kept them from recognizing Him (restrained their eyes)." luke 24:13-16

Jesus appeared to these two before He even appeared to the eleven disciples! why do you think that is? He was giving an illustration of personal restoration. it was also a confirmation of the restoration of the edenic covenant that had been broken so long before.

these two weren't talking about the weather, hurricanes, storms. they weren't talking about their aches and pains, physical issues. they were meditating on and discussing the crucifixion and Jesus' life. He HIMSELF, not an angel, appeared to them to reveal Himself in the Word. that is why their eyes were restrained at first, so that they could see Him in the Scriptures and so that you from a distance of earthly time could see Him in the Scriptures as well.

I want you to have a personal emmaus everyday! whenever you meditate or speak God's Word, Jesus Himself will draw near to you and you will be restored. you will feel His depth of love for you and that love is inherently attractive. it draws people toward the One who loves. it is a powerful and solid Bridge.

"very early in the morning, while it was still dark, Jesus got up, left the house, and went off to a solitary place, where He prayed." mark 1:35

"Father (Abba), forgive them for they know not what they do." luke 23:24

of the seven all-encompassing utterances by Jesus at the Cross, this may be the most stunning. here, at His most vulnerable, painful moment Jesus has the temerity and strength to intercede for those who slay Him, and by implication, all of us. His Blood speaks of better things and calls out for our eternal and complete Forgiveness. all the sin, sickness, shame, sorrow, and suffering of the world (that's a mouthful, say them out loud, never mind, don't speak them!) is heaped upon His Body- and His first thought in that moment is to cry out to save us from being held responsible. oh, how incredible! it is literally breath-taking, His lack of Self concern and Self-focus. through surrender to Him, you cannot sin yourself out of this imparted Righteousness!

He is the Man, the Man of all Sorrows, and the Man of all Perfection!

every knee shall bow to His glory and honor one day. every knee is already bowing, whether they know it or not, for He exists in the Timeless, Placeless Eternity.

"i delight greatly in the Lord. for He has clothed me with garments of salvation and arrayed me in a robe of righteousness, as a bridegroom adorns his head like a priest, and as a bride adorns herself with jewels." isaiah 61:10

"surely today you will be with Me in paradise." luke 23:43

as He was flanked by two thieves at the Cross, one thief cried out in faith for salvation.

that one man was able to see behind and beyond the veil of misery and death- even at the very moment of death one can cry out and I will rush there at that very instant. I have many times! I want to speak about these sufferings as they are such important and transformative moments in human history.

you have seen horrific things because of the internet- beheadings, people falling from buildings, children murdered and murdering, and even more unspeakable abominations.

look beyond this vale of tears. look at Me! if you can't see Me clearly enough, just call out, yes, call My Name! get down on your knees, are you desperate for Me, as when you are extremely hungry or thirsty? turn off all devices...lay out prostrate on the floor. come and cry, come and worship, in your private room or space at home, seek Me! close the door and meet Me in the silence.

"but the Lord is in His holy Temple, let all the earth be silent before Him." habakkuk 2:20

"and there was silence in heaven for about a half an hour." revelation 8:1

"I thirst. a jar of wine vinegar was there, so they soaked a sponge in it, put a sponge on a stalk of the hyssop plant and lifted it to Jesus' lips." john 19:28,29

"I looked for sympathy but there was none, for comforters, but I found no one. they put gall in My food and gave Me vinegar for My thirst." psalm 69:21

physical anguish and pain are sometimes overwhelming. the chronic pain that keeps you awake at night, the hunger pangs of a starving child, the mortal coil exerting its primary survival instinct. then, there is the anxiety and constant fluctuation of the soulish realm, where your mind, will, and emotions reside.

just know, the corruptible body you inhabit will one day lose its nature of suffering. you will put on your glorified new body and you will walk, run, dance, swim, sing, shout, clap, hug, and fly! you will be free of any earthly encumbrances. any mental torment, any emotional scars will be transformed into badges of honor. all these things you have experienced and overcome will have led you to greater honor and appreciation for and from Father God. can you feel Me smiling within you now as you make the right, holy choices time after time? I am so proud of you son, daughter!

"but whoever drinks the water I give him will never thirst again. indeed, the water I give will become a fresh, bubbling spring within them, giving them eternal life." john 4:14

"son, behold your mother. mother, behold your son." john 19:27

have you ever experienced the closeness of bonding with your child or children? there is much spiritual growth generated by sleepless nights with a sick child. it would take many years of devotion and monastic practice to equal that! have you cared for aging parents or been with loved ones as they transition from this earthly realm? there is no more compassionate endeavor than to be with someone near or at that time of their life when they transition. I see the dignity of life that you give them by being with them and holding their hand.

here, Jesus expresses deep affection, such as you have known, if you are blessed. it has been said that a more profound love produces a greater grief. imagine the love between Jesus, His mother mary, and His closest disciple john. aspire to those impenetrable types of relationships in your life, unconditional, uncontainable Love.

It is My highest Gift and Attribute!

"your love has given me much joy and comfort, my brother, for your kindness has often refreshed the hearts of God's people." philemon 1:7

"My God, My God, why have You forsaken Me? (Eli, Eli, lama sabacthani in aramaic)" matthew 27:46

"My God, My God, why have You abandoned Me? why are You so far away when I groan for help?" psalm 22:1

in this period of mental torment and anguish, for a time, Jesus was totally vulnerable, stripped, and alone. in His condemnation of sin, God the Father necessarily turned His Back on His Son, on His Own Self. at the Cross, Jesus willingly took your complete punishment and suffering. oh, I can't even write this without Great Tears and Grief. it was a moment like no other.

I Knowingly and Purposefully stood aside as the King of Glory, My Manifested Glory, was tormented unto death, all the sins of the world, Past, Present, and Future- a heavy, unthinkable burden fell on Him as a penetrating and piercing fist. I had to look away. I had to Cry. there was no other way.

"rather, we will speak the truth in love, growing in every way more and more like Christ, Who is the Head of His Body, the Church, from Whom the whole Body, joined and held together by every joint, does its own special work, helping the other parts grow, so that the whole Body is healthy and so that it builds itself up in love." ephesians 4:15,16 "it is finished." john 19:30

after Jesus released these victorious words from His parched lips, He voluntarily laid His Head down upon His Chest. it was not resignation. it was surrender to God's Infinite Will. He had effectively put away death by stepping into it. it's hard to even put this moment into words, but if you can, sit in silence with Me for just a moment here. don't open your Bible, don't write, don't look around.

complete silence is really the only thing that can encapsulate this holy moment. sit and wonder as you did when you were a child.

there is no answer to find here; My Voice Itself is the "brittle silence" at the mouth of elijah's cave and, by extension, your cave. another translation says, "after the fire, a sound of sheer silence."

the quieter you become, the more you will hear.

"what did you come here for, elijah?" 1 kings 19:13
"so, let us do our best to enter that rest." hebrews 4:11

"Father (Abba), into Thy Hands I commit My Spirit." luke 23:46

luke records this as the final Word of Jesus- not desperation, but contentment. I'll tell you more about it when you get here- you wouldn't be able to process it now. there's so much that was said and not said, that happened and didn't happen- don't worry, I will share all of it with you! it was beyond what the Word you have can explain- it was amazing. no words you have can describe the sacredness. the Glorious One, Jesus, is within Me and I within Him and within you as Infinite Love. I am the Cloud in the pupil of your eye and I can see into the very window of your soul! I am the Fire within your very heartbeat!

be content with that hope for now!

"for i find protection in You alone. i entrust my spirit into Your Hand." psalm 31:5

"Jesus answered by saying to them, you don't know what you are asking. can you drink this bitter cup of suffering I am going to drink?" matthew 20:22

this is going to sound all backwards I know, because nobody enjoys suffering. spiritually, you should know and feel at rest, already assured of your eternal standing, place, and condition which gives you the advantage over anything- you are already spiritually seated!

however, physically, you must still stand and fight in the faith. you may be suffering physical pain and/or mental burdens. remember, you will physically and mentally rest entirely when you get here with Me.

stand up now though!

fight and destroy strongholds!

never compromise!

I will help you decide which battles are worth taking a stand for and when to step back and allow things to take their course, trusting Me to fight and work it out for you. it's a fine line. love will be a guiding principle. if it isn't loving and you don't feel My Peace, let it go.

"dear friends, don't be surprised at the fiery trials you are going through, as if something strange is happening to you. instead, be very glad- for these trials make you partners with Christ in His suffering." 1 peter 4:12,13 "my soul, wait silently for God alone, for my expectation (hope) is from Him." psalm 62:5

silence is a balm for your soul. carve out some time each day for complete silence- first thing in the morning (My favorite time to be with you!), during an afternoon break, or at night before you get ready for sleep. just sit, recline, or put the legs up and listen. inhale and exhale deeply. find the quiet hush of holiness. if you'd like to open your Bible to read a bit first, then your mind will be filled with My thoughts and not your own as much. however, I want to be with you and not just have you read the Book I wrote!

you will find strength in that witness and after this has become a habit, which will take some discipline, you will begin to notice that you look forward to this time with Me.

even God waited for the Holy Spirit before He created. genesis 1:2,3 says, "the earth was formless and empty, and darkness covered the deep waters. and the Spirit of God was hovering over the surface of the waters. THEN God said, let there be light, and there was light." (emphasis Mine!)

even Jesus waited to begin His formal ministry until after He had been appointed and anointed by Me at His baptism.

come to that Oasis of Calm and Rest!

"be still and know that I am God." psalm 46:10

"there is much more we would like to say about this, but it is difficult to explain, especially since you are spiritually dull and don't seem to listen. you have been believers so long now that you ought to be teaching others. instead, you need someone to teach you again the basics about God's Word. you are like babies who need milk and cannot eat solid food. solid food is for those who are mature, who through training have skill." hebrews 5:11-13

are you spiritually mature or do you just want Me to tell you things that tickle your ears? I want you to grow up into a fully mature Christian, a leader not a follower, a strong and commanding testament to My Power in you! don't take offense easily if someone says something to you, don't criticize others who are doing the best they know how, don't compare yourself to others, and finally, stop complaining all the time! it just makes things worse. alright- you can laugh now cause you've probably done all these things at some point! if you're feeling anger or despair, hold that close to the vest, not in denial, but just prioritizing. press on with what I have called you to. you can tell Me about the frustrations- I love to listen, but you don't have to dwell on the anger or grief with everyone you know. get a concordance. do word studies on the solid food of the Bible. study Jesus- His life, His words (I put them in red for you!), His miracles (especially if you need a healing), His ministries, and His Passion! do a word study on faith, on hope, on strength, on prayer. go deep-I'm passing the ball to you.

"dear brothers and sisters, when i was with you i had to talk to you as though you belonged to the world or as though you were infants. i had to feed you with milk, because you weren't ready for anything stronger." 1 corinthians 3: 1,2 "do you not know that your body is the temple of the Holy Spirit Who is in you, Whom you have been given from God, and you are not your own." 1 corinthians 6:19

I want to richly inhabit your life- if you allow Me to! I will not force you though- I will not overwhelm your own free will. I know the world offers many bright, shiny objects and exciting experiences. I, on the other hand, want to woo you with My Promises.

I promise I will guide you and keep you safe.

I promise to make you laugh, to give favor for the things that you enjoy doing.

I promise to love you, no matter what, good days and bad.

I promise to never leave you, even when you feel most alone, especially then.

I promise to strengthen you with My mighty Right Hand.

I want to give you your dreams, the desires of your heart, but more than that, I want to give you Myself.

"take delight in the Lord and He will give you the desires of your heart. commit everything you do to Him. trust Him, and He will help you. He will make your innocence radiate like the dawn. be still in the Presence of the Lord." psalm 37: 4-6 "and He said to me, My grace is sufficient for you, for My strength is made perfect (shows up best) in weakness! therefore, most gladly i will rather boast of my infirmities, that the power of Christ can work through me. for when i am weak, then i am strong." 2 corinthians 12:9,10

do you have a sense of a cloak over your life, a protective covering from Me? in 2 kings chapter two, elisha asks for the Double Portion of Spirit from elijah, and in response, I allowed him to see the chariots of fire and elijah being translated right in front of his eyes. then, elisha picks up elijah's mantle, his cloak. you are not ordinary- you are eminently called and necessary to My Kingdom's fulfillment.

I am your Primary Covering! through prayer, draw the Bloodline around your life, your home, your family, your dreams, your very body. Jesus' Blood has a Voice louder than the blood of abel.

your secondary covering is your husband if you are female. your next covering, for male and female, is the local church leader you reside under. this is invaluable advice- don't ever get separated from the Body. I prefer you to stay rooted, but if I do call you for service somewhere else, let there be no gap in your attendance.

these "cloaks" of anointed authority offer you stability, instruction in godliness, and My Holy spiritual power. stay under the Covering- the Blood, the sacred marriage union, the local Body- I cant stress this enough in these Last Days.

"our sufficiency is from God." 2 corinthians 3:5

"therefore, we who have fled to Him for refuge can have great confidence as we hold to the hope that lies before us. this hope is a strong and trustworthy anchor for your souls. it leads us through the curtain into God's inner sanctuary. Jesus has already gone there. He has become our eternal High Priest in the order of melchizedek." hebrews 6:18-20

melchizedek is a king from the times of abraham who was a prophetic foreshadow of Jesus. his name means "king of justice" and since he came from salem, he is also the forerunner from the "city of peace," jerusalem. Jesus Christ is your Intercessor Forever in the order of melchizedek. Jesus Himself is the King of Kings, the Lord of Lords, and the Prince of Peace. He is going to bring down justice to the earth for those who think they have "gotten away" with murder or WORSE- yes, there is worse, unfortunately. "vengeance is Mine" and I will repay. I have a day of vengeance planned and it is coming soon. proclaim the year of My Favor, and also that Day of Justice. I will provide weapons of war. I will exact payment for your suffering- "put on a garment of praise for the spirit of heaviness."

"He is the kind of High Priest we need, for He is holy and blameless, unstained by sin. He has been set apart from sinners and has been given the Highest Place of honor in Heaven." hebrews 7:26

"and we, who with unveiled faces all reflect the Lord's glory, are being transformed into His likeness. and the Lord, Who is the Spirit, makes us more and more like Him as we are changed into His glorious image." 2 corinthians 3:18

do you desire deeper understanding of the Lord's glory? the gift and miracle of understanding comes from being in the Glory Zone- from turning inward toward Me!

worship releases the supernatural to operate on your behalf! do you believe that? if so, you will press in with all your energy and dance like david did! or stand still, as moses did before the burning bush- as long as your heart is ecstatic! be on the Front Line! lift up your hands and voice in the Sanctuary!

daily, come alone, as esther to the king, as mary to the Tomb, as elijah to the cave, and as joseph to the well. come, wherever you are- I am there in the Midst of it All.

don't put the veil back on- as moses did when his face radiated from being in My Presence. let everyone see that you and I are forever intimately connected!

"but whenever someone turns to the Lord, the veil is taken away. for the Lord is Spirit, and wherever the Spirit of the Lord is, there is freedom." 2 corinthians 3:16,17 "that joy is mine and it is now complete. He must become greater and i must become less. the One Who comes from above is above all." john 3:30,31

"your attitude should be the same as Christ Jesus: Who, being in very nature God, did not consider equality with God something to be grasped (to cling to) but made Himself nothing, taking the very nature of a servant. and being found in appearance as a man, He humbled Himself and became obedient to death- even death on a cross. therefore, God exalted Him to the highest place and gave Him the Name that is above every other Name." philippians 2:5-9

read this carefully. take it apart and dissect it word by word and you will see why Jesus is Preeminent!

He willingly and purposefully humbled Himself even though He is the Creator of the entire universe. He was obedient and subservient in the face of impossible fear and grief. He set His face to look at the end goal, which was your full forgiveness and eternal life. He set Himself apart, alone, so that you would be set apart, sanctified, in full communion, communication and union, with God.

"that at the Name of Jesus every knee shall bow in heaven and on earth, and every tongue confess that Jesus Christ is Lord, to the glory of God the Father." philippians 2:10,11

"I have cut off nations; their strongholds (fortified fortresses and towers) are demolished." zephaniah 3:6

I offer full and compete forgiveness! the seventy times seven expression means Infinite! in fact, I am Forgiveness itself- it is My very nature. remember this as we speak here of sensitive subjects.

forgiveness can help you keep from being controlled by the past. it is a strength that breaks the chains of bondage to those who do wrong to you. the more heinous their behavior, the stronger that bond of evil tries to hold you to them. take a sledgehammer to that chain, that stronghold. refuse to be connected to that anymore.

you have the necessary weapons to destroy strongholds and soul ties. strongholds are faulty human reasonings, deceptive teachings you have embraced, habitual emotional and addictive choices, and generational patterns. soul ties are physical attachments to others through emotional and intimate bonding outside of marriage.

set yourself free with the freedom Christ gives! how? seek intently to understand and wield the authority you have in Jesus (fasting and prayer often help). lift up the Sword of My Word, especially speaking the Promises aloud (the enemy hates that as it reminds him of his humiliation in the desert by Jesus). displace the strongman by focusing on Jesus and firmly establish My Presence in your body, in your home, and in each moment of your life. choose your words and actions carefully.

"if satan opposes himself and is divided, he cannot stand, his end has come. in fact, no one can enter a strongman's house and carry off his possessions unless he first ties up the strong man. then he can rob his house." mark 3:26,27 "your people will rebuild the ancient ruins and raise up the age old foundations; you will be called Repairer of Broken Walls and Restorer of Streets with Dwellings." isaiah 58:12

notice how I've taken on many duties as I inhabit and work through your voice and hands? I help you in all restoration. wherever people dwell, there is a spark of possibility and I will never give up on one single person. do you have this type of heart for the harvest field? some call others "lost", in fact, that even became a "cool" worldly title- lost... a thing to aspire to for the world. I don't call you that term, you are a miracle waiting to happen!

I am primarily interested in reaching out to hurting people in the "highways and hedges." will you come with Me to those places, where there are those who are marginalized? will you come to public venues where people congregate? I will bring people there to speak with you.

there's a Change coming! there is widespread revelation and revival available even in this moment. don't wait for the masses to catch on- go and start the revival now, today!

"arise, shine, for your light has come, and the glory of the Lord rises upon you." isaiah 60:1

"but when they did not find them, they dragged jason and some other brothers before the city officials, shouting, these men have caused trouble all over the world, turning it upside down. and now they are here disturbing our city also." acts 17:6

your faith is going to be tested multiple times, I assure you. I'd much rather say to you that it's all going to be smooth and easy, but I'm sorry child, that just isn't the case, as you well know. I could immediately, at this very moment, banish satan and his evil, and I will one day soon, but you know what? then you wouldn't know that you have the power and right to stand up to him, like david to the lion, the bear, and finally, through knowledge of former victories, to goliath himself. send satan fleeing yourself! cut off his head! turn him out of your life, crush him under your heel decisively. become the strong warrior I intended and created you to be!

and while you're at it, turn away from the world's leading that follows self-focused teachings, crying, "i'm entitled to have this free will, i'm entitled to do whatever i want." some people you have to place a firm boundary line against, a plumbline, that cannot be crossed. if not, they will drag you down with them, as the drowning person who pulls the rescuer under. don't be afraid to say no. I will help you know when to engage and when to let go.

oh, and can you turn the world upside down a little bit today?

"the God of peace will soon crush satan under your feet." romans 16:20

"how you are fallen from heaven, o shining star, son of the morning! you have been thrown down to the earth, you who destroyed the nations of the world. for you said to yourself, i will ascend to the heaven and set my throne above God's stars…i will climb to heaven and be like the Most High." isaiah 14:12-14

the battle has been going on for a long, very long time. I'm actually getting really weary of it; so grieved at seeing My beloved ones suffer. it needs to come to an end soon. I tell you, the evil has surpassed the days of noah. it is Enough. I'm tired of the arrogance of satan and his constant lies and ministrations in front of My Face- schemes and tactics, his blatant agendas and ulterior motives. I am going to establish the Millenial Reign and you who are pure-hearted and innocent will lead the Revolution! don't be trapped by the cynicism and jaded lifestyles of the world. stay fresh and new, as if you just spent an hour floating and laughing in a clear, calm ocean! I am going to use you in such glorious ways!

"yes, He told them, I saw satan fall from heaven like lightning." luke 10:18

"i will both lie down in peace, and sleep; for You alone, O Lord, make me dwell in safety." psalm 4:8

how did you sleep last night, My child? I know there are many things on your mind, for you see, I created your mind to function as it does- to analyze, prepare, organize, and remember much minutiae! that's the powerful survival instinct that even the youngest child possesses.

I have said of children "of such is the Kingdom" and unless you think as a child does you won't be able to fully grasp the simple, yet profound, truths of My grace, protection, and love. when children are tired, notice how they can fall soundly and peacefully asleep almost anywhere. this is because they trust their parents and are able to fully let go and relax. have you noticed how children also live entirely in the moment, fully present for each new thing?

sleep the sleep of a baby tonight. I will be on guard all night long, as I have no need of slumber nor sleep. pleasant dreams to you, My child!

"for the Lord gives His beloved sleep." psalm 127:2 (claim it tonight by saying this verse out loud as you close your eyes) "of all the commandments, which is the most important? Jesus replied, listen, o israel! the Lord your God is the One and only God. you must love the Lord your God with all your heart, and with all your mind, and with all your strength." mark 12:29

be conscious of the fact that you have My Personal attention and that I want you to be healed more than you want to be healed!

so, come to Me. pray until you feel My Presence so strongly that all your problems are left on the floor. say "i don't worry about what will happen- i trust You, Lord."

it's alright to just sit with Me and not say anything as well! you will notice a pure and real connection with Me that comes from us spending time together!

"look at his woman kneeling here. when I entered your home, you didn't offer Me water to wash the dust from My feet, but she has washed them with her tears and wiped them with her hair. you didn't greet Me with a kiss, but from the time I first came in, she has not stopped kissing My feet. you neglected the courtesy of olive oil to anoint My Head, but she anointed My feet with rare perfume." luke 7:44-46 "his Master was furious and said, go quickly into the streets and alleys of the town and invite the poor, the crippled, the blind, and the lame." luke 14:21

samuel, samuel!
martha, martha!
simon, simon!
zaccheus, lazarus, john!
daughter- insert your name!
son- insert your name!

all these people were/are called personally and individually by God and by Jesus. I am personally calling YOU!

they each had a particular need- some knew their need, some didn't. I know each one of you by your personal name. even if you think someone else has your name- they don't! I know even the little derivative of your name that makes you smile, a little nickname between us! I know what makes you happy, I know when you have had a bad day, when you have had enough, and I send angels to help you, to give a hedge of protection around you so no more attacks can come until you build back up. hundreds of thousands of angels come the moment you speak- you command them now by faith.

"he explained to me, daniel, i have come here to give you insight and understanding. the moment you began praying, a command was given. and now i am here to tell you what it was, for you are very precious to God. listen carefully so that you can understand the meaning of your vision." daniel 9:22,23 "what are you, mighty mountain? before zerubbabel you will become level ground." zechariah 4:7

zerubbabel led the israelites back from exile (nehemiah 7:7) and as the governor of israel, he helped to rebuild My Temple and My Holy Altar.(ezra chapter 3) this return from babylon was initiated by cyrus, the king of persia, who is a prophetic type and shadow of your modern day leaders.

zerubbabel's first priority was to rebuild the altar and restore the holy sacrifices. after that, for eighteen years, he faced opposition of every kind- scheming governmental lies and great spiritual attack. just remember, the bigger the problem, the easier it is for God to act, or more precisely, the more He will come to your aid!

just keep trusting Me. the victory is "not by might or power" but by My intervention and anointing on the situation you are in. read that again slowly please. study what happened here- as you study and meditate on these stories, I will give you more specific instructions.

joy is My new wealth for you.
health is My new success for you.
kindness is the new cool on earth
as it is in heaven.
amen.

"Jesus told them, I tell you the truth, if you had faith even as small as a mustard seed, you could say to this mountain, move from here to there, and it would move, nothing would be impossible." matthew 17: 20

"foxes have dens to live in, and birds have nests, but the Son of Man has no place to even lay His Head." matthew 8:20

here's how you do it- keep on moving forward and be a walking concordance- your Sword at your side at all times! you are equipped with the most powerful weapon of all- the Word of God!

I definitely don't want to give the enemy too much focus or power, as he craves both, but I do want to equip you so you aren't caught unawares. watch each others' backs- set someone, and maybe even everyone, up on the wall for your family! have everyone be joined in agreement as prayer warriors. there's strength in numbers when it comes to prayer and worship. don't attach too much to the world or the world's opinions. reread My Promises over and over, speak them out and claim them in faith as you say them. be very courageous, knowing that you are loved and that I will fight for you always.

"don't be afraid of them. remember the Lord, Who is great and awesome, and fight for your brothers, your sons and your daughters, your wives and your homes... from this day, those who carried materials did their work with one hand and held a weapon in the other and each of the builders wore his sword at his side as he worked. but the men who sounded the trumpet stayed with me." nehemiah 4:14,17, 18 "posterity will serve Him; future generations will be told about the Lord. they will proclaim His Righteousness to those yet unborn- for He has done it. (it is finished!)" psalm22:30, 31

there is a partnership between psalm 22, 23, and 24. psalm 22 is a revelation of the Cross, psalm 23 is the song of the Waiting period, and psalm 24 is the prophetic celebration of the victorious Resurrection! this verse above encapsulates the events on that good friday and the whole psalm sings the song of the Cross. this three day period is the most remembered and exalted event in history. see how the ancient prophecies were all fulfilled here by the Royal Descendant of king david. the roman soldiers didn't even know that they were fulfilling Scripture. they cast lots for His garment, His bones weren't broken, they mocked and scourged Him, and His hands and feet were pierced. this piercing was prophesied in psalm 22 before roman crucifixion was even thought of.

for over two thousand years, one generation after the next has told of Yeshua Ha-Mashiach's glorious Victory. continue that legacy- exhorting your children and grandchildren to make Him Lord of their lives. of all the things you buy and give them- food, clothing, gadgets, college educations- this is the best gift you can ever give them- knowledge of the Lord Jesus as their Redeemer, Savior, and Friend, for it avails them of eternal life.

"train up a child in the way that they should go and when he is old he will not turn from it." proverbs 22:6

"My life is poured out like water, and all My bones are out of joint. My heart is like wax, melting within Me…they have pierced My hands and feet. I can count all My bones. My enemies stare at Me and gloat." psalm 22:14,17

this Messianic psalm was fulfilled to the letter. I would like you to read all of psalm 22 aloud to yourself. psalms is located at the center of the Bible for many reasons- and it also makes it easy to find! open to it now please.

after you have read all of psalm 22, sit quietly and let it resonate within you. notice how you feel. aren't you grateful for Jesus and what He went through, His willingness to come at a time in history when He knew He would meet one of the most painful deaths possible- crucifixion? He wanted you to know that He was willing to give the utmost, everything He had and was, for you. the enormity of the full removal of all sin for eternity demanded a bold and powerful finality. that it was! feel it in the depths of your spirit!

"yet it was the Lord's good will to crush Him and cause Him to suffer grief." isaiah 53:10

"the Lord is my Shepherd, I have everything I need." psalm 23:1

once you have full realization from psalm 22 of what has been given for you, it makes this psalm even sweeter and richer. in the time of waiting in your life, your Shepherd keeps watch day and night, feeds you, and when you go astray, He personally comes after you!

He provides everything for you. does this mean you are dependent on Him and that you need Him? absolutely! that is not a criticism or drawback- it is not a crutch, as the world interprets it. you need Him- and let Me tell you, child, He needs you. I don't need you to DO anything for Me, as "I own the cattle on a thousand hills", but I want to be in a real Relationship with you! I can't create or manufacture that true love. only YOU- freely and purely, can give that to Me! will you?

"every good and perfect gift comes down from God our Father, Who created all the lights in heaven. He does not change nor cast a shifting shadow." james 1:17

"blessed is the man who listens to Me, watching daily at My doors, waiting at My doorway. for whoever finds Me finds life and receives favor from the Lord." proverbs 8:34,35

"He makes me to lie down in green pastures (He lets me rest in green meadows). He leads me beside still waters (peaceful streams)." psalm 23:2

I show you how to rest in green fields so that you can live fully! I don't just want your tacit recognition of that- show Me the size of your dreams and let Me help you accomplish them for the kingdom. take those steps of faith. I am leading you beside calm, quiet waters, even more, I AM the Quiet Waters! I am the Lush Meadow! I'd love nothing more than for you to come apart to that peaceful place with Me. no one can reach you here- you're off the grid! no one can bother you- your head gently rests on My shoulder and I reach over and put My Hands on each side of your face, whispering your name and telling you how happy you make me, how very proud I am of you in all you have been through and how you have never turned from Me!

turn to Me especially in the evening hours as you lay upon your bed. you may sense Me there, I hope- for you are never alone, My child. notice how infrequent are any bad dreams, for I send you beautiful dreams.

rest- rest deeply. "no one shall hurt or subdue in My holy Mountain", where the verdant fields of flowers and soft dewy grasses grow.

"those who look to Him are radiant." psalm 34:5

"He restores my soul (He renews my strength)." psalm
23:3

afterwards, when you go out from the Throne Room to the
world, you will be refreshed and invigorated! My primary
purpose is to uplift and point to Yeshua, Jesus, but My
secondary purpose is to encourage and strengthen you! since
you haven't yet manifested your glorified body, I understand
how challenging life can be, particularly as your body begins
to mature. also, it seems that the more people you love, the
more possibility of some challenge or attack occurring to
someone you love. it may even seem easier to keep from
loving too many people so that you won't be hurt.

that is not My way for you. all these things will bring My
power to the forefront and I have promised you that you will
never face more than you can bear.

"and God is faithful. He will not allow the temptation to be
more than you can stand. when you are tempted, He will show
you a way out so that you can endure." 1 corinthians 10:13

"He leads Me in the paths of righteousness, for His Name's sake (bringing honor to His Name). yea, though i walk through the valley of the shadow of death, i will fear no evil, for You are with me." psalm 23:3,4

I am leading you all through your life, once you surrender to Me. even when you make wrong choices and seeming mistakes, I am constantly turning them around to your good. you can have complete confidence today, no matter what you "seem" to be facing in the natural. I am greater than the physician's diagnosis. I am greater than your physical limitations that are presenting. they are symptoms only. I am greater than any situation at all.

and it's alright to ask, why the valley? right when you are walking through it, I will show you that it is just a shadow, it isn't real. you fear it because it appears unknown and because it separates you temporarily from those you love who have graduated into My Presence. if you study carefully, it isn't unknown! I have told you many particulars about heaven-search for them. I've told you about your new body. I have given you much hope! we will have all eternity together in the New Jerusalem!

"he persevered because he saw Him Who is invisible." hebrews 11:27

"Your rod and Your staff they protect and comfort me."
psalm 23:4

david grew up as a shepherd boy, playing his harp and worshiping Me in the grazing fields. the imagery he wrote here of the rod and staff are spiritual principles I taught him in those long days and nights we had together. it helped to mold him into a confident leader. he needed to be able to stand up to the wolves and other predators that attacked relentlessly, especially in the dark nights. he overcame and killed the lion and the bear and this boosted his faith that I would help him in any situation. thus, when goliath came along, he was looking unto Me and not the puny giant. that's what My rod is for- it is not an instrument of correction. it is to give a beat down to the devil! oh, and a bigger beat down is coming for him. it seems to be a long time coming in the natural, but I am tarrying for just and certain purposes, though that doesn't make sense to you now. I honor you for believing what I tell you.

my staff has a "crook" or handle on it so that I can gently draw you back when you get too far to the fringes. it's not good for you to be too far from Me! edge your way in, if you have to. use those sharp elbows I gave you and say "excuse me, excuse me, move aside please- i need to be near my Shepherd!"

"my soul finds rest in God alone." psalm 62:1

"You prepare a table before me in the presence of mine enemies." psalm 23:5

you know how you feel when you're really really hungry? close your eyes a moment and remember some of those delicious meals you've had in your lifetime! don't they taste the best when you've really worked hard, worked up an appetite, and have waited all day to sit down to a lovingly prepared meal? or remember, maybe you've attended a joyous wedding banquet, a special celebratory meal. after the sacred vows, but before the dancing, comes the magnificent dinner! I am preparing it for you even now!

this part makes Me grieve for I have invited everyone and don't want to turn anyone away- outside are those who look on but have no desire to enter and celebrate. the implication of refusing to come doesn't resonate with them- they disinvite themselves. I wish that you, as their friend, had been bold enough to ask. please, I'm asking you for a personal favor- kindly tell them how much I love them. phrase it with all humility and respect, then continue in loving relationship with them no matter what their response.

"a gentle answer turns away wrath." proverbs 15:1

"You anoint my head (You honor me by anointing my head) with oil; my cup overflows with blessings." psalm 23:5

it's hard to even put this into words- again, words just aren't adequate to convey how much love I want to pour over you. have you held your child or grandchild yet? maybe a cherished niece or nephew? have you felt that close bond and the feeling of wanting to protect them from any harm or danger? that's just a miniscule amount of how I feel for you!!

I don't want you to ever be in pain, or to have your heart broken- I want you to see all the beauty I have created just for you and I want you to have blessings and favor that overflow your cup and pour out all over the table and into your lap and onto the floor- as over the head of aaron, running down his beard, and so much oil it is even flowing down onto the hem of his robe!

stop sighing! you are going to be honored and anointed- you are even in this moment honored and I give you My Blessing! all that I have is yours, My son, My daughter, My beloved, My beautiful, strong, precious one!

"she is clothed with strength and dignity; she can laugh at the days to come." proverbs 31:25

"surely goodness and mercy will follow me (surely your goodness and unfailing love will pursue me) all the days of my life." psalm 23:6

have you been out in a storm? have you ever been walking with lightning all around, or with insults hurled from all sides, or with bombs falling?

look behind you where you are sitting. right now in the natural, turn, and look behind you. what did you see? did you sense anything in the spiritual realm? I am there! I am your Rear Guard- I'm bringing up the cotillion. I am protecting the place where you didn't see it coming. I am both Preceding and Following you. I am actually pursuing you like the most ardent Lover of your soul, every single day of your life. every tiny raindrop that falls nurtures the tender leaf, bud, and fruit that is growing in you.

I see it all! I'm not unaware, as you may perceive Me to be. I see you!

"He feels pity for the weak and needy, and He will rescue them. He will redeem them from oppression and violence, for their lives are precious to Him." psalm 72:13,14 "and I will dwell in the house of the Lord forever." psalm 23:6

if you can imagine the most spectacular residence you've ever seen, visited, or dreamed of- your home in heaven is a million times more glorious than that! I can't put into human words a terminology stronger than that. if you would be more comfortable with simple digs, then your home will be relaxed and real. if you like ornate, then I will make it resplendent for you. whatever will make your heart smile- I know you are all very different and have unique tastes so, believe Me, there will be no cookie-cutter homes in heaven. and oh, there will be colorful gardens exploding with profuse flowers. there will be the open heavenly sky, unobstructed views in all directions, dignified mountains- can you dream of the sounds, sights and scents of your heavenly home?

I'm so anxious for you to be here with Me so you can experience all I have prepared. we will talk and celebrate, sing and laugh every single day- I love you!

"today if you hear His Voice do not harden your hearts as you did in meribah." psalm 95:8

"the earth is the Lord's and everything in it. the world and all its people belong to Him for He laid the earth's foundations on the seas and built it on the ocean depths." psalm 24:1,2

this psalm of david is not only a battle cry but also looks forward with visionary foreknowledge to Mashiach's future entry through the eastern gate to reign forever. I am the One with the Keys that open the Door- that final Door!

this psalm is the Son-day, the day of the Brilliant Resurrection- a reflection of the fulfillment of all the prophecies- every comma, period, and sentence that must be fulfilled before the Day of the Lord comes.

"who may climb the mountain of the Lord? who may stand in His Holy Place?" psalm 24:3

I have chosen you to come and stand because of your unwavering faith. I have loved you with an everlasting love! I have chosen you!

"the Lord called me before my birth; from within the womb He called me by name." isaiah 49:1

"open up, ancient gates! (lift up your heads, o ye gates!) open up, ancient doors, and let the King of Glory enter!
Who is this King of Glory?
the Lord strong and mighty,
the Lord Invincible in battle.
open up, ancient gates!
open up, ancient doors, and let the King of Glory enter.
Who is this King of Glory? The Lord Almighty
(El Shaddai, the Lord of heaven's armies)
He is the King of Glory." psalm 24:7-10

notice how I repeat here in psalm 24 "open up!" and I repeat "Blessing and Honor and Glory and Power to You, O God, Forever." no other words than what is revealed here suffice. I stand beyond words that could explain how Holy, Righteous, Perfect, All-Knowing, All- Powerful, All-Loving and Eternal God Is! to You be Blessing and Honor and Glory and Power Forever! amen and amen!

"so the king sent out a second horseman. he rode up to them and said, the king wants to know if you come in peace. again jehu answered, what do you know about peace?" 2 kings 9:19

"Jesus told him, stand up, pick up your mat,and walk."
john 5:8

there is nothing trivial or insignificant in My Word. I specified here that this man was lame for thirty eight years. that is brutal- thirty eight years. Jesus asks him, would you like to get well? after thirty eight years, of course he wanted to be made well. the Lord asked not because He didn't know, but because He wanted the lame man to articulate what he wanted and then He wanted him to activate his faith by standing up and picking up his mat.

I manifest to you when you materialize the intention- open your heart, the ancient gate, by praising Me with singing, by walking toward the next thing, the next person I bring to you with confidence and overt authority.

My dream for you, My original Interpretation of Life, is Perfection. all the excellencies of Jesus were revealed in creation and in the gift of free will. because of your redemption, the shattering of that dream in eden is no more! life is now an astonishing Adventure for you- challenges and all! stand up and walk!

"He looked around at them one by one and then said to the man, stretch out your hand. so the man held out his hand and it was restored!" luke 6:10

" jonah went in the opposite direction to get away from the Lord and the Lord arranged for a great fish to swallow jonah and he was inside the fish for three days and three nights." jonah 1:3,17

rise each morning with an awareness of My fresh supernatural favor! be courageous today as you face unknown events with confidence. here, jonah had pride- he didn't trust Me and furthermore, he believed he could hide from Me! he was afraid of the reaction of the people of ninevah, so he ran away as far as he could. his arrogance led him to believe he didn't need to listen to what I specifically asked him to do.

I'm going to ask you to do something for Me today. trust Me to give you all the words you need. you are like a little child, just learning to speak, and that innocence is attractive to others. be child-like with people. take the risk to speak about Me! look for the adventures in life, that will turn your perspective to Me and intrigue others as to where your joy emanates from.

"indeed the right time is now, for today is the day of salvation!" 2 corinthians 6:2

"don't let your mouth make you sin. and don't defend yourself by telling the temple messengers that the promise you made was a mistake. talk is cheap- fear God instead." ecclesiastes 5:6,7

I'm talking here about respectfulness. if you have respect for Me, you will readily admit mistakes. mistakes aren't always sin, they're part of being human, so don't beat yourself up over them too much. I can even use the mistakes you make to draw you closer to Me.

however, it is good to reflect on why you made the mistakes and how the next time you can make a better choice, with My discernment and help. you will choose with more wisdom as you mature in the Word.

the storm occasionally comes up very suddenly, which is why you prepare ahead of time. you know you will be tempted or tested. you can know what those parameters are, even something as innocuous as a misspoken word of complaint can open the door to the enemy. it is not always conspicuous- sometimes it is just a small thing. don't let satan use your mistakes- let Me transform them into thoughts of forgiveness and grace- just enough grace, just enough for today!

"Father, Lord of heaven and earth, thank You for hiding these things from those who think themselves wise and clever, and for revealing them to the childlike. yes, Father, it pleased You to do it this way." matthew 11:25

"two people together are better off than one, for they can help each other succeed. if one person falls, the other can reach out and help, but someone who falls alone is in trouble." ecclesiastes 4:9,10

I have told you that "wherever two or three are gathered, I am there among you." don't despise My small things- My heart is for one of the tiniest nations in the world- israel. part of My plan is that you will learn how to get along with others even when they are incorrigible. I'm not condoning bad behavior, but no one on earth ever gets it right all the time. so even though others can be really irritating, keep being kind- kindness, lovingkindness, is My high standard. you don't have to tolerate anyone taking advantage of you- set boundaries for sure- but also know that I breathed life into each soul! there is an organic worthiness because I lovingly created them. every person has the potential to be a force for good in the world. look for that spark of divinity and give them a chance- for My sake!

"he who refreshes others will himself be refreshed." proverbs 11:25

"for a triple braided cord is not easily broken."ecclesiastes 9:12

as the Third and somewhat elusive Member of the Trinity (although not really, that's just your perception of Me!), I like to think I have the best sense of humor; however, Father God did create the anteater and other hilarious species (like humans)!
a joyful mind is very ordinary and relaxed. it is curious about things- think of the mind of a child, so easily distracted and yet able to hone in and focus on every little detail, like the small sound of a bird or the airplane as it moves overhead. as adults, you've become so accustomed to things that you've lost the wonder of it all.

try something different! splash cold water on your face, laugh at the stars, sing in the shower, paint a picture, write your thoughts down for posterity, swim in the deep part of the ocean, walk slowly in the rain, dance in the rain! I've called you to be different, a unique people- find what that means for you, child!

"a cheerful heart is good medicine." proverbs 17:22

"the Lord said to gideon, you have too many warriors with you. if I let all of you fight the midianites, the israelites will boast to Me that they saved themselves by their own strength." judges 7:2

the fighting, the war, is real and necessary, but the outcome is predetermined because of the accomplished victory. I just want you to be courageous and to understand that I am fighting for you. you don't have to do it all in your own strength. and you don't have to back down from adversaries- in fact, you shouldn't back down from the fight, as that just emboldens the enemy.

trust in My ability, as this is My battle! when I sent the angel to gideon, he was threshing wheat (souls) by hand in the bottom of a grape press, a pit where grapes are pressed to make wine (judges 6:11). he was steadily pressing in! when I was presented to simeon, anna was nearby at the exact moment to see Me in the flesh (luke 2:36).you do your part and I will hold good to My Promises, brave warrior!

"this is what the Lord says, don't be afraid! don't be discouraged by this mighty army, for the battle is not yours, but God's. tomorrow, march out against them…you will not even need to fight. take your positions, then stand still and watch the Lord's victory. He is with you." 2 chronicles 20:15,17 "and God confirmed the message by giving signs and wonders and various miracles and gifts of the Holy Spirit whenever He chose." hebrews 2:4

I am constantly coordinating people and things to help to sustain a safe, harmonious world. this is My Perfect Will. on the other hand, for the time being, My Permissive Will allows certain consequences of things to occur.

layered beneath these is the Alignment principle when you choose to come into agreement with My will for your life, known or unknown. I realize how difficult it is to surrender control of that. when you become truly invested in our Relationship on a daily basis, you will begin to see much more favor occurring in your horizontal relationships, your health, your job, and your life.

when that occurs, sing praise songs!

have honest, raw conversations with people about important things. slow down and observe- walk somewhere, everywhere if you can! appreciate the everyday miracles that are happening all around you.

"commit to the Lord whatever you do, and your plans will succeed." proverbs 16:3

"not to us, O Lord, not to us, but to Your Name goes all the glory for Your unfailing love and faithfulness." psalm 115:1

I am a Person, albeit a supernatural Person, with thoughts, emotions, and deep feelings- especially for you! of course, I enjoy hanging out with the angels, but they are beings who were specifically created to worship and send messages, to do My bidding as needed.

you, however, were created with an entirely free will! oh how inconvenient that is sometimes! but also, your love, which comes unbidden and profusely to Me, makes Me so happy!

I am so proud of you- I see all your struggles and challenges and I love you immensely! I can't wait until I can replay all the wonderful, triumphant moments of your life, and rejoice with you, both of us smiling at the memories! the best is yet to come!

"He said, they are My very own people. surely they will not betray Me again. and He became their Savior. in all their suffering, He also suffered and He personally rescued them. He lifted them up through all the years. but they rebelled against Him and grieved His Holy Spirit." isaiah 63:8-10

"God is with us. His outspread wings protect the land."
isaiah 8:8

I am your Deliverer!

I want to explain what this means practically for you. Jesus has already completed the finished work of your eternal salvation. the enemy can't touch your spirit. that is precisely why he keeps trying to attack your body and mind. I don't want you to over analyze this, but there is a spirit, a demon actually, of "infirmity" or sickness. even as a believer, you can have a bondage- it is not eternally corruptible, but can cause much pain and sorrow in your life. I want to deliver you from that. you don't have to live in debilitating depression, immoral or unequally yoked relationships, addiction of any kind, suffer under a religious spirit, or any other type of bondage.

I am the Chain Breaker. I am capable of breaking any soul tie no matter how strong. these fleshly things don't serve you. I can break them definitively and permanently. ask Me, come to Me humbly, and ask Me, as the woman who had suffered for eighteen years came humbly and reached for Me.

"fear of the Lord is the foundation of wisdom (the beginning of understanding)." proverbs 9:10

"look at My Servant, Whom I uphold, My Chosen One in Whom I delight; I will put My Spirit on Him and He will bring justice to the nations. He will not shout or cry out or raise His voice in the streets. a bruised reed He will not break and a flickering candle He will not put out." isaiah 42:1-3

do you feel alone or tired today? I understand. come to Me and let Me comfort you. there is no circumstance that can come between you and I, once together. I am the shady bench under the poinciana tree. I am the wings of birds flying over and covering you with protection.

well, you may respond, then why did that accident or illness happen to me or to someone I love? I'm so sorry for your pain- this will not last forever. it is a terrible yet momentary place that I will help carry you through. this world in its present form is passing away, so look beyond these occurrences. I have protected you so many times that you don't know of, and I will continue throughout your entire span of years, or days, or hours.

"he will have no fear of bad news; his heart is secure, he will have no fear." psalm 112:7

"a faith and knowledge resting on the hope of eternal life, which God, Who does not lie, promised before the beginning of time, and at His appointed season He brought His Word to light through the preaching entrusted to me." titus 1:2,3

God appoints times and seasons and He can bring you into a new season of health and grace. it may be you are wondering why a physical challenge continues- it can be a season of trusting and resting in the Lord. it may be a new season for you- but it is the same unchanging Source- God!

why do you need seasons in your life, you may ask? oh, I know you have a lot of questions, I've heard all of them, and don't worry they will all be answered one day! have you ever gotten so used to something that God blessed you with, something you may have even prayed specifically for- a marriage, your home, a job, children- that you start to complain about it? you start to find lots of faults with it over time? seasons teach you humility and appreciation. I want you to be continually thankful, not just when things are going your way. don't compare and criticize- just enjoy and be grateful- extremely grateful- for all that you have!

"be joyful always, pray continually, and give thanks in all circumstances, for this is the will of God in Christ Jesus."
1 thessalonians 5:16,17

"again He said, what is the Kingdom of God like? it is like a mustard seed, which is the smallest seed you plant in the ground. yet when planted, it grows and becomes the largest of all garden plants, with such big branches that the birds make nests in its shade." mark 4:30-32

work the new ground! plant those seeds- I will water them, I will fertilize, and I will even cause them to grow when I discern a willing heart. I have prepared the ground for you- go and sow!

look at your agenda for today. I'm not saying you can't plan and work for your family, food, home, and other nice things. just have balance between the temporal and the eternal! as paul said, "consider everything a loss compared to the surpassing greatness of knowing Christ Jesus as Lord" philippians 3:8. I can't say it any better than that.

"work hard to show the results of your salvation, obeying God with deep reverence and awe. for God is working in you, giving you the desire and the power to do what pleases Him." philippians 2:12,13 "for i have learned how to be happy whatever the circumstances. i know how to live on almost nothing or with everything. i have learned the secret of being content in any and every situation, whether with a full stomach or empty, with plenty or little. for i can do all things through Christ, Who gives me strength." philippians 4: 12-14

a child always demands- they have no sense of their parents' hurts or struggles. you know this to be true. the mature person I desire you to be is patient, waits their turn, is sensitive, and doesn't make excuses. get over yourself! I say that somewhat jokingly, but also in all seriousness. I want you to put on the raiment of holiness and not always have to be searching for the next new thing, materially or spiritually.

a baby is carried constantly. a child still needs to be held by the hand and told where to go. in contrast, an adult is "sent." go where I am sending you today, I have important work for you that only you can do! I can use you, how amazing! I <u>will</u> use you!

"instead, speaking the truth in love, we will in all things grow up into Him Who is the Head, that is, Christ." ephesians 4:15

"then the angel showed me the river of the water of life, clear as crystal, flowing from the Throne of God and of the Lamb down the middle of the great main street of the city. on each side of the river grew a tree of life, bearing twelve crops of fruit, with a fresh crop each month. and the leaves were used as medicine for the healing of the nations." revelation 22: 1,2

see, all the places you have been injured or operated on, all your scars, will be badges of honor for you in the Kingdom. you won't look at yourself the same way anymore- there will be no earthly mirror to reflect your "flaws" to you. actually, the balm of gilead, the healing properties of which I have told you, will completely transform the way you see everything. you will have complete confidence, complete clarity when you see me face to Face.

try to understand that the issue, whatever it is, has already been solved for you! say solved out loud right now- solved!

"a word aptly spoken is like apples of gold in settings of silver." proverbs 25:11

"then i looked, and there before me was the Lamb, standing on mount zion." revelation 14:1

can you close your eyes and envision this scene? if you can do this, it will turn your earthly perspective in a complete 180. this is not a fantastical dream- it is a prophetic pronouncement of what will surely come to pass. the imminence of the Day of the Lord reveals a perspective of history. I want you to see with My eyes, I want you to have the benefit of My eternal outlook. that is why I am working in you daily to give you these abilities! aren't you tired of depending on approval from the world? it's alright to have dreams and goals in the natural, just keep them in perspective, as part of My purpose for your life. don't let them become overwhelming to you.

I'm happy when you enjoy yourself and your dreams- have fun today! laugh, sing, eat something delicious, hug lots of people! live life to the fullest!

"on that day, His feet will stand on the mount of olives, east of jerusalem. and the mount of olives will split apart, making a wide valley running from east to west." zechariah 14:4

"at that time men will see the Son of Man coming in the clouds with great power and glory. and He will send His angels and gather His elect from the four winds, from the ends of the earth." mark 13:26

Jesus spoke this to His disciples so that they would tell you. in Scripture there is a heavy focus on the close of the Age. so, while I indeed want you to have an enjoyable life with great purpose and growth, also keep an eye on things that happen in the world which seem unusual. I enjoy the order of numbers and using dates to convey ideas. I also love to use strong confirmation so that you can know beyond a shadow of a doubt that I am telling you something. if you have a sketchy feeling about something or someone, then don't do it! but if you have My peace, then go ahead!

buy that home!

marry that equally yoked person!

have children!

start that business!

I love you and I want your life to reflect the culminating joy of heaven! I will lead you with My peace.

"but i am like an olive tree flourishing in the house of God. i trust in God's unfailing love forever." psalm 52:8

"brothers, think of what you were when you were called. not many of you were wise by human standards, not many were influential, not many were of noble birth." 1 corinthians 1:26

don't get offended by others.
it's okay to be beautiful or handsome, it's okay to be rich, it's okay, but don't let it make you proud.

it isn't the reason or your confidence of why you obtain favor or blessing from Me. there's no glory in the flesh- please hear that. remember, God doesn't look upon your flesh or recognize it as attractive. He looks upon your heart. the glory, My glory, comes when I come upon you! God has something called "radiance" and it shows up best when you are just being ordinary. people can tell by your face how long you have been in relationship with Me. I can tell by your heart- tender and open.

there's a supernatural radiance that comes after spending a season with Me.

"look to the Lord and be radiant!" isaiah 60:5

"through their faith, the people in days of old earned a good reputation." hebrews 11:39

abel, enoch, noah, abraham, sarah, isaac, jacob, joseph, moses, joshua, rahab, gideon, daniel, david, samuel, all the prophets, mary, all the disciples, all the apostles, all the church to the present time!

what a great Hall of Faith we are included in. as you read these names, I hope their life histories rise up to inspire you! if not, get yourself a good concordance and get into the Word for it is dramatic and powerful history.

one day your name will be written on the Hall of Faith scroll! can you imagine that? can you imagine standing in the company of such giants of faith? don't forget, they all, admittedly, had their flaws. none of them were perfect, so you stand in good company!

press on! keep going. keep your eyes on the prize. I will never steer you wrong, because I love you! you are engraved on My Hand and in My Heart.

"by faith we understand that the entire universe was formed at God's command, that what we now see did not come from anything that can be seen." hebrews 11:3

"so, take a new grip with your tired hands and strengthen your weak knees. mark out a straight path for your feet, so that those who are weak and lame will not fall but become strong." hebrews 12: 12,13

you have a huge responsibility to the generation coming behind you! and I'm not just talking about your children and grandchildren, but all those whom I bring for you to mentor and represent Me to. train them, and be a transparent role model for them so they can come to the same place of faith where you stand. set an example, be an example of grace. it doesn't happen by osmosis- they need to hear and <u>see</u> and, by hearing and seeing, <u>know</u>. faith is that confident knowing-ness.

I'm proud of the legacy you are leaving for your children- they are imprinted with My Name because of you. all the physical things you do for them will pass away, but the love you share with them will go on forever. those relationships will never end, only becoming clearer and better, including yours and Mine! I've got you in My Grip, My beloved one!

"for God's gifts and His call are irrevocable." romans 11:29

"therefore, since we are surrounded by such a huge cloud of witnesses to the life of faith, let us strip off every weight that slows us down." hebrews 12:1

I know you have someone very close to you that has graduated to heaven. I want to speak with you about that person, or persons, without being insensitive- especially if it was a child. I know nothing takes this pain away- not time, not faith that they aren't suffering, nothing. so I am not discounting your pain or trying to sweep it under the rug, hear Me.

all I want to say to you is that they are watching from heavenly grandstands, cheering you on, proud of you, and interceding for you to do well and be strong. one day soon, in the twinkle of an eye, you will be reunited and the intimacy of that relationship will be fully restored. I have big plans for you and everyone that you love! it won't be long, child. there are far far better things coming for you than anything that you leave behind. I save the best for last.

"the righteous man leads a blameless life. blessed are his children after him." proverbs 20:7

"God calls those things that are not as though they were. (visible, tangible, in our own eyes)" romans 4:17

don't limit Me!

gideon was a mighty man of valor. he asked and asked of the Lord. he never lost his conscious sense of his own weakness, for he knew his power wasn't of himself. yet, still he had doubts in his fleshly mind, and wanted a sign of the golden fleece.

God left some of the flesh nature in you. that was His decision in this plan so that you would have a paradox to contemplate and to overcome by My strength. the flesh is not the body, though it uses the body. the flesh involves the body and the soul (mind, will, and emotions). your body and your mind will one day be transformed and glorified. the flesh is the part of you that loves to sin- but that is not you. you are the Righteousness of God in Christ- stand in that even though your weakness may still be apparent. your weakness is how I work in you! read that again, speak it out loud please.

"the same power that raised Christ from the dead dwells in us." romans 8:11

"now many nations have gathered against you. they say, let her be desecrated, let us see the destruction of israel. but they do not know the Lord's thoughts or understand His plan. they don't know He is gathering them together to be beaten and trampled like sheaves of grain on a threshing floor. rise up and thresh, o daughter of zion!" micah 4:11-13

I am the Threshing Floor!

the threshing floor is the place where the grain is winnowed. it is thrown into the air with a type of instrument, much as worship instruments powerfully winnow. the wind then separates the light husks, the useless chaff, and they are blown away. the threshing ground is where you come to separate, to sanctify, from the world and its superficial pursuits.

to rise up and thresh also prophetically refers to the work that must be accomplished before the end will come. yes, the sanctification work of Jesus is finished, yet the harvest is ripe and I need you to tread, to march, to staunch the evil with the loudness of your praise and the fullness of your worship. be fierce! bring your full attention and energy- it's time to press in!

"swing the sickle for the harvest is ripe. come, tread the grape for the winepress is full." joel 3:13

"He is ready to separate the chaff from the wheat with His winnowing fork. then He will clean up the threshing area, gathering the wheat into His barn but burning the chaff." luke 3:17

this spiritual life is going to cost you something. you're not just here for your own pleasure. this minute of reading the powerful prophecy above changes you- did you feel it? do you feel the eternal consequences attending every action you choose? people's lives hang in the balance. oh, hear Me and let your life count for eternity!

how, you say?

tell that neighbor or family member today what I am doing for you. tell them that you care for their future. look for people I am intersecting you with each day and open your mouth about faith, and hope, and My love. I know sometimes it will feel unusual or uncomfortable, but I will prepare the open door and the solid ground of the threshing floor. It will be Me speaking today- be bold. thresh!

"david replied, i have come to buy your threshing floor to build an altar to the Lord there...i insist on buying it, for i will not present offerings to the Lord that have cost me nothing." 2 samuel 24:21,24 "now you have every spiritual gift you need as you eagerly wait for the return of the Lord Jesus Christ." 1 corinthians 1:7

God the Father is the One Who sets the determined time for the Messiah's return. watch and pray for there is a crown of glory awaiting those who are eager for that time! are you expectant for His arrival?

"we have these treasures in earthen vessels."

nothing virtuous or mighty is in the flesh, in the fish or barley loaves- it has little to do with you or your clay pot. think of the clay pots you have, they can be dropped, broken, and are then discarded. so your body is transient, a temporary container for your eternal spirit.

yet you, the clay vessel, have purpose and beauty to Me and I chose not to discard you! I will quicken (change) your mortal body at that last day.

"listen! your watchmen lift up their voices; together they shout for joy. when the Lord returns to zion, they will see it with their own eyes." isaiah 52:8

"lay seige against it, and heap up a mound against it; set camps against it also and place battering rams against it all around." ezekiel 4:2,3 "the Lord will mediate between nations and will settle international disputes. they will hammer their swords into plowshares and their spears into pruning hooks. nation will no longer fight against nation, nor train for war anymore." isaiah 2:4

these prophetic announcements are coming to pass in this century. I have told you that you are the benjamin generation.

today, do what you can do to keep the world pristine, pure, and beautiful! pick up that piece of trash, don't use a plastic straw or bag, turn the a/c up a little, walk. know that your stewardship is having a profound effect, as I watch and applaud you for caring for the earth and the people that I created. that means so much to Me, as I created you to be stewards of the earth. it gives a good testimony.

yet, the bulk of your time should center on eternal issues. the Replacement Principle is coming to pass and the Millenium will settle all concerns. there will be no more global warming nor war. there will be gardens, lavish meals, holy mountains, clear rivers, humble service, ecstatic worship, beauty, and unconditional love forever and forever. amen.

"nation will not take up sword against nation, nor will they train for war anymore. every man will sit under his own vine and under his own fig tree, and no one will make them afraid, for the Lord Almighty has spoken." micah 4:3,4 "gideon said to God, if You will save israel by my hand as You have promised- prove it to me this way- look, i will place a wool fleece on the threshing floor tonight. if there is dew on the fleece but the ground is dry, then i will know that You are going to help me rescue israel as You promised." judges 6:36,37

there are four things that you need in order to live physiologically-
air to breathe
water to drink
food to eat
light

these are the four things I provide for you spiritually as well as physically.
I am the Ruach- the Spirit-filled breath of Life.
I am the Living Water, rivers of which pour out of your body.
Jesus is the Bread of Life, giving His very body for you.
Jesus is the Light of the World, bringing clarity and truth to all situations.
you have all of these inside of you, provided by Me for all eternity. light the fire of acknowledgment!

" he placed trumpets (ram's horns) and empty jars in the hands of all of them, with torches inside." judges 7:16

"he that dwells in the secret place of the Most High shall abide under the shadow of the Almighty." psalm 91:1

what was your first thought of the day today?

I have seen that the world, and your world, have become overly busy and noisy. there's always too much to do and too much over stimulation of your nervous system and senses. I want to call you away to silence- to a quiet corner of your life.

silence is the protective border of My Robe that I wrap around you.,

even in situations where you are around others, sometimes not speaking, not saying anything, is the best thing to do.

let silence be your protective mantle today as you dwell with Me in the Secret Place. again, I AM the Secret Place! you are always with Me. I am always with you- when you are enjoying family, when you are receiving chemo, when your child is sick or having a tantrum, when you have an accident, when you feel alone, when you rejoice, when you are afraid, when you are sleeping- I am in all those places with you. practice noticing My Presence all day long by turning your thoughts toward Me.

"stand in silence in the Presence of the Sovereign Lord." zephaniah 1:7

"when the Lamb broke the seventh seal on the scroll, there was silence throughout heaven for about a half an hour." revelation 8:1

your eternal home, Heaven, is a place of balanced times of noise and silence, loud praise and transfixed worship, activity and rest. so, too, your life should have a balance to it. I want you to examine your activities, especially when you feel like you need to rush places or when you start to feel overwhelmed or tired. beware! be aware! this is the enemy's trap to get you distracted and conflicted and out of awareness of My quiet strength within you. the secret to having it all is knowing that you already do, through Me!

as soon as you sense you are getting tired or frustrated, step away for a moment into the Word, come and rest with Me. I will fill you again, giving you hope and new energy to continue.

now go, be a warrior!

"for the Lord takes delight in His people; He crowns the humble with salvation." psalm 149:4

"and they have overcome by the Blood of the Lamb and by the word of their testimony." revelation 12:11

this is such an important verse that I'd like you to earmark this page so that you can read it again and again throughout the year. Jesus' death and Resurrection, His Blood contract with you when you accept it by faith, is the utmost important thing in all of life- past, present, and future. it is THE defining historical event, no question. it is more important than family, than friends, than career, than any possession. His triumph imparts complete and eternal Righteousness to you.

when you implicitly believe that, your life, your actions, your words, and your very thoughts become different and new. what you speak about to others takes on new meaning and authority- authority to heal, to bind demonic influences, to provide financial disbursement, to open hearts to Me. I gave you that authority! testify, testify, testify with boldness today about what I have done for the world and what I have done for you!

"i also pray that you will understand the incredible greatness of God's power. this is the same mighty power that raised Christ from the dead." ephesians 1:19

"then another angel came from the temple and shouted to the One sitting on the cloud, swing the sickle, for the time of harvest has come, the crop on earth is ripe." revelation 14:15

this life is meant to be a celebration! I know there are still daily issues and challenges that confront you. that's why I'm really proud of your perseverance and ability to choose correctly (most of the time!). I see how hard it is sometimes when you have pain and I promise I'm going to make it all up to you. you will say one day, "it was all worth it."

remember when you looked forward to your wedding day or the birth of a child? that is the level of joy multiplied infinitely that you will experience for all eternity! I have given you foretastes of that perfection in many moments of your life. hold onto those glimpses. Jesus is coming with multitudes of angels very soon so live this moment in happy expectation and with the blessed hope of His appearing!

"be strong and take heart, all you who hope in the Lord." psalm 31:24

"i saw heaven standing open and there before me was a white horse, whose Rider is called Faithful and True. with justice He judges and makes war. His eyes are like blazing fire and on His head are many crowns. He has a name written on Him that no one knows but He Himself. He is dressed in a robe dipped in Blood, and His Name is the Word of God." revelation 19:11-13

this is Jesus! close your eyes and envision His appearance, full of Light and eyes like Fire! all the prophets foretold Messiah's appearance. because He is timeless, He is already here in this now moment. He is a Warrior, fierce and protective. He is passionate. (see the blazing eyes!) He is interested in justice for those who have suffered horribly in life.

there are the everyday mundane moments in life, and then there are the high point moments- weddings, childbirth, vacations, birthdays, a delicious meal, intimate moments with others. this prophetic announcement is the ultimate high moment that makes a shadow of the best joys you have known in life.

this moment <u>will</u> arrive soon- every eye will see it. prepare for that day!

"You are my Hiding Place; You will protect me from trouble and surround me with songs of deliverance. selah." psalm 32:7

"and the devil, who deceived them, was thrown into the lake of burning sulphur." revelation 20:10

I want you to know that I am going to finally deal justice to the one who lies to you, steals from you, and daily tries to take your earthly body from you. he is after your marriage. he is after your children's health and peace. he is after your soul. he is an evil coward. some of his attacks are blatant, but most are subtle, deceptive, usually using the method of surprise. thus, you need to be on alert and cover your family and yourself each day with a protective prayer.

don't forget though, I have his number and it will soon be called. until that day, I call you to stand and fight with Me. his judgement was already sealed at the Cross and because you are in the Third Day, the Resurrection Day that entirely conquers death, you are fighting from a place of strength and victory.

the "catching away" will happen at any moment, so be ready! attach lightly, if at all, to the world, as one traveling through on a connecting flight. you don't unpack at the airport; you travel through as lightly as possible!

"the end of a matter is better than the beginning, and patience is better than pride." ecclesiastes 7:8

"and He carried me away in the Spirit to a mountain great and high, and He showed me the holy city, the New Jerusalem, coming down out of heaven from God. it shone with the glory of God and its brilliance was like that of a very precious jewel, like a jasper, clear as crystal." revelation 21:10,11

love doesn't always manifest the way you think it should. it shines like a diamond, like many diamonds that turn this way, and then that, to reflect the sun. it floods like an ocean, filling the places where your footsteps carved a path. love is often a battle, and when it comes, your life will never be the same.

talk to Me! talk with Me! be vulnerable- tell Me it all. I want to hear about everything you feel and are. and then you can leave those hard things with Me and I will deal with them. go and shine on, My diamond.

"do you not know? have you not heard? has it not been told you from the beginning? have you not understood since the earth was founded? He sits enthroned above the circle of the earth, and its people are like grasshoppers. He stretches out the heavens like a canopy, and spreads them out like a tent to live in." isaiah 40:21,22 "the Spirit helps us in our weakness. we do not know what we ought to pray for, nor how to pray, but the Spirit Himself intercedes for us through wordless groans." romans 8:26

I understand your heart, both its desires and concerns. I know sometimes when you pray that you don't feel you have the right words or even know what to pray. I can take even your sighs though, even your groanings, and present them to the Father since I am One with the Father and I always pray according to His Will.

yes, you can say "Thy Will be done" or "I ask for Your Will in this situation." if that seems inadequate or you are more deeply concerned about a person or situation and can't quite let go, allow Me the honor of praying with you, through you and in you. just come quietly and if tears or sighs attend your thoughts, just allow them. I know how you feel and I also know God's Heart- as you and I pray together, you will find peace.

"therefore, since we have been made right in God's sight by faith, we have peace with God because of what Jesus Christ our Lord has done for us." romans 5:1

"where the Spirit of the Lord is, there is freedom."
2 corinthians 3:17

I want you to be fearless and I impart that through freedom! your very existence is tied up in your moment by moment, day by day free choices. your thoughts are <u>alive</u>, very much alive, and they lead unfailingly to your decisive actions.

allow Me to help you choose correctly. I am in you, dwelling in your quiet heart and mind. I told you that I will give you checks in your spirit so you will know when you are venturing out of My Will for your life. My intention is not for you to suffer. remember- everything is innately connected. so stay close to Me, keeping very aware as you choose. you will feel your heart on fire sometimes. choose well in those moments! ask for wisdom and discernment and listen carefully by slowing yourself down and getting really quiet.

"it is for freedom that Christ has set us free." galatians 5:1

"therefore, do not worry about tomorrow, what you shall eat or what you shall you drink, or what shall you wear. these things dominate the thoughts of unbelievers, but your Heavenly Father already knows your needs. seek the Kingdom of God above all else, and He will give you everything you need." matthew 6:31-33

I hope you are plugged into My local Body of Christ- at least once a week you need to be there. it is the Catalyst for My Presence. My Shekinah Glory and the sense of My Presence is there most strongly. it is not just a bunch of ritualized actions. and let Me clarify, it doesn't matter what anyone else is doing, whether lifting hands or clapping or saying amen during the Word- you participate. you press in! don't even look around at anyone else, who is there or what they are doing. focus only on Me! as you sense and participate fully in My Presence, more faith is released to you.

when you feel led to pray for someone, ask and then wait a moment to speak. don't lay hands on them too quickly. wait for My Presence and let Me give you the words, My words, to speak. there will be a supernatural weight, a heaviness or a lightness. there will be a palpable sense there, an opening, and the person you are praying for will feel My love, My healing, My wisdom. I will impart as you pray together (let the other person pray as well). I will work in hearts to increase faith. faith manifests miracles and patiently respects My timing. My plans are only for your highest good- I know that is sometimes hard to understand, especially when you are in the midst of trials. be content for you are greatly loved!

"at the moment i have all I need- and more!" philippians 4:18
(written from prison by paul)

"for me, to live is Christ and to die is gain." philippians
1:21

your Heavenly Father loves you so much, favored child!
you are a precious daughter to Me! you are a strong, warrior
son in My eyes! I love you so much that I am relentless in My
pursuit of you.

let Me brag on you a little, as you do your children and
grandchildren. you stand for your convictions! you refuse to
compromise, I saw that! you speak and make decisions from a
place of authority. you aren't influenced by the world, even
when they are in the majority. you are loving and kind to
everyone.

now, come into the private silence with Me- I'm still here-
I've always been here, on the Front Porch, waiting for you!

"the apostles left the high council rejoicing that God had
counted them worthy to suffer disgrace for the name of Jesus.
and every day, in the temple and from house to house, they
continued to teach and preach the message that Jesus is the
Messiah." acts 5:41,42

"even as peter was saying these things, the Holy Spirit fell on all who were listening to the message." acts 10 :44

I can impart spiritual proprioception to you if you ask Me to- the ability to see and know yourself in space and time, but also beyond space and time into eternity. in effect, you become entrained in Me. entrainment is the complete synchronization with someone or something. in other words, who you spend time with, hang with, is who you will become most like, as clocks lined up on a wall eventually start ticking and chiming in harmony and conjunction with one another.

so, it's your choice once again. do you want to be aligned and balanced in My Divine Will for your life? come into agreement with My Word, My promises, and My prophesies for your life. I will fill you completely with My love and grace and it will block out anything that brings you down.

"O God, You are my God, earnestly I seek You; my soul thirsts for You, my body longs for You in a dry and weary land where there is no water." psalm 63:1

"unless you become like a little child, you cannot enter the Kingdom of heaven." mark 10:15

I want you to experience life fresh and new everyday, like a child does. I've explained this to you before, but here's a new take.

children have a brilliance, a genius to their actions. they think outside of the box because no one has yet told them "no" or how to conform. they have complete trust and confidence, unashamed of their freedom, their appearance; they don't care how their hair or their clothes look. most importantly, they love unconditionally, which is probably their most magnetic quality.

welcome children into your life- watch them with awareness as you can learn a great deal from them. pattern your way of loving after them.

"about that time the disciples came to Jesus and asked, who is the greatest in the Kingdom of heaven? Jesus called a little child to Him and put the child among them. then He said, I tell you the truth, unless you turn from your sins and become like little children, you will never enter the Kingdom of heaven. so anyone who becomes as humble as this little child is the greatest in the Kingdom." matthew 18:1-4 "as they were walking along, He asked them, who do people say I am? well, they replied, some say john the baptist, some say elijah, and others say You are one of the other prophets. then He asked them, but who do you say I am?" mark 8:27-29

He asked them questions, as He asks you brand new questions each day. who is Jesus to you personally? your vertical relationship with Jesus is your most important priority in life. it is much more important than your horizontal relationships on earth. yes, these earthly relationships have eternal consequences and I am pleased with your ministry for the Kingdom. however, I want you to also spend time cultivating our Relationship by spending time with Me daily and sharing your innermost thoughts and feelings with Me. grow as you go and just like on the emmaus road- keep on walking with Me.

call to Me! recognize Me in those routine moments. I'm calling you to derive passion from time spent alone with Me today.

"the Sovereign Lord is my strength! He makes me as surefooted as a deer. He enables me to go to high places." habakkuk 3:19

"the fruit of the righteous is a Tree of Life, and he who wins souls is wise." proverbs 11:30

the longer amount of time you have been blessed to be on this earth, the more I hope you turn away from the mirror and look instead into others' faces, lives, and towards others' interests. I put specific people into your pathway each day. I know sometimes it feels like you are maneuvering through an overgrown jungle with a machete trying to find the right path.

I am the Path! I am constantly confirming Myself to you. constantly! it wasn't random that I began creation in a Garden. that Tree of Life still stands at the Center and draws you to Me for sustenance daily. come and eat of the Tree of Life and then, nourished, see Me working in every detail of your life, large or small. see Me in everything, and more importantly, everyone. you will be sharing the gospel of grace for their sake and not your own.

"and let us not grow weary in doing good, for in due season we shall reap if we do not lose heart." galatians 6:9

"we grow weary in our present bodies and we long to put on our new bodies like new clothing, for we will not be spirits without bodies. while we live in these earthly bodies, we groan and sigh, but it's not that we want to die. rather, we want to put on our new bodies so that these dying bodies will be swallowed up by life. God Himself has prepared us for this, and as a guarantee He has given us His Holy Spirit." 2 corinthians 5:2-5

I want to ask you something important and I want you to really meditate on it and see what action you can take today. there has been an increase in hopelessness, depression, and suicide in the world, corresponding to the increase in the devil's activity as his time grows short. people sometimes isolate themselves away and hide their true feelings behind a smile. I want you ask you if you can be really sensitive today to what others are feeling, especially those closest to you. listen carefully to their emotions as you talk together. look in their eyes and see if you can say encouraging things to help them feel better.

the enemy is upping his game, planting thoughts of worthlessness and shame in people. I need you to help Me guide people skillfully toward faith and hope in these last days. speak that encouraging Word! hold out hope like a bright candle, a burning flame. have a distinct passion for Me that is contagious to others.

"but i keep praying to you Lord, expecting the time of Your favor." psalm 69:13

"learn a lesson from the fig tree. when its branches become green and soft and new leaves appear, you know summer is near. in the same way, when you see all these things happening, you will know that the time is near, ready to come." matthew 24: 32,33

I want to have a first hand experience with you. I want you to have a First-Hand experience with Me! I am preparing you, as a chosen generation, for the close of this Age. this is not second hand revelation I am offering- get up close to the Front here! I know it is sometimes loud and personal up front, but it's where I pour out the Anointing. no one can go on vacation for you, no one can whisper to your beloved in the night for you, no one can chew your food for you, like a baby- and you wouldn't want them to anyway! I am inviting you to come and have a personal and intimate Relationship with Me. do you want that? do you want to love Me as I do you?

please don't sell or throw away your birthright, as esau did. it is your Double Portion and Inheritance Blessing! your birthright is your position as My child!

"look, i'm dying of starvation, said esau. what good is my birthright to me now? but jacob said, first swear that the birthright is mine. so esau swore an oath, thereby selling all his rights as the firstborn to his brother jacob." genesis 25: 32,33 "and a Man wrestled with him until dawn…but jacob said, i will not let You go unless (until) You bless me. then the Man said, let Me go for the dawn is breaking." genesis 32:24,26

I have to admit something to you- don't laugh- sometimes I wake you up in the middle of the night just because I want to spend time with you (oh, okay go ahead and laugh!) this story of Me wrestling with jacob is a classic- it's not always that I want to impart or caution or contend with you- sometimes I just want, or I will say need, to be with you. do you ever miss Me? do you ever wake up on your own and want to listen for Me, talk in a whisper to Me, or just be together?

what joy for those who choose to come near with undivided attention! wait quietly without trying to go back to sleep…I am there with you in the stillness of the night hours.

" i lie awake thinking of You, meditating on You through the night." psalm 63:6

"is there anyone among you in trouble? let them pray. is anyone happy? let them sing songs of praise. is anyone among you sick? let them call the elders of the church to pray over them." james 5:13,14

there's a wealth of untapped resources available for you! many of them are accessed through the Body of Christ. corporate worship is exceedingly powerful, communion is a vital connection with My healing power as well as an expression of love, and then, also, your local pastor or pastors have authority to bring blessing over your life as they lay hands and pray for you. seek that blessing as often as you need it!

My child, you can also daily access these other efficacious weapons of Mine- private worship should be a profound daily desire within you, like food. is it? in some texts, to "worship" is translated "to kiss", establishing it as an intimate act.

you can take communion daily by yourself (well, it's not really solo because I am there!) or with your spouse as you impart to each other. have your Word open and available around your home- you can have multiple Bibles, aren't your blessed?! talking with Me- prayer- is a continual outpouring, you to Me and Me to you, throughout your day. esther came many times before king xerxes (pronounced zerk-sees! funny name, right?) seeking favor. keep your prayer and worship weapons at the ready every moment! I pray that you hear My heart clearly and loudly as I am your Heart-Knowing God!

"queen esther replied, if i have found favor with the king, and if it pleases the king to grant my request, i ask that my life and the lives of my people will be spared." esther 7:3

"come unto Me all ye that labor and are heavy laden and I will give you rest." matthew 11:28

stretch yourself out in the Hammock of My grace! you can rest now! rest gives Me the opportunity to provide for you supernaturally.

after all that spiritual battle, it's so important to take the time to rest. I will give you seasons of grace with no attacks or temptations. appreciate those times! curtail any and all complaint, and instead say "thank You" over and over. enjoy the company of your family. celebrate with them over a good meal, as a communion. light candles. dance to some meaningful music and hold each other for a long time. take a swim, go to a concert together, take an evening walk. spend the day in your pajamas. all these ways to rest, and more, I have established in your spirit. you are totally unique in all the world, so find what makes you feel free and light. pursue that! you will know what that is when your sense of time passes into a beautiful timeless state. also, you will probably be effortlessly smiling!

go find the bliss I have designed for you, My friends!

"so let us do our best to enter that rest." hebrews 4:11

"and elisha said, borrow as many empty jars as you can from your friends and neighbors. then go into your house with your son and shut the door behind you. pour olive oil into the jars, setting each one aside when it is filled!" 2 kings 4:3,4

soon every one of the widow's containers was filled to the brim! if you go to second kings in your Bible, you will be blessed and you will see that the exclamation point is there. I am asking you to read this short story for yourself. right here, right now I am asking you to open your Word and read this for yourself. even so, I will be there!

okay, thank you for obeying, welcome back. now I can reveal more through your obedience.

the widow had a desperate need. I am there in those times as I hate when you suffer. it grieves Me. My tears rain down from heaven. I want so much for you to be content and joy-filled in your relationships and in your work. I understand and empathize when you are separated by death from a spouse or close friend. Jesus wept at lazarus' tomb because He loved him and didn't want the family He cared so much for to suffer. I give great grace and abundant mercy to widows, widowers, children, babies, and also to you in specific areas of need.

come to Me- share your needs and believe for a miracle. I'm still in the miracle business today!

"so come boldly to the throne of grace that you may receive mercy and find grace to help you when you need it most." hebrews 4:16

"the Lord took hold of me and i was carried away by the Spirit of the Lord to a valley filled with bones...so i spoke the message as He commanded me, and breath came into their bodies. they all came to life and stood up on their feet- a great army!" ezekiel 37:1,10

read ezekiel chapter thirty seven in entirety, but only if you want to activate God's favor in your life! strong prophetic visions still hold power and importance today.

DON'T DRY UP! "your leaf shall not wither" and I will give you back, yea, repay you a hundredfold, for the years the locusts have eaten. it is I Who prepares these miracles and recompense for you. understand that even though Jesus only lived thirty three years on your earth, He has been with Abba Father since before Creation and knows how challenging life is.

I know what it feels like to be physically tired and to lose the energy and vigor of youth. let Me impart a Truth to you-spiritual power can renew you physically. abraham had a child at ninety! caleb was as strong at eighty five as he was at forty. depend on Me for your physical renewal. I want to bless and protect you!

"today i am eighty five years old. i am as strong now as i was when moses sent me on that journey and i can still travel and fight as well as i could then." joshua 14:11

"but caleb tried to quiet the people as they stood before moses. let us go at once to take the land, he said. we can certainly conquer it." numbers 13:30

I know things look like big giants sometimes. give the good report in all situations! I want to hear your faithful testimonies ring out! let Me comfort you and reassure you that I am bigger, stronger, and <u>much</u> greater than he that is in the world. in fact, satan knows the truth- that I created him. I brought him into this world and I will take him out soon.

can you sense that things are accelerating in the natural? storms, earthquakes, volcanic eruptions, wars and rumors of wars; all these are increasingly sudden and strong birth pangs, which are necessary. I have given you the sign of the twelve young men in a cave in thailand with their leader, the boys who were trapped in the cave and then rescued. one man gave his life in the rescue.I am giving increasingly intense signs- can I be any clearer?

keep your lamps full of oil- keep the wick trimmed and burning brightly. keep your gifts operating at the highest capacity! the Prince of Peace is standing at the altar to greet you, My Bride, because He loves you!

"at midnight, they were roused by a shout, look the Bridegroom is coming! come out and meet Him! all the bridesmaids got up and prepared their lamps." matthew 25:6,7 "for prophecy never had its origin in the will of man, but men spoke from God as they were carried along by the Holy Spirit." 2 peter 1:21

I am the Original!

find what makes you different. I have never been afraid to go apart from the multitudes. I am not a copy of someone else and neither are you! it's time to take a vacation from the world, from social media, and the pressure of always answering every noise and taking a multitude of pictures to document your life. what you look at creates comparison in your mind and comparison is a grace killer. if you want to compare something- compare the miracles and glory of Jesus. compare the mercy and truth that go forth from My throne. compare My wisdom to the world's.an original sound in the world causes thousands, millions of echoes.

I came in as a Lamb and am going out as a Lion- what a contrast!

"coming in and going out" you will be blessed. meditate on this- "coming in" refers to taking the time and delight for being in the Lord's Presence. that's why david was a "man after God's own heart." after being with Me, you are able to "go out" with joy and peace. I made you to be an original!

"so God created human beings in His own image." genesis 1:27

"all authority in heaven and on earth has been given to Me. therefore, go and make disciples of all nations, baptizing them in the Name of the Father, and of the Son, and of the Holy Spirit, and teaching them to obey everything I have commanded you. and surely, I am with you always, even to the very end of the age." matthew 28:18-20

this is Jesus' Great Commission, His last recorded words in the gospels of matthew and mark. in luke, Jesus instructs the disciples to wait for Me to come. someone's last words are very important, but especially His. if you turn to the last page in this book even (I know you want to!) you will see the last words in the Bible- also very important!

stay focused on what's important to Me, which is souls for the Kingdom and your preparation for eternity. I'm helping you to stay focused right now as you meditate on this writing. if you knew you wouldn't see someone for a long time, what important thing would you say to convey your final thoughts and emotions to them? put this book down and think about that for a moment here.

thank you for doing as I asked. every time you <u>immediately</u> follow My suggestions, I will bring a blessing and a deeper revelation of Jesus. He is the most important One and His priority while on earth was to give the news of grace and free eternal life out to the world. He lived healthfully and gave healing, He gave love and respect, He was focused on the eternal.

"as He is, so are you, in this world." 1 john 4:12

"the last enemy to be destroyed is death." 1 corinthians 15:26

I hardly know where to start to explain to you how sorry I am for all the pain and loss you are experiencing. it wasn't My Perfect Will for death to occur, but I'm not going to create more blame or guilt at this time. Father God told Me to tell you, He doesn't begrudge you your grief or tears. even though you have the hope of heaven, I understand you still feel deep pain and separation at the loss of that person you love.

you are in the Waiting Period between My Promise and its' fulfillment. I'm not going to sugar coat anything or say it's alright when it's clearly not. I hear your sadness. I also hear your strength. you don't have to pretend you're not sad. remember, I also felt the excruciating pain of loss at martha and mary's home in bethany when lazarus died. immediately after that resurrection miracle, Jesus went on to jerusalem and faced the horror of His own death. He conquered death completely at the Cross and spoke of your complete freedom from death and its attendant sorrow, a future event, in the present tense participle, saying "it is finished."

that day is coming soon, My child, when you will see that reality fully manifested.

"oh, death, where is your sting?" 1 corinthians 15:55

"but one of the twenty four elders said to me, stop weeping! look, the Lion of the tribe of judah, the heir to david's throne, has won the victory. He is worthy to open the scroll and its seven seals." revelation 5:5

a lion lives in a lifelong committed group called a "pride." they travel together, eat together, sleep together, and hunt together. when attacking, the older lion will roar and the prey usually turns in fear and runs into the ambush of the young lions behind him.

I established you to be in a community, called a church. there, I will regenerate you and reveal more of Jesus. He is the Messiah, the Anointed, the Only Begotten Son of God, the Lamb, the Word, the King of Kings and Lord of Lords, the Prince of Peace, the Advocate, the Good Shepherd, the Way, the Truth, and the Life, the Door, the Gate, the Bread of Life, the Light of the World, the Vine, the Resurrection and the Life, the Author and Finisher of your Faith, the Savior of the World, your High Priest, the Alpha and Omega, the First and the Last, the Horn of Salvation, and the Chief Cornerstone.

He is flawless. He is lovely. He is perfect in every way.

the Lion of the tribe of judah is roaring- run toward the roar!

"i was glad when they said, let us go to the house of the Lord." psalm 122:1

"martha, martha, the Lord answered, you are worried and upset about many things, but only one thing is needed. mary has chosen what is better, and it will not be taken away from her." luke 10:41,42

mary was sitting at the Lord's feet, listening to Him speak. david, the rich and famous king, also found the most important place to be- in the temple where God's Presence was.

of all the significant and very worthy things you have to do today, this time right here is the most valuable. it is priceless and eternal. <u>I am not an item on a list!</u> I am a Person and I want to be with you!

first you were a child, then you matured into a teenager, and then you became a young adult. you weren't overly concerned, or even aware, of your parents' emotions or problems because you were so focused on your own needs. now, as a hopefully mature adult, you can see and appreciate with a different perspective those things that are most important in life. actually, it's not things- it's people- messy, inconvenient, infuriating, funny, and lovable people. be with Me intensely, in the moment, and then go out and do the same thing with them!

"the one thing i ask of the Lord, this is what i seek- to live in the house of the Lord all the days of my life, delighting in His perfections and meditating in His temple. for He will conceal me when troubles come; He will hide me in His sanctuary. He will place me on a high Rock." psalm 27:4,5

"I will never leave you nor forsake you." matthew 28:20

it's the middle of the night kind of loneliness that gets you, a coming home to an empty house kind of loneliness, a bone tired at the end of a long day tiredness. this is life in all of its ordinariness. long after the children are grown and gone, you remember nostalgically the chaos, the missing shoes, the hand prints on the windows, the mess. it's the mess, the tears, the intertwined connections that matter.

see how
fearfully
and
wonderfully
I created you to live, in a horizontal fashion
interwoven
with others
continually
eternally
purposely
intentionally
gracefully
vertically
Loved!

"but i focus on this one thing: forgetting what is past and looking forward to what lies ahead, i press on to reach the end of the race and receive the heavenly prize for which God, through Jesus Christ, is calling us." phillipians 3:14

"look! I stand at the door and I am constantly knocking. if anyone hears My Voice and opens the door, I will come in and share a meal together as friends." revelation 3:20

see how I don't force you to do anything. no one wants someone to love them like a robot. I want you to open the door of your heart and love Me of your own volition.

eating together is a very ordinary thing. that's why I fashioned your body to need regular nourishment. it's a time when you can stop your work and effort and just be with those you love- and with Me! thank you for inviting Me to your table as you speak grace over your meals.

one day soon, we are going to enjoy a sacred wedding banquet, a meal, together. it will be better than the most delicious food you have ever eaten in your life! and just like in the upper room, when Jesus washed the feet of His disciples, Jesus will be serving you! He will serve you all the food that you love- fruits, acai bowls, grilled vegetables, yes, but also all those things you felt you couldn't eat as they were not good for you.

isn't it mind blowing? how cool is He, the totally humble and original Servant! listen for My Voice at the banquet- I will be the One that is singing over you!

"for as the lightning flashes in the east and shines to the west, so it will be when the Son of Man comes." matthew 24:27

"there is therefore now no condemnation for those who are in Christ Jesus." romans 8:1

everybody needs a Personal Savior!

the book of romans is paul's definitive writing. in romans, he uncovers the "salvation road", the salvation plan through grace. he comes to the conclusion that all men sin and come short of God's glory. of course you do! give up the illusion that you can be good enough to save yourself! within yourselves there is nothing but ulterior motives and self-centeredness (I still love you though).

then, in romans 5:8, paul details that even while you were a sinner, Jesus chose to come and die for you. within Jesus, there is nothing but perfection and righteousness. and now, through His grace, His Righteousness is placed on you. your new identity is in Christ Jesus.

My eye is forever looking at you with favor because My eye is forever upon Jesus and His Righteousness! I will help you see that truth more and more as you proclaim it. proclaim the "acceptable year of the Lord." luke 4:19

"the Lord searches every heart and understands every motive behind the thoughts." 1 chronicles 28:9

"and God raised us up with Christ and seated us with Him in the heavenly realms." ephesians 2:6

I am the Omnipotent One.

again, here I am speaking in a timeless manner. you are already seated in heavenly places! you were destined to reign as "a chosen people, a royal priesthood, a holy nation." everything that is happening in your life has meaning and is preparing you for the time when you will be making totally compassionate, judicious decisions, judging not in a self-righteous fashion as the world and even yourselves sometimes do now. this is the Wisdom that solomon received- yet even he only reigned forty years when he allowed his flesh to take him off course and submit to worshiping other gods (I had to remind you again as solomon had all wisdom and still fell into sin.)

close your eyes and see if you can lucidly envision a time in eternity when you will be asked to lead a mighty team of worshipers, or delineate seasons or times of service for vast multitudes, or organize the construction of a large edifice or building, or hold sleeping babies and help them thrive, or direct angels.

all your work here on earth seems temporal, but it is preparation for where and what I will need you to accomplish in heaven.

"since then you have been raised with Christ, set your hearts on things above, where Christ is seated at the right hand of God. set your minds on things above, not on earthly things, for you died, and your life is now hidden with God in Christ." colossians 3:1-3

"I looked for someone who might rebuild the wall of Righteousness that guards the land. I searched for someone to stand in the gap." ezekiel 22:30

it isn't random that this passage came on this day. it definitely was not planned in the natural. I am looking all over the whole earth, at all times throughout history, and there you are. I see how you are clinging to My Word and My Promises, sometimes by your fingernails. I see how you serve. I see how you worship with intensity. I see how you love others, starting foundations to help them, sharing your heart with others who grieve, seeking Me on anniversaries, rebuilding your family.

of all the seven billion people on earth at this moment, in My Omnipotence, I am able to love you uniquely and personally. I know you have a hard time grasping how that can be so- even in your finite capacity to love as parents, see how you love them each differently, but with just as much intensity and devotion. you would give your life for them.

know that I see you and I am so proud of your courage when you feel lost. I hear your secret sighs that no one else hears. I am so sorry for the grief you have experienced. I see you in those private moments. I cry with you, when you feel alone. I love you.

"for the eyes of the Lord search (scan) throughout the earth, to and fro, to strengthen those whose hearts are fully committed to Him." 2 chronicles 16:9

"where can i go from Your Spirit? where can i flee from Your Presence? if i go up to the heavens, you are there; if i make my bed in the depths, You are there. if i rise on the wings of the dawn, if i settle on the far side of the sea, even there You will guide me." psalm 139:7-10

I am Omnipresent!

you are never really alone, even though at times you may feel that way. feelings aren't a strong basis for truth, but in those times, I'm not offended if you ask for a sign. I am responsive that way and I adamantly love to confirm My Presence and importance in your life.

so, "test Me" and see if I will not throw open the windows of heaven with "coincidences" and seemingly random comments or occurrences. if you are alert, you will notice My unfailing Presence every moment of the day!

"simon peter answered Him, Lord, where would we go? You have the words of eternal life." john 6:68

"O Lord, you have searched me and You know me. You know when i sit and when i rise; You perceive my thoughts from afar off. You discern my going out and my lying down. You are familiar with all my ways, before a word is on my tongue You know it completely." psalm 139:1-4

I am Omniscient!

All wise, All knowing, Perfect, Infinite, Eternal, the Comforter and Consoler, the Intercessor, the Restrainer, the Teacher, the Counselor, and your Guide.

I guess what I'm trying to tell you is, don't worry if you feel like you can't figure it all out. I will help you! the things you can't understand I am asking you to trust that I have plans that will come to fruition. I have a Perfect Will and a Permissive Will. I will only permit these things for a short while longer and then, finally, all things will be set right. that Day is coming soon.

I pray for you that your faith will not fail. I am willing, but your flesh is weak. I know you will lose your cool sometimes-don't "weep bitterly" at that time, just ask for My forgiveness and begin again. I will honor you and restore you.

your sins are all forgiven once you trust Me.

"for what I want to do I do not do, but what I hate I do." romans 7:15

"He got up, rebuked the wind,and said to the waves, quiet! be still! then the wind died down and it was completely calm." mark 4:39

I am Perfect Love.
trust My Favor.
I am coming straight for you.
speak the following out loud right this second-
"i am greatly loved by You.
i am highly blessed because of that love.
Christ is my Holiness.
Christ is my Righteousness.
Christ is my Peace.
amen and amen."

"whoever drinks the water that I give him will never thirst, indeed, the water I give will become a fresh, bubbling spring within them, giving them eternal life. please, sir, give me this water so that i won't get thirsty and have to keep coming here to draw water." john 4:14,15 "every good and perfect gift is from above, coming down from the Father of heavenly lights, Who does not change like shifting shadows." james 1:17

I am Immutable, Unchanging Spirit!

when I promise something, you can be certain I will do as I say. I am not a man "that I should lie." I have told you and shown you how much I love you, haven't I? you can take that at face value because it is Absolute Truth.

you are My beloved, l'dodi in hebrew. I created the entire world just for you to enjoy. think of all the blessings I have given you. contentment flows from meditating on the excellent, good things in life, not the bad.

your love for Me may change.

My love for you will never change.

learn to respond correctly. your faith and your broken heart will lead to blessing. the world says because you are imperfect, you will not be blessed. the Lord says you will receive the hundredfold blessing for all you have lost.

" I the Lord do not change." malachi 3:6

"He was despised and rejected- a man of sorrows, acquainted with deepest grief. we turned our backs on Him and looked the other way. He was despised and we did not care." isaiah 53:3

for a time in the natural Jesus was separated from God. He willingly came to earth and because I chose more simple conditions for Him to live in, He had to sweat. He had to walk dusty roads, lay His head on a rock to sleep. He chose to be mocked, He chose to be whipped, beaten severely, scourged in fact. He chose nails, large spikes, to pierce His tendons at the wrist. stop and look right now at your wrists and the two tendons that lie there. put your finger in that area,such a delicate area. He chose to be stripped almost naked, bleeding. He chose to hang on a Cross for three hours in the noonday heat, in agony, unable to breathe, suffering, profusely bleeding from His side, utterly alone and forsaken. He bore all our sins. He chose it.

"and being found in appearance as a man, He humbled Himself and became obedient unto death- even death on a cross." phillipians 2:8

"come, let us return to the Lord. He has torn us in pieces, but He will heal us. He has injured us, but He will bind up our wounds. after two days, He will revive us. on the third day, He will restore us, that we may live in His Presence." hosea 6:1,2

"revive us and we will call on Your Name," you say. I pray that you do call out to Me often! that's what I'm waiting for, standing ready each day to fill you if you but call to Me.

sing, "all my fountains are in You."

cry, "You hold the Keys of Life."

call out, "give me the Living Water."

self-focus and self- interest stop this Revival. I know you don't want to appear weird or fanatical to people. when you arrive here, ask john the baptist, elijah, isaiah, john, peter, and paul if it was all worth looking strange for!

I want to light a holy Fire within you that no amount of rain can ever quench. in fact, the Latter Day Rains will only make you burn hotter and brighter!

"will You not revive us again, that Your people may rejoice in You?" psalm 85:6

"I'm going there to prepare a place for you, that where I am there you may also be." john 14:2

you can't see or understand fully what this means right now in your present form. the Door to God opens when you know that you don't and can't know everything right now.

I've tried to describe the perfection of heaven in revelation. words don't do it justice. they are a pale facsimile, for heaven is beyond any words anyone could ever say.

maybe you've never even opened the Bible, much less the book of revelation. turn to the back of your Bible now, the next to last chapter, chapter twenty one and read verses twenty one through twenty five.

this is the best description I could give to the apostle john in a lucid vision. when you read it I hope you can remember the last time you did something for the first time- remember your first love? if you are a believer, remember your first love for the Lord, your first realization of what He did for you. thank Him! thank Him! thank Him! you can never thank Him enough!

"the twelve gates were made of pearls, each gate from a single pearl. and the main street was gold, pure as glass. i saw no temple in the city, for the Lord God Almighty and the Lamb are its temple. and the city had no need of sun or moon, for the glory of God illuminates the city and the Lamb is its light. the nations will walk in its light, and the kings of the world will enter the city in all their glory. its gates will never be closed at the end of the day, for there is no night there." revelation 21:21-25 (just in case you didn't turn to it!)

"for you did not receive a spirit that makes you a slave again to fear, but you received the spirit of sonship. and by Him, we cry, Abba, Father. the Spirit Himself testifies with our spirit that we are God's children." romans 8:15,16

Jesus cried out "Abba" in the garden of gethsemane. because you are sons and daughters of God, Abba sent the Spirit of His Son into your hearts, the Spirit Who calls out Abba!

what is the name you use or used to call your natural father? as a child you called out "daddy" and in the streets of jerusalem children still run after their fathers calling, "Abba!"

God wants you to have this close relationship with Him. if it feels unusual to call Him "Daddy" then practice saying it until it becomes comfortable, a natural outcry from your spirit. or, if you must, just say "Dad" or "Papa", which you probably started saying as a teenager to sound more grown up. I want you to have a special Name for Me that you call Me by, as I do you.

"going a little farther, He fell to the ground and prayed that if possible the awful hour awaiting Him might pass Him by. Abba, Father, He cried out, everything is possible for You. please take this cup of suffering away from Me. yet, I want Your Will to be done and not Mine." mark 14:35,36 "what good will it be for a man if he gains the whole world, yet forfeits his soul?" matthew 16:26

I want to ask you a question today. who are you? what is your identity rooted in? is it your job description, your place in your family, your bank account, your personal appearance? how do you define yourself to others when they ask? these are trick questions as your identity is not in things. let Me propose to you that your identity is in Christ, more so is Christ.

spend your time finding those practices and purposes that help you receive and live the abundant life that Jesus promised. it is forgiving, ongoing love and dependence on God, a vital and precious personal Relationship.

you may have heard this expression so many times that it has become a cliche. I am the Anti-Cliche! so, examine your personal relationships and tell Me how they function and deepen- isn't it through time and experiences together? doesn't it involve each person in the relationship reaching out to the other and sharing important things?(face to face, if possible) that's what I am asking of you! spend time with Me, talk with Me, let's share experiences! I want to be in a real relationship with you!

"but what about you, He asked? who do you say that I am? simon peter answered, You are the Christ, the Son of the Living God." matthew 16:15,16

"He said to them, therefore, every teacher who has been instructed about the Kingdom of heaven is like the owner of a house, who brings out of his storeroom new treasures as well as old." matthew 13:52

I am the New Treasure!
sell everything you have, turn away from every distraction, see that nothing interferes with acquiring this Treasure- an authentic connection with Me! you may say, "but You're invisible!" yes, in the natural for now I am- but My Voice is very obvious for those who have spiritual ears and want to hear. I fully manifested at one time in the body of Jesus Christ and I am manifesting now in you as you believe. your part is to be available and very aware of My thoughts and movements in your life. I challenge you- look for Me in new, fresh ways everyday. I love to surprise you! I confirm Myself in many ways- through the Bible primarily, but also through godly counsel, through circumstances, and through a sense of My Peace within you.

"store up for yourselves treasures in heaven where moths and rust cannot destroy and thieves do not break in and steal. for where your heart is, there your treasure will be also." matthew 6:20

"Jesus answered, it is written: man does not live by bread alone, but by every Word that proceeds from the mouth of God." matthew 4:4

I work in conjunction with the infallible Word of God. I will never ask you to do something that is questionable or disagrees with the Bible. in fact, when you are out in the desert, as Jesus was here, the Word that you have memorized will be your comeback and strength.

if you are reading this, most likely you have a heart and a passion for the Lord; Bible knowledge is second to that. you may know someone who is stuck in depression or fear. they may not know that their sadness is but a wall between two lush gardens, one wild and one landscaped, one known and one as yet unknown.   it is there that the Word can be a healing cloister, a comfort.

maybe you know someone, even a believer, who doesn't like to read or finds the Bible dry or confusing. will they let you read to them, especially children, teens, or the elderly? can you write a card, letter, or email including a particular Scripture I give you for them? get creative as you share the Word with others, especially in their times of sadness or grief. show them how powerful it can be to hear My Promises and how, when you have the Word hidden in your heart, you can cry out to Me any time you need.

"the Scriptures say, you must worship the Lord your God and serve Him only." matthew 3:10

"Jesus said to the servants, fill the jars with water, so they filled them to the brim. then He told them, now draw some out and take it to the master. they did so and the master tasted the water that had turned into wine." john 2:7-9

this was the first of Jesus' miraculous signs. He condensed time to create an expensive wine in a moment. the text says it "revealed His glory and the disciples put their faith in Him." let's meditate on this event. would it take a miracle or an undeniable sign, a supernatural event, to convince someone of Jesus' deity? what are the purposes for miracles? when Jesus was on earth, He performed many healing miracles and God has not changed since. He wants to make you whole.

there are horrific tragedies in life. no child should ever be hurt, period. no person should have to go through abuse or dire illness. poverty is terribly wrong. war is evil. I grieve for the fallen state of the world and the suffering that comes from that. I want to help you know that it's not anything you did wrong if you don't receive the miracle in the way you believe you need. it's not that you're not good enough or didn't pray hard enough or the right way. this is a very hard thing to understand and you probably won't until you reach here. I'm asking you to trust Me and know that I am with you.

"so don't worry about tomorrow, for tomorrow will bring its own worries." matthew 6:34

"how many loaves do you have? Jesus asked. seven, they replied. He told the crowd to sit. when He had taken the seven loaves and given thanks, He broke them and gave them to the disciples." mark 8:5,6

I am the Seven Loaves, multiplied by grace for your needs! I am the Five Smooth Stones, plucked from the stream by david to slay goliath. I am the Abundant Overflow for your need- you're not alone!

in the feeding of the five thousand, the seven loaves and two fish show Jesus' compassion towards the peoples' hunger. ask, seek, knock! persevere in prayer. bang on the door until it opens. I can't tell you that it will be solely because of your efforts, but I can tell you that faith moves mountains and opens doors and windows that seemed nailed shut. it's not always easy- all the platitudes in the world don't help in the face of bitter anguish. that's when you and I will stand together the strongest, facing the adversary down, standing tall, and miraculously rising above.

"and everyone assembled here will know that the Lord rescues His people, but not with sword and spear. this is the Lord's battle and He will give you to us." 1 samuel 17:47

"when the disciples saw Him walking on the water, they were terrified. in their fear, they cried out, it's a ghost! but Jesus spoke to them at once. don't be afraid, He said. take courage. I am here!" matthew 14:26,27

when I describe the wonders of God's love in a term you could grasp, I say "as high as the heavens" or expound on the depths, the vastness of the ocean. here, Jesus demonstrates His authority over any created thing. the wind and the seas obey Him. the dimensions of time and space collapse at His command. sickness and even death flee in His Presence. the Bible as an historical record verifies all these truths.

Jesus' ministry of healing and miracles began after I descended on Him as a dove. that is also where you access a calling and purpose in your life! Jesus said to you, "you will do greater things than these!" grasp that a moment! you have the same power in you!

you may ask how to access this power. you access anointing (spiritual power from the Lord for a certain situation) through faith. faith begets prayer, prayer begets relationship, and Relationship with Me develops favor. if you are truly established in relationship with the Lord, then your life will be different. you will have different priorities and even conversations. you will have an indomitable spirit. lay hands on people- miracles are still occurring daily!

"we believe that we are all saved the same way, by the undeserved grace of the Lord Jesus." acts 15:11

"very early on sunday morning the women went to the tomb, taking the spices they had prepared. they found the stone had been rolled away from the entrance." luke 24:1,2

I could speak all day about the life, ministry, legacy, and glory of Jesus! the culmination of His purpose was His Resurrection. it showed His victory over sin and death, so it was in a whole different category from the other miracles. it transports Him, and us in the future, to the other dimension beyond our earthly encumbrances. yet, in His glorified Body, He spoke and listened, ate, touched and was touched, embraced and encouraged his frightened disciples.

close your eyes again- a theme with Me! breathe in deeply, exhale slowly. can you feel the eternal life within you, how valuable and fierce it is, how very vulnerable and precious?

"to live is Christ, to die is gain." phillipians 1:21

"and we who are left will be caught up together in the air to meet the Lord and thus shall we ever be." 1 thessalonians 4:17

there are many theories and assumptions about the rapture. I reveal information about this time again and again so you will be prepared. use only the Word as your source for wisdom here, as you should for most things in life. don't worry about the details of timing too much except to be excited to see Me!

the Church is My best and most powerful designee on earth. in the Bride of Christ are all the blessings and favor, protective covering, fellowship, and grace that I meant for the world to have. she has been influenced by the world somewhat, and yet she stands. are you committed to a local Body, even though she is not yet fully perfected? this pleases Me greatly! if you are a lone ranger Christian please reconsider. definitely stay in your Word daily and keep filled up with My grace and truth- but be a vital part of a local Church.

I am the Restrainer! for now I am holding back, but once I am removed from the world, evil will be totally unleashed.

stay awake- watch and pray.

" behold, I come like a thief in the night." 1thessalonians 5:2

"i was glad when they said, let us go to the House of the Lord." psalm 122:1

there's much to be said for the traditions of the Church, even the liturgies and sometimes ritualistic observances, if they are done with a heart for Me. hold to the stories that I preserved for you to learn from and have reverence for the Bible. meditate on the important moments of Jesus' life. I'm asking you, pleading with you, to carefully study the gospel of john in particular. I exhort you to immerse yourself in it. "faith comes by hearing", paul wrote in romans. reading is also hearing. read out loud to yourself and hear My Voice through your own intonations and expressions!

I will call you and lead you to the Body you are meant to serve in! be faithful. be rooted and planted there, this will save you a host of problems. each time you transplant, it is as when a shrub is uprooted. it will recover, but it is better to grow deep, meaningful roots and relationships. I will firmly tell you if I need to use you somewhere else.

"let us not give up meeting together, as some are in the habit of doing, but let us encourage one another- and all the more as you see the Day approaching." hebrews 10:25

"this is the meaning of the mystery of the seven stars you saw in My right hand and the seven gold lampstands. the seven stars are the messengers of the seven churches and the seven lampstands are the seven churches." revelation 2:20

reread yesterday's meditation. I know it was a challenging one, but it is necessary. the Church is prolific and filled with power, yet constantly comes under extreme attack. I want you to defend Her. defend your leaders, pitch in where you can, suggest and help with not too much criticism. persevere to the end. you will grow to great maturity and faith within the Body, much more so than as a lone-wolf, vulnerable to attack. the Shepherd will seek you out if you venture away, but He'd rather you stay secure in the fold.

"won't He leave the ninety nine others in the wilderness and go to search for the one that is lost until He finds it? and when He has found it, He will joyfully carry it home on His shoulders." luke 15:4,5 "do not let your heart be troubled." john 14:1

I don't think you quite understand the significance of a royal wedding. it is full of history, pomp, and circumstance. there is traditional music, a whole symphony and a choir even, an abundance of flowers, guests dressed their finest- and at the center of it all is one man and one woman.

this is a prophetic glimpse of the excitement there will be when we are united together. it will be a celebration such as no one has ever seen! at the birth of a child the birth pangs and delivery are quickly forgotten in the welcoming of the beautiful miracle of the baby.

everyone will be there, yet, as at a wedding, I, the Groom, will welcome you personally. there is a calm hush just before you arrive. you are the one that brings the light to My eyes as I await you. I have been standing and waiting now for a long time! can you imagine that Jesus may be nervous as He awaits the culmination of everything He purchased you for? as the Bride arrives, everyone gasps- the time is so filled with joy and possibility! I am marrying, not for duty or protocol, but for love!

"I am the Rose of Sharon, the Lily of the Valley." song of solomon 2:1

"arise, My fair one, My beloved and come away. look, the winter is past and the rains are over and gone." song of solomon 2:10,11

marriage is a way of life made holy by God, a joyful covenant. it is a type and shadow of heaven, a breath-taking show of unity, made sacred by My blessing. it is the most vital picture of your Relationship with Me.

at the foot of the Cross, mary, Jesus' mother, john, His closest friend, and mary, a disciple, were blessed to witness such love. they were chosen, but they also chose of their own free will to be there to witness Love Come Down. Jesus began and completed the revolution movement and even today I am still in that revolution business.

I AM the Revolution itself.

I have the power to manifest revival and change the world and I am honoring you and using you to do it, for I have faith in you and love you! thank you for choosing to be at the foot of the Cross and at the empty Tomb.

"place me like a seal over your heart, like a seal on your arm. for love is as strong as death, it flashes like fire, the brightest kind of flame. many waters cannot quench love, nor can rivers drown it. if a man tried to buy love with all his wealth, he would be utterly scorned." song of solomon 8:6,7

"does not My Word burn like fire? says the Lord."
jeremiah 23:29

fire generates energy in the natural. in the spiritual, fire is evocative of passion. I am the Fire!

I am calling on you now. "I came to set the world on fire, how I wish it were already ablaze!" luke 12:49 I want you to be passionate about loving others and making the world a better place. the passion of true love exhibits this fervor and focus.

ask Me to fill you with determination and purpose and I will! I have made you for a certain purpose that no one else can fulfill. you are specifically suited to help in certain areas. there are many wonderful things that will not be done if you don't do them!

so, if you are tired even before the day begins, I am asking you to take a new grip with your creative hands and to stand up on your strong knees! get that fire shut up in your bones!

"therefore, I have set my face like a flint to do His Will."
isaiah 50:7

"as the men watched, Jesus' appearance was transformed, so that His Face shone like the sun, and His clothes became white as light." matthew 17:2

this is the Transfiguration. I came as a Voice out of the cloud, exactly as I came at His Baptism. I tangibly gave Him the initiative to begin and continue His ministry. both times, I wanted to express that Jesus was God the Father's Beloved Son.

when you are in My Presence, your face will also radiate. you will feel a lightness, your smile will appear naturally bright, your eyes will be relaxed and clear. I told you, you will feel chills, you will feel goosebumps on your skin or the hairs on your arms and the back of your neck will stand up! sometimes I put a warmth in your heart or your heart will start to beat faster, a volcano of emotions!

these emotions and feelings are not always present, but it is powerful when they are. God the Father created you in His image, so you have emotions and that is good! the process is challenging as life ebbs and flows with many emotions. express them freely, as a child does, not attaching too much to happiness or sadness, just experiencing them fluidly.

"i have the daily burden of my concern for all the churches. for who is weak without my feeling that weakness? who is led astray and i do not burn with anger?" 2 corinthians 11:29

"deep calls to deep in the roar of Your ocean, all Your waves and breakers have swept over me." psalm 42:7

the anointing flows where the Blood is!

sorry, not sorry, but you can't make this happen. you CAN be obedient and available, for many of the best things that happen to you in life will be unexpected, like waves in the ocean. waves of grace and mercy follow each next step I show you. love each next person I put in your path today. it seems so random but it is not random at all, in fact, there is nothing in life that is random. there is no such thing as luck.

when you get frustrated, just remember- it will all make sense one day, when you see the front side of the exquisite tapestry that you have woven day by day with your life choices.

I'm so proud of you!

"be silent before the Lord, all humanity, for He is springing into action from His holy dwelling." zechariah 2:13

"for you died to this life, and your real life is hidden with God in Christ." colossians 3:3

Father God put you <u>in</u> Christ!
to protect you- psalm 91
to hide you from attack- ephesians 3:9
to give you the address of heaven- john 14:2
you are safe!

"when i looked again, i saw a man with a measuring line in his hand. where are you going? i asked. he replied, i am going to measure jerusalem to see how wide and how long it is." zechariah 2:1,2

"for I am not ashamed of this good news about Christ, for it is the power of God at work...it tells us how God made us right in His sight. this is accomplished from start to finish by faith." romans 1:16,17

"He said to me, My grace is sufficient for you." 2 corinthians 10:9

there is a rhythm in My moments with you, mostly a quiet rhythm. I love when you read your Bible. I love when you sing to Me and play your drums, guitars, pianos, violins. I love when you pray, telling Me all about your feelings and concerns for yourself and others.

then, after, I am waiting, just waiting for you to be still and quiet and to build that bridge between the natural and the supernatural- in the Holy of Holies in complete silence, if there can be. can you prostrate your body? prostration brings humility. I suggest for you to have a special place to meet with Me- a chair, a mat, a special corner. it will hold the space for Me to come. God the Father speaks very clearly when His Book is open- keep it near and maybe just put your hand on it if you are too tired to read.

then just listen...

"come, let us worship and bow down. let us kneel before the Lord our God, our Maker. for He is our God. we are the people He watches over." psalm 95:6,7

"He will not crush the bruised reed or put out a flickering candle. He will bring justice to all who have been wronged." isaiah 42:3,4

there is much violence in the world today. there always has been, but it has increased so much that I know you can't help but be aware of it. can you try to keep your mornings sacred and calm and not turn on your phones or televisions immediately? it is a bad habit. I want you to come to Me <u>first</u> and I will guard your heart and emotions that way.

I am the Hedge around about you, if you will allow Me to be. I know there are things you want or feel you need to know. I'm asking you to trust Me when you can't understand immediately. the enemy wants to distract you and steal both your time and your peace.

instead, be an intercessor, be a forerunner! be a watchman on the wall today for this generation.

"those who sow in tears will reap in songs of joy." psalm 126:5

"he is like a tree planted by the streams of water, which yields its fruit in season." psalm 1:3

whatever your gift is, if you use it, it will multiply. this is essential to know so that you will be motivated to continually operate in those areas, any and all, that you are gifted in. leaders will usually have administrative abilities, those with the gift of helps will have compassion for others, a tender heart. if you have financial blessing, you will probably be gifted with a generous heart. if you have the gift of healing, lay hands and pray for many people, when they allow you to or ask you to. if you have been given the gift of wisdom, share and interpret the Bible.

as you use your gifts, you will experience blessings, health, and favor from God.

"i pray that you may prosper and have health, even as your soul prospers." 3 john 1:2

"i lift up my eyes to the hills, where does my help come from? my help comes from the Lord, the Maker of heaven and earth. He will not let your foot slip. He Who watches over you will not slumber, yea, He Who watches over israel will neither slumber nor sleep." psalm 121:1,2

you can sleep peacefully each evening. I am watching over you and your family. your legacy of faith reaches out to cover and protect over them, from one generation to another. this is My Promise to you.

if you should awaken I can use that time with you. david would praise and pray as he laid on his bed in the evenings. lift up your hands and bless Me then. if you arise, put the legs up, elevated and supported against the bed or a wall. breathe in My Presence in the night hours. see Me in your mind's eye- I can give you wonderful spiritual abilities and visions! you will be at the Throne of the Lord of Hosts and then just go straight on and Jesus is there! as you repeat My Name or a verse you have recalled, I will come very near with My soothing hand on your forehead. feel your brain relax with that gentle weight of My Hand.

"God gives His beloved sleep." psalm 127:2

"You have seen me tossing and turning through the night. You have collected all my tears and preserved them in Your bottle (wineskin). You have recorded every one in Your Book (scroll). the very day i call for help, the tide of battle turns." psalm 56:8,9

I am with you in the quiet hours of the night when the pain of the loss (es) or chronic physical pain you are suffering pierces you so badly. if you have been separated from someone you love, when you reunite with that person or persons, time will cease to exist and it will be as if you had never been apart at all. to know this type of profound love is a precious gift. many don't get that opportunity.

in these hard, almost unbearable times, have much silence around you. lean on My promises in the Bible and repeat them to yourself over and over. remember when I helped you in the past with challenges and testify to others of how I brought you through.

meditate on My Sufficiency.

in these moments, I am Enough! I pray for you to know you have enough!

"He will wipe every tear from their eyes. there will be no more death or sorrow or crying or pain. all these are gone forever!" revelation 21:4

"teach me to number my days, to realize the brevity of life, so that i may gain a heart of wisdom." psalm 90:2

of the 80-85 years you live
-<u>26</u> are spent sleeping
 59
-<u>12</u> are spent working
 47
-<u>10</u> are spent cooking and eating
 37
-<u>10</u> are spent on tv and internet
 27
-_<u>6</u> are spent driving
 21
-_<u>3</u> are spent grooming
 18
-_<u>3</u> are spent cleaning
that leaves 15 years to live!

time is a concept the world uses to measure age. you are timeless and eternal spirit, but use your time on earth well.

"so, be careful how you live. make the most of every opportunity in these evil days. don't act thoughtlessly, but understand what the Lord wants you to do…be filled with the Holy Spirit. sing psalms, hymns, and spiritual songs to the Lord." ephesians 5:15-19 "after two days He will revive us; on the third day He will restore us, that we may live in His Presence. let us acknowledge the Lord, oh, that we might know Him! He will come to us like the winter rains, like the spring rains that water the earth." hosea 6:2,3

my prophets are calling this the time of the Latter Day Rains. there is an increased outpouring of spiritual gifts, fruits, and power! if you are open to receive that, then revival can truly spread across this earth.

are you interested in Me and what I'm doing? are you excited about this Moment of Mine? are you ready for what's next?

I want to pour over you and into you, in season and out of season. this is how revival comes, just as simply as that, each person using every ounce of their energy to spread My love to the world.

open your mouth right now and say "YES!"

did you do it? say a big yes out loud right now. the world is in "no" mode. don't be like the world. it is your agreement with Me that propels the Revival and a Revolution of grace. esther 4:14 says you were born "for such a time as this." you were born at this time to impact many lives for eternity.

"in those days I will pour out My Spirit upon the earth. your sons and daughters will prophesy. your old men will dream dreams, and your young men will see visions." joel 2:28

"the Spirit interprets the Word." 2 peter 1:20

I want to share with you what I am talking about here- the Scripture is given, or you read it, and as you hear and allow it to penetrate through meditation, I will speak to you. you will hear thoughts of wisdom and feelings of peace that are clearly not self-generated. God the Father's Words have a creative unction- they manifest My Presence, especially when they are read out loud. have you noticed that the most effective preachers keep their Bibles physically very near them as they preach?

I know, I know the Bible is on your phone now. I inhabit the words, not the device. still, the phone is not quite the same thing as carrying the actual Book. plus, it's very distracting when the Word is on your phone. carrying an actual Bible gives you a protective anointing and makes you refer to it much more often. it is also a witness to the world and a great conversation starter! if you truly knew how powerful this was, you would carry your Bible everywhere the way most do with their phones. check in with Me in Scripture, in your mind, more often than you check your phone. I will bless you for that understanding action.

"how can a young person stay pure? by living according to Your Word. i have tried hard to find You- don't let me wander from Your commands. i have hidden Your Word in my heart that i might not sin against You." psalm 119:9-11 "the rain and the snow come down from the heavens and stay on the ground to water the earth. they cause the grain to grow, producing seed for the farmer and bread for the hungry. it is the same with My Word. I send it out, and it always produces fruit. it will accomplish all I want it to and it will prosper anywhere I send it." isaiah 55:10,11

the more you pour out, the more supply comes to you.
everything flows down from the Head, Who is Christ Jesus.
blessings flow down from your generosity to others.
grace falls down on you, like rain.
don't complain when it rains-
receive!
receive My abundant mercy and grace.

"how wonderful and pleasant it is when brothers live together in harmony. it is as precious as the anointing oil that was poured on aaron's head, that ran down his beard, and onto the border of his robe." psalm 133:1,2 "but in that coming day, no weapon formed against you shall prosper and you will refute every tongue that accuses you. these benefits are enjoyed by the servants of the Lord; their vindication will come from Me, says the Lord." isaiah 54:17

the devil is the accuser, who constantly tries to get you to believe lies about yourself and others- don't listen to him! the world brings every distraction it can into your life, especially when you are trying to be with Me, have you noticed? be wise with your time. these come against you- the enemy, the world, and your own flesh that has its desires and agenda. stay Christ-focused!

I am steadily looking and working each day for your highest good. I can see everything from that eternal perspective, looking down at the whole picture of the big blue marble you call home. I run interference for you so that you don't have to focus on when the next shoe is going to drop. instead, it can be your birthday everyday! have that mentality! move through life with an easefulness, trusting that I have your back, My child!

"all these blessings will come upon you and accompany you if you obey the Lord your God. you will be blessed in the city and blessed in the country. the fruit of your womb will be blessed, and the crops of your land...your basket and your kneading trough will be blessed. you will be blessed when you come in and blessed when you go out...the Lord will make you the head and not the tail, you will always be above and not beneath." deuteronomy 28:2-6,13 "then the Lord said to isaiah, take your son, shear-jashub (meaning "a remnant will return") and go out to meet king ahaz at the end of the aquaduct of the upper pool, near the road leading to the field where cloth is washed. say to him, keep calm and carry on." isaiah 7:3,4

you may have thought the world originated this thought. other translations say "keep calm and don't worry," meaning the same thing. I have told you many times to stay in a restful state and believe Me for your deliverance. all I ask is that you continue on and rest in Me!

I understand there is a hesitancy when you are walking into an unknown situation or the way seems too difficult. I don't expect you to get it perfect all the time. just like a child learning to walk, there will be missteps, even falls, but I will hold your hand as you walk and I will be there to catch you when you try to run ahead of Me.

"if you do not stand firm in your faith, you will not stand at all." isaiah 7:9

"and we take captive every thought to make it obedient to Christ." 2 corinthians 10:5

here, the apostle paul is pleading with those in corinth, and with us, to come up to a higher place of thought and being.

peaceful thoughts.

peaceful words.

peaceful hearts.

I am not the meditation police. you make the decision, the choice, to retrain your thoughts, although when you are close to Me that is so much easier! restrain your thoughts from purely worldly and self concerns. sanctify your thoughts, set them apart. in other words, don't dwell on or engage with unclean thoughts.

you know that this world and all that is in it is passing away, right? it's happening right in front of your eyes. you can't "own" anything, not even your own body. spend your time on eternally consequential thoughts and pursuits; on people and not things.

all that being said (good expression, I like it!) nothing you do can change the all-encompassing love I have for you!

"when the Son sets you free, you will be free indeed!" john 8:36

"and when He brings out His own sheep, He goes before them, and the sheep follow Him." john 10:4

hold My Hand- I am in front of you leading the Way. remember when you had a small child or grandchild? maybe it was in the past, but I gave you memory areas in your brain, so I know you can call up the image of them reaching for your hand whenever you got near the street. if you were blessed, they wanted to hold your hand for many years. in the same manner, reach for My Hand when you are in precarious situations. I will lead you!

we talked before about hearing and knowing that you hear My Voice- that involves wanting to hear, taking the time to shut out the world and listen, and astutely discerning what is from Me and what is counterfeit spirituality from the world or the devil (hint: it usually has a kernel of truth to it just to confuse you). it sounds overwhelming, but really it is very simple- "My sheep know My Voice." stay close to the Shepherd! (ps- I want you to feel that when you are in church that you are in your element! get comfortable there- it will feel weird at first, just keep going!)

"then peter got down out of the boat, walked on the water and came toward Jesus. but when he saw the wind, he was afraid and, beginning to sink, cried out, Lord save me! immediately, Jesus reached out His hand and caught him. you of little faith, He said, why did you doubt?" matthew 14:29-31 "he picked up five smooth stones from a stream and put them in his shepherd's bag." 1 samuel 17:40

I am the Five Smooth Stones!

I needed more time with this revelation. in the natural, there's no way david could have defeated goliath, but he had hope in God. the stones weren't supernatural in and of themselves, they were just regular stones. it was david's prayer, heart, and intention that infused them with power.

hope says with faith, "I am 100% sure this will work out for my highest good!" not 100% sure of yourself, or your goodness, but 100% sure of God!

maybe you're still afraid- young david was as he looked at the giant. joshua and caleb were as they saw the giants in canaan. daniel was afraid as he advanced toward the lions.

the Lord shut the lions' mouths- He will do it for you too! God is no respecter of persons, but answers the call of faith.

"then david ran over and pulled goliath's sword from its sheath. and david used it to kill him and cut off his head." 1 samuel 17:51

"but they delight in the Word of the Lord, meditating on it day and night. they are like trees planted along the riverbank, bearing fruit each season. their leaves never wither and they prosper in all they do." psalm 1: 3

be anxious for nothing, My child. don't lose one ounce of your faith! I know every moment of your whole life. I see you as that large, blossoming tree, standing immovable even if the banks should begin to erode. keep your earthly relationships strong and steady, but even more, be secure in your vertical taproot that you have sent down deep into our Relationship.

that is why I am upholding you! the scorching heat will not wither you as you and I walk together in the cool of the morning before the sun blazes- and then we close the day together even as it was in eden. how I love to be with you!

"blessed is the man who trusts in the Lord, and whose hope is in the Lord. for he shall be like a tree planted by the waters, which spreads out its roots by the river, and he will not fear when the heat comes; but his leaf will be green, and he will not be anxious in the year of drought." jeremiah 17: 7,8 "the Holy Spirit expressly (clearly, strongly) says, in the latter days some will abandon the faith and follow deceiving spirits and doctrines (false teachings) taught by demons." 1 timothy 4:1

life is a challenge, yet as your loving Creator, I want you to have a paradisical life! how can I reconcile that dichotomy to you? "in this world, you will have troubles"- attacks from the enemy, irritations, problems with relationships, and physical issues with your body.

I'm sorry that things are so hard- I am. soon all disease and death, all evil, all crime will be abolished forever. I get angry at the hypocrisy and the faithlessness of people. you may be angry also, it's alright, but don't sin. "speak the truth in love."

I can't wait to rid the world of the evil one and all his vile, horrific schemes. I'm asking you to believe that I will use what you have had to face for increase. increase of blessing in your life, increase of your faith and respect for Me, and increase in all your relationships, for life is at its core about relationships.

"but take heart, for I have overcome the world." john 16:33

"oh, that You would burst from the heavens and come down! how the mountains would quake in Your Presence!" isaiah 64:1

there are times when My nature is very laid back. there are also times when I am assertive. this shows the resiliency that is inherent in My character. just know that I will always protect you and I would like you to cultivate the same stamina that I have.

when you were a young parent, remember how you could stay up all night to feed or comfort your baby if they were upset? be just that conscious of the needs of the world and dedicated to helping- so many are hurting and feel alone.

I want you to be saturated with My love, saturated by My Promises, saturated in My Presence. then go and impact the world with that expressive love!

"once again I will shake not only the earth but the heavens also. this means that all of creation will be shaken and removed, so that only the unshakable things remain." hebrews 12:26,27

"I was ready to respond, but no one asked Me for help. I was ready to be found, but no one was looking for Me. I said, here I am, here I am! to a nation that did not call on My Name." isaiah 65:1

seek the counsel of the Lord first. seek Me before you make any decision, particularly a momentous one that will affect your eternity. who you are yoked to in marriage is extremely important. pray for that unforgettable person that I have for you! use great discernment and prayer and then, once committed, stay strong by keeping Me at the center of the relationship and praying together daily.

jehoshaphat (meaning "the Lord judges"), king of judah, sought insight and internal guidance from the Lord and also from the Lord's prophets and he found godly success. (study 2 chronicles chapters 17 and 18). pray about how this applies to you today. I chose these stories to help you glean by example.

"give honor to marriage, and remain faithful to one another, and keep the marriage bed pure." hebrews 13:4

"this is what the Lord says: Heaven is My Throne and the earth is My footstool. can you build Me a temple as good as that? could you build Me such a resting place?" isaiah 66:1

your firm foundation is built upon My Grace and My Truth. My Justice sent Jesus, and My Mercy operates daily in your favor. however, it is My Righteousness that availed the judgement for sin- sins of commission and sins of omission. My holy Justice required and accomplished the crucifixion, the judgement for your sin, the penalty falling on Jesus. God the Father is a Righteous Judge- He determines outcomes from the Throne. oh, come to His Mercy Seat- where the cherubim look down on the Blood- no longer with flaming swords like at the entrance to eden, but with winged protection for you.
blessed are your eyes for they can see!
blessed are your ears that are open to hear!
blessed is your heart that willingly receives My Grace!

"look! I am creating new heavens and a new earth, and no one will even think about the old ones anymore." isaiah 65:17

"and in Him you too are being built together to become a dwelling in which God lives by His Spirit." ephesians 2:22

in a natural family, there are varying states of dysfunction, and there are no perfect families, because of your fallen state. there are many examples of this in the Bible- cain murdered abel, jacob deceived esau, absalom betrayed david, solomon condoned idol worship, james and john jockeyed for position with Jesus. have you thought about the fact that I chose to place you in the certain family you are in? I am the One Who chose your parents, your siblings, your children. I chose which spirit would indwell each person. the world has a false teaching that you chose your family- no, it was I who saw what you would need to grow and mature.

your spiritual family is a different matter. My child, these are the people you can choose to be in your life to inspire, mentor, and encourage you. they speak strength and Scripture into your life and you enjoy being around them. I instituted the church to bind you together in the Kingdom. together, as you pray for one another, take communion together, cry together, laugh and worship together, I work encouragement, forgiveness, and humility.

find a way! find a way to let go of resentment if there is any. families are the biggest challenge in life because they know all about you, and you about them. find a way to make peace with everyone!

"this is a trustworthy saying, and everyone should acknowledge it; Christ Jesus came into the world to save sinners- and i am the worst of them all. but God had mercy on me so He could use me as a prime example of His great patience with even the worst sinners." 1 timothy 1:15,16 "for no matter how many promises God has made, they are all "Yes" in Christ. and so through Him, the resounding "Amen" is spoken by us to the glory of God." 2 corinthians 1:20

lift up your voice and say amen! I am right near to you, closer than you can intuit. I am as close as the sound of the amen even! call Me on My Promises- tell Me "You said so!" I am bringing Revival- a Revival in the world and a Revival in your personal life and Relationship with Me. you will hunger to speak with Me as soon as your feet hit the ground in the morning, or even before!

I want you to lose track of time when you are in My Presence. talk to Me about what you need today, a sincere prayer about even the small things that are bothering you. I have promised to hear and answer you.

I hear you- you are so important to Me!

I hear you- your concerns are My concerns!

I hear you.

"and so dear brothers and sisters, i plead with you to give your bodies as a living and holy sacrifice- the kind He will find acceptable. this is truly the way to worship Him." roman 12:1

"how the king rejoices in Your strength, O Lord! he shouts with joy because You give him victory. for You have given him his heart's desire; You have withheld nothing he requested." psalm 21:1,2

I find great delight in giving you the desires of your heart- in seeing you laugh, dance, and sing, just as you enjoy making your own children happy! you know, I created this entire world for you to enjoy and appreciate! search for the things and the people who uplift you and spend time with them! and then go uplift others. family and strong family bonds are one of My best gifts to you. let's go into this concept even deeper- I chose who would be your parents so they would shape your character. if your parents weren't loving enough to you, or at all, I am sorry, My child. that was their bad choice, not My Will for you. try to let that go and forgive, as difficult as that may be.

I chose which children would be yours because I knew specific personalities that would complement and challenge yours, bringing you lots of maturity and growth, right? I chose your natural brothers and sisters, if you have them. they shared many things with you as you were growing up (or not!) and are there to teach you profound lessons. so, unless there is severe abuse, I am asking you not to disown them. forgive and stay in relationship with them.

I love how you try to pray in accordance with My expressed Will and I will try My best to give you what you ask, if it is in your best interests. trust Me to know and determine that and be content with what I have given you!

"he who walks with wise men will be wise." proverbs 13:20

"the Kingdom of Heaven will be like ten bridesmaids who took their lamp and went to meet the Bridegroom. five of them were foolish and five were wise. the five who were foolish didn't take enough oil for their lamps, but the other five were wise enough to take along extra oil." matthew 25:1-4

I'm waiting for you each day to come to Me for your extra oil! the world gets in your head and drains you with comparisons and distractions, constant barrages on your peace of mind, head games. do you really think you will find satisfaction in the things the world offers?

instead, come to the Fountain that flows with Anointing Oil! the oil is the power and confidence you need to deal, to endure to the end.

you've heard generalities of how to approach Me, but I want to get more specific with you here. turn off your phone and any other controllable noise. sit or recline. close your eyes and breathe that deep breathe a few times. and then just say My Name. maybe you've only had a peripheral relationship with Me, in your mind, not in your heart. do you have a special Name for Me? God, Abba, Jesus, Papa, Father, Dad, Holy Spirit- what Name do you speak when you speak to Me? call to Me like I am calling to you- by name! then just BE with Me, speaking honestly and listening in the silence. you will hear Me. you will know.

"I have called you by name, you are Mine." isaiah 43:1

"as the sun went down that evening, people throughout the village brought sick family members to Jesus. no matter what their diseases were, the touch of His Hand healed every one." luke 4:40

just touching the hem of Jesus' garment heals, being in His Presence brings the anointing. that's why I suggested to you to get alone somewhere, but also, after you've really known Me, you can be in a crowd, lights bright, music around, and still have the knowledge that I'm there. no matter where you are, you can be focused intently on Me.

especially when you are having a good time, I am there! are you guys having any fun there on earth? I want you to feel alive- living each moment and reaching out from that place of confidence, like a musician who hones his craft through practice and then delights in sharing that gift. you applaud at a concert. clap your hands and abandon yourself in worship as well! I will come and heal you as you sing in genuine faith and "first time" love for Me.

remember the story of the men who tore off the roof to let their paralytic friend down into Jesus' Presence? I want you to RAISE the roof! get the anointing from Him and then lift the roof off the place where you are. more on this story later, it's a beautiful one!

"sing together everyone! all you honest hearted people- raise the roof!" psalm 32:11

"early the next morning, Jesus went out to an isolated place. the crowds searched everywhere for Him and when they finally found Him, they begged Him not to leave them. but He replied, I must preach the good news of the Kingdom in other towns too, because that is why I was sent." luke 4:42,43

Jesus often withdrew to the wilderness to pray. and He often went away from the multitudes to draw strength from prayer and time alone. even though I created you to be in relationship with others, it's okay if you need to take time to yourself to replenish. in fact, it is necessary.

follow Jesus' example in all things. He had a mission and a focus- to announce God's loving plan and people were attracted to that. people love being around those who are confident and easy to relate to. see how they begged Him to stay with them. He was passionate about healing, uplifting, and encouraging others.

you do the same!

"but his officers tried to reason with him and said, sir, if the prophet had told you to do something very difficult, wouldn't you have done it? so you should certainly obey him when he says simply, go and wash and be cured. so naaman went down to the jordan and dipped himself seven times, as the man of God had instructed him. and he was healed." 2 kings 5:13,14 "now fear the Lord and serve Him wholeheartedly. throw away the gods our forefathers worshiped beyond the euphrates and in egypt and serve the Lord alone. if you refuse to serve the Lord, then choose this day whom you will serve. but as for me and my house, we will serve the Lord." joshua 24: 14,15

I need you to make a decision- that is why I gave you free will, so you would be able to choose for yourself. in these last days, people have gone further and further away from My standards. I know it is impossible for anyone to keep the law perfectly, which is why I gave the plan of Grace through Christ Jesus. nevertheless, true faith leads to greater sense of morality. there is an accompanying sense of humble repentance when you get way off the mark.

those lines are being wiped away and things are becoming sanctioned and permissible that are a stench to My nostrils. turn your eyes away from the deceits of the world. I will let you know in your spirit clearly when something is not of Me. don't compromise when you hear those directives.

"solomon built such shrines for all his foreign wives to use for burning incense and sacrificing to their gods. the Lord was very angry with solomon, for his heart had turned away from the Lord Who had appeared to him twice. He had warned solomon specifically about worshiping other gods, but solomon did not listen to the Lord's command." 1 kings 11:8-10 "but at midnight, paul and silas were praying and singing hymns to God and the prisoners were listening to them. suddenly, there was a massive earthquake, and the prison was shaken to its foundations. all the doors immediately flew open and the chains of every prisoner fell off!" acts 16:25,26

the first portion of this Scripture is amazing, that these men would be worshiping and joyful as they were chained to a wall and probably beaten and starving for Who knows how long (I do!)

the second portion, though, is completely astounding and makes Me even more proud. they were consciously giving testimony to God's love and peace by their worship, as Jesus did to the thieves at the Cross. the other prisoners and even the guards themselves came to salvation and eternal life because of paul and silas' heroic actions here.

I'm asking you to do the same! no doubt you are not in a prison cell, although there are some Christians who are. I'm not minimizing the challenges you have or suggesting you don't have any issues-I know you do- I know every second of your suffering. I'm asking you to give a sacrifice of praise today. thank you for that obedience and belief in what I ask.

"you will live in joy and peace. the mountains and hills will burst into song, and the trees of the fields will clap their hands!" isaiah 59:12

"those who seek the Lord lack no good thing." psalm 34:10

"Jesus said, everything is possible for him who believes. immediately, the boy's father exclaimed, i do believe, help me overcome my unbelief!" mark 9:23,24

the father here was desperate for his son to be healed. I certainly didn't cause that, or any, illness, but I did use it to strengthen his faith. with fear and trembling, the man pleaded with Jesus for his son's healing. have you been there? at these times when you feel most helpless and alone, please draw closer to Me and allow Me the honor of lifting your faith to higher levels, like an upward vortex that spirals ever upwards toward Me!

what if the necessary miracle doesn't occur exactly as you thought it should. I hear you- I understand your frustration and pain. having anger at that point, having a doubt, is not sin, but dwelling on and manufacturing more doubt and fear can be. don't discuss or over analyze the issue or problem. at some point in any area of challenge, you must move on, as God told moses. He asked moses why he was coming to discuss something- and He said, " just tell the people to move on." this thing you're facing will generate a legacy, maybe a piece of art or music, an empathy and strength of character. it will certainly give you a powerful testimony. in some way, you will help others through this.

"for i am the least of the apostles and do not even deserve to be called an apostle, because i persecuted the church of God. but by the grace of God i am what i am, and His grace to me was not without effect." 1 corinthians 15:9,10 "but stephen, full of the Holy Spirit, looked up to heaven and saw the glory of God, and Jesus standing at the right hand of God. look, he said, I see heaven open and the Son of Man standing at the right hand of God. at this they covered their ears and, yelling, they rushed at him, dragged him out of the city, and stoned him." acts 7:55-58

here, Jesus was respectfully standing from His Throne for stephen! what an honor! paul was present that day and at this time in his life, he thought it was important to kill people who disagreed with his opinion and the opinion of the law. the very fact that paul completely changed after his damascus road encounter with Jesus proves the power of knowing the truth. afterward, he dedicated thirty years of his life to planting churches, spreading the hope of the gospel, and eventually becoming a martyr for Christ, beheaded.

today, can you dedicate some time to tilling new ground, get your hands dirty! dedicate to planting good seed in ground that may seem infertile, nurturing those people who show tender sprouts of faith or interest sprouting up. I am honored by your worship, but I don't really need it. your worship does glorify God, but mainly strengthens you in your walk, focusing you on Me. I have millions of angels to worship Me, My child. however, I do love and need your passion for sharing with others about Jesus as you serve and love them. be fearless like stephen!

"and saul was there, giving approval for his death." acts 8:1

"it was in the year king uzziah died that i saw the Lord. He was sitting on a lofty Throne, and the train of His robe filled the temple." isaiah 6:1

no one gets tired in the Throne Room. whenever you quiet yourself and come into My full manifested Presence, I bring you vast reserves of healing and energy! I equip you for the day that I have called you to. you are not moving by your own power or resources, but by My mighty Right Hand. I prepare Shade for you, not to cast dispersion as the world throws shade, but to cool and comfort you. My Robe of Righteousness wraps you in resplendent beauty and cushions you from any of life's heartaches, softening the disappointments, and abandonments.

come and let Me encircle you and enfold you, My tired one.

"since we are receiving a Kingdom that is unshakable, let us be thankful and please God by worshiping Him with holy fear and awe. for our God is a consuming fire." hebrews 12:28,29

"I have come to bring fire on the earth and how I wish it were already ablaze! but I have a baptism of suffering ahead of Me and I am under a heavy burden until it is accomplished." luke 12:49,50

here, Jesus is speaking about the consuming fire of faith. it has a cleansing and purifying effect, purging out any thoughts or behaviors that don't align with the One Person, Himself, Who can unite us with God. there is no other path.

there are many ways that people hear about or experience Jesus and many paths to finding your individual personal faith in Him. some of those paths involve suffering. some of those paths are legacies from previous generations. I can see into your heart and I know whether you are hungry and searching for truth and into those hearts I plant seeds of knowingness that you allow to blossom into faith in Jesus. all paths lead to one Person because of His ultimate Sacrifice of Himself and His unmatched Resurrection. no one else can ever replace or stand above Him.

"then Jesus turned to the crowds and said, when you see clouds beginning to form in the west, you say, here comes a shower. and you are right. and when the south wind blows, you say, today will be a scorcher. and it is. you fools, you know how to interpret the weather signs of the earth and sky, but you don't know how to interpret the present times." luke 12:54-56 "nothing will hurt or destroy in all My Holy Mountain, for as the waters fill the sea, so the earth will be filled with people who know the Lord." isaiah 11:9

think of times when you are feeling bad. maybe that is right now as you are reading this. now, think back and remember how those feelings have passed before, although they try to overwhelm you. how fleeting and transitory are emotions!

as an example, remember when you may have carried a child in your womb, or if you are a man, if your wife was going through that. the birthing process is just the culmination of many months of sacrifice and then the labor comes. you wonder if you can bear another contraction. then, finally the baby crowns and arrives. all the pain was worth the reward.

if you lost a child in some manner, I want to express My sorrow personally to you. as you face these serious issues, or watch those you love who must do so, concentrate on moving through with grace- not rejecting Me, but drawing even closer, anticipating My reward. that reward is closeness with Me and then abundant relief and peace in Heaven for eternity. I love you, child.

"yes, everything else is worthless when compared with the infinite value of knowing Christ Jesus my Lord. for His sake, i have discarded everything else, counting it as garbage, so that i could gain Him." phillipians 3:7,8

"He will make a Highway for the remnant of His people."
isaiah 11:6

I am the General Contractor and the Engineer on this most important project! it was begun with the ancient prophets and was continued by john the baptist. I need more modern day voices that ring loud and clear! the infrastructure is crumbling, the bridges are collapsing. yet, look with open eyes at My supply, not at the world's resources. you are the generation of the double portion blessing- the remnant generation!

yes, I will tell you of things that are entirely new. listen, and you will understand in your inner man. righteousness will roll over you like undulating waves of the ocean. truth will whisper in your ear like the soft incoming tide against the sand.

listen Remnant! it is happening now. there is nothing small or insignificant in the Kingdom.

"make a straight highway through the desert for our God. fill the valleys, level the mountains and hills. straighten the curves and smooth out the rough places." isaiah 40:31

"without faith it is impossible to please God, because anyone who comes to Him must believe that He exists and that He rewards those who earnestly seek Him." hebrews 11:6

I am the Rewarder of you who diligently search for Me!

I see what your priorities are and I understand you have many things you must do in order to survive physically- to eat, drink, have a place to live, a home. but listen, shema, a lot of the things you spend so much time on are luxuries, illusions that are so transient you don't even consider them the day after you purchase them. you're wasting precious time chasing things. instead, seek closeness with Me today!

your level of faith determines the amount of respect and therefore time you give to Me. be interested in developing more and deeper faith! shift your priorities to the eternal, where I wait for you to come. come and close your eyes. breathe with Me.

do you realize you are being held by the nail pierced Hands? do you realize He has you in His strong grip? those Hands created the whole world and took up that Cross. this is not a joke, this is not a game you are in- this is My Plan! I gave My Life for it, for you to be strong and free and holy.

"by faith, we understand that the universe was formed at God's command, so that what is seen was not made out of what was visible." hebrews 11:3

"the days are coming, says the Lord, when the reaper will be overtaken by the plowman and the planters by the one treading grapes. new wine will drip from the mountains and flow from all the hills; I will bring back My exiled people israel; they will rebuild the ruined cities and live in them. they will plant vineyards and drink their wine; they will make gardens and eat their fruit." amos 9: 13,14

I am looking for fruit in your life. you are planting things in this world and you should be bearing fruit!

if you're not growing and changing, you're stagnating. is your life too compacted down, too busy? go and do something you thought you would never do. as the vine needs to be lifted up to bear fruit, literally on a trellis, so spiritually you need to be lifted up to new ground, new places for your roots to grow. fertilize your life by changing things up. get quiet, get loud, sing, paint, dance, walk, love, go out and impact the world for Me. be fertile!

"it is a land with prosperous cities that you did not build. the houses will be richly stocked with goods you did not produce. you will draw water from cisterns you did not dig, and you will eat from vineyards and olive trees you did not plant. when you have eaten your fill in this land, be careful not to forget the Lord, who rescued you from slavery in the land of egypt." deuteronomy 6:11,12 "walk in the Spirit, and then you will not fulfill the lust of the flesh." galatians 5:16

walk refers to your lifestyle. what does your daily life primarily consist of? think about your everyday activities. to walk "in" Me means to be guided and and controlled by Me- living in submission to Me everyday. this entails spending time with Me daily at a consistent time and place, as well as a moment by moment relationship where you are aware I am in you.

walking in Me also refers to growing within. get the Word on the inside of you, saturating your thoughts, emotions, and attitudes. this is the main way that I work- through the Word permeating your mind. ask Me to bring it alive to you. regular study of the Bible is so vital, whether it's verse by verse, chapter by chapter, or another method.

continue in constant prayer- whether you sit, walk, or recline- take that time to come and talk and listen with Me. if you press in, walking with Me, then you won't be as interested in worldly pursuits, not altogether. you won't be just looking for more pleasures and activity. I'm expecting something from you today. it flows from time walking in Me and it's developed in your life as you mature.

"I am the Vine and you are the branches. he who abides in Me, and I in him, bears much fruit; for without Me you can do nothing." john 15:5

"attending Him were mighty seraphim, each having six wings. with two wings they covered their faces and with two they covered their feet, and with two they flew. they were calling out to each other,

Holy Holy Holy is the Lord of Heaven's Armies!

the whole earth is filled with His Glory!" isaiah 6:2,3

this is a prophetic foreshadowing of the Messiah and of the very Mercy Seat Itself. there is an elegance to the description of angels in the Bible. cherubim guard and protect. I described the two cherubim who hover over the Mercy Seat, looking down at the Blood. here, seraphim worship God. many angels function as messengers to humans or they rush to your aid. angels are not human though.

you have a very different purpose to fulfill here on earth, as well as in eternity. do you want to be please Me or do you want to be popular? that question is going to come up a lot as you live in the world. some will think you are too intense, but don't tone yourself down because of that. I made you with that boldness and I admire when you are your authentic self! you were born at this time for a spiritual purpose to fulfill, something no one else can do! continue in that unique plan as I unveil it.. I'm so proud of you!

"jacob found a stone to lay his head against. as he slept, he dreamed of a stairway that reached from the earth up to heaven. and he saw the angels of God going up and down the stairway." genesis 28:11,12 "john replied in the words of isaiah the prophet, i am the voice of one calling in the wilderness, prepare the way of the Lord." john 1:23

john the baptist is a great friend of Mine. he will really tell you some stories! everyone considered him to be eccentric; he ate locusts- they were dipped in honey, but still!

the main thing I love about john's personality (even to this day!) is his boldness. he doesn't care what anyone else says or does. he didn't care what people thought, he followed exactly what I told him to do.

when I see you face to Face, I would love to announce the same thing about you! be a voice for a confused and perverse generation. use your fingers to make war, as david proclaims in the verse below. use your fingers to fight harmful cultural standards and to proclaim truth. I allowed the internet to proliferate so that the gospel would reach the entire world. the most remote places have access to My message of grace and hope through Jesus. post about Me! it is such a wide open mission field! have an urgency- reach out with boldness today!

"God arms me with strength, and He makes my way perfect. He makes me as surefooted as a deer, enabling me to stand on mountain heights. He train my hands for battle; he strengthens my arm to draw a bronze bow." psalm 18:32-34

"God made Him to be sin for us, He Who knew no sin, that we might become the Righteousness of God in Christ Jesus."
2 corinthians 5:21

this is such an important Scripture that I feel the need to go more in depth with this. in the reading of it, I hope the technicality doesn't throw you off, so let's dissect it. that's how to study the Word. break it down and meditate on it.

Father God came up with the Plan to send Jesus to earth, before He even created earth, to take away the guilt and condemnation that He knew would fall on you for your sinful actions. He put your sin upon Him, so Jesus literally became your sin in His Body at the Cross.

"He knew no sin." in Him there was no sin. Jesus was born totally sinless. even though He was able to be tempted, He never succumbed to temptation and even though He was True Man, His Divine Nature kept Him from any impurity.

"that we might become the Righteousness Of God"- this is the Divine Exchange- when you acknowledge the sacrifice of Jesus, you take on Jesus' complete Righteousness as your nature and character. the punishment for your flaws was paid in full and you now have "Right Standing" or Righteousness with the Lord.

"in Christ Jesus"- it is only through Jesus' life, death, and resurrection that you can gratefully accept this gift. there was no other way. there can never be another way. you cannot follow any other path that will make you good enough, holy enough, or pure enough to be in union with God. it takes humility to receive such a gift without feeling you have to do anything for it. you have been made totally Righteous in My Eyes!

"those who sow in tears will reap with songs of joy. he who goes out weeping, carrying seed to sow, will return with songs of joy, carrying sheaves with him." psalm 126:5,6

I want you to realize that your suffering and trials are accomplishing much. sheaves of souls are standing, moving in the fields with the winds of change. as you travel from place to place, you have the freedom of meeting new people and some you will only see one time. that is such a huge responsibility, to be quick enough to say one Word which will have eternal impact.

in the natural, you may be in pain- difficult,chronic pain. this produces more self-focus. it is easy in that situation to believe that the whole of life will be painful. when you are sad, everything seems tinged with sorrow. you cannot dwell here.

in the spiritual realm, just the opposite is true. life is always more than the moment you are in right now. it is an eternal celebration that will confirm the goodness of My Plan. being a Christian means that you recognize that you need a Savior, you need forgiveness, you need My love. help people to see that in a gentle way, My witnesses.

"Jesus replied, I am the Bread of life. whoever comes to Me will never be hungry again." john 6:35

"as long as it is day, we must do the work of Him who sent Me. night is coming, when no one can work. while I am in the world, I am the Light of the world." john 9:4,5

Jesus is speaking to the brevity of life here. "a day is as a thousand years" to Him and since His death has been two thousand years, you are in the Third Day. time is short.

in your youth, you felt a sense of immortality and invincibility, didn't you? since nothing bad had happened to you yet, you felt nothing ever would. you had your whole life in front of you with many possibilities in your mind. then, after you have an illness, or an accident, after someone you love died or your first heartbreak came, you started to become cynical and jaded. I never intended this to be the way, but it occurs in a fallen world.

even though Jesus physically left the world two thousand years ago, He is still vibrantly here, alive in you. thus, you carry His Light within you to shine to others wherever you go. this sacred mantle He placed on you makes it all worthwhile. have a sense of My imminence- night is coming. truth be told, night is already here. wake up! it's almost time!

"the house to be built for the Lord should be of great magnificence and fame and splendor in the sight of all nations. therefore, i will make preparations for it. so david made extensive preparations before his death." 1 chronicles 22:5

"as they went, a woman who wanted to be healed came up behind and touched him, for she had been bleeding for twelve years and could find no cure. coming up behind Jesus, she touched the fringe of His robe and immediately the bleeding stopped. who touched Me? Jesus asked." luke 8:43,44

what great faith this woman had, and Jesus recognized it! no one walked in greater authority and grace than Jesus, yet He was never too busy, never too high and mighty to help someone who approached Him. He turned to look at her and called her "daughter" !

this is a great story to read and meditate on. whether you need a miracle at this time or not, this story affirms the power that Jesus walked in- and the same power that He offers to us. this is the hope that you have to give the world- the enduring truth about the path to eternal Relationship with God.

how do you specifically access this power and authority? you get it from Jesus, the same as this woman did. act as if you have been bleeding for twelve years and need Him that much! walk, yes run, hard after the Lord! literally reach your hand out to Him. make Him your first priority everyday!

"together they stayed there a long time, boldly bearing witness to the truth." acts 14:3

"now there was a man of the pharisees named nicodemus, who came to Jesus at night and said, Rabbi, we know You are a teacher who has come from God and no one could perform the miraculous signs You are doing if God were not with Him. in reply, Jesus declared, I tell you the truth, no one can see the Kingdom of God unless he is born again." john 3:1,2

this is one of the most often used Christian phrases- "born again." yet, it was initiated from the Lord Himself. use this phrase with the exquisite power and authenticity that He did! it isn't jargon- it is a true representation of how your heart and mind are totally renewed once you come to trust Jesus as your personal Savior. that phrase, personal Savior, is also a popular Christian tenet- and yet it is sound doctrine. the weapons mentioned in ephesians chapter six are also doctrinal and still spiritual reality.all Scripture is alive and true. what I'm trying to say is, that it all depends on how you convey being "born again" to someone who doesn't know that life-saving experience yet. say it with complete, unconditional love and I will open their hearts, if they are willing.

"create in me a pure heart, O God, and renew a right spirit within me. cast me not away from Your Presence and take not Your Holy Spirit from me. restore unto me the joy of Your salvation and make me willing to obey You." psalm 51: 10-12 "when the Lord saw her, His heart went out to her and He said, don't cry. then, He went up and touched the coffin and those carrying it stood still. He said, young man, I say to you, get up! the dead man sat up and began to talk." luke 7:13-15

this was the only son of a widow. I purposely gave this example so that you would feel compassion. that is My desire- for your heart to go out to others, as Mine does.

be a good listener! even if you can't offer material aid to someone, you can offer encouraging words to make them feel better. you can let them know that they are not alone. you can ask them if you can pray for them. your prayer, as a person made righteous by Christ, has great effect. give what you can by way of ministry of prayer, and praying in the Spirit privately, to anyone who needs. be a good listener- be a friend to those who need you, to those who need Me.

"peter said, i don't have any silver or gold for you. but i'll give you what i have. in the Name of Jesus Christ, get up and walk! then peter took the lame man by the right hand and helped him up. and as he did, the man's feet and ankles were instantly healed and strengthened. he jumped up, stood on his feet, and began to walk!" acts 3:6-8 "but caleb tried to quiet the people as they stood before moses. let's go at once to take the land, he said, for we can certainly conquer it! but the other men who had explored the land with him disagreed. we can't go up against them. they are stronger than we are! so they spread the bad report about the land." numbers 13:30-32

unbelief causes rebellion and negativity whereas faith brings the good report and hope. here, joshua and caleb saw the abundance and the fruit of the new land, not the giants or the obstacles. they refused to dwell in fear. I want you to see the opportunities of a land flowing with milk and honey. I will continue to network you with people who will help you in all aspects, business and personal, people who will pray for you, and speak My Word to you.

be strong and courageous- go up and take possession of the land, as joshua did. he later became the successor of moses and actually did lead the people who weren't rebellious protesters, the new generation, into the Promised Land.

"so, joshua ordered the officers, go through the camp and tell the people to get their provisions ready. in three days you will cross the river jordan and take possession of the land the Lord your God is giving you." joshua 1:10,11 "your faith is being tested as fire tests gold and purifies it- and your faith is far more precious to God than mere gold; so if your faith remains strong after being tried in the test tube of fiery trials, it will bring you much praise and glory and honor on the day of His return." 1 peter 1:7

peter knows a thing or two about trials and faith. listen to him! you have heard Me say that without faith you won't ever be able to please God. this is the essence of faith- it is essentially trusting that what I say is true. no one would want to live with a husband or wife that they can't trust. you can trust what I have said and the Relationship that we have.

that's all well and good when everything is going good in your life, you may say. if you are reading this and have food and water, a nice home, you probably can appreciate that you have a blessed life on the whole.

if this came into your hands and you are searching for truth, some truth that will make sense to you, please don't turn away! keep digging in My Word- today is the day when I am calling you!

"faith is the confidence that what we hope for will actually happen; it gives us assurance of things we cannot see." hebrews 11:1

"faith comes by hearing, and hearing by the Word of God." romans 10:17

I want to show you what real love is, especially if you haven't known or felt it in your life yet.

I will never leave you.

I will love you unconditionally, whether you are sick, poor, tired, or even angry at Me.

when you are faithless, I will remain faithful. learn to see that I am with you all the time. I'm sitting here right now with you! be conscious of this! learn to see Me. if you are conscious of Me, you won't be afraid of anything. live your life knowing this above anything else that you trust in. you are hearing it now. boldly say amen right now!

"look, my lord, here is the woman now, and this is her son- the very one elisha brought back to life! is this true? the king asked her. and she told him that it was. so he directed one of his officials to see to it that everything she had lost was restored to her, including the value of any crops that had been harvested during her absence." 2 kings 8:6

"while appollos was at corinth, paul took the road through the interior and arrived at ephesus. there he found some disciples and asked them, did you receive the Holy Spirit when you believed? they answered, no, we have not even heard that there is a Holy Spirit." acts 19:1,2

if you are reading this, most likely you at least have heard ABOUT Me. I want to bless you with more than just knowing though. I want you to have the experience of knowing what it is to be "filled" by Me. I will do this continually and daily as we walk together.

I am so glad that you are interested in having a Relationship with Me because I want that also! I want you to be involved with Me daily! I need you also to be concerned that there are many people who don't know Who I am.

mostly everyone has heard of Jesus, even if they, sadly, reject Him. a majority of the world confesses that they believe in "God." but, hardly anyone speaks about Me because I move more supernaturally and My nature is much more nebulous. if you have read this far, I am overjoyed at your faith and discipline. flow profusely in the gifts and fruits so that others will be interested in finding out about your Source- Who is Me! tell them Who I am! show them Who I am through your love!

"we love because He first loved us." 1 john 4:19

"no one pours new wine into old wineskins. if he does, the wine will burst the skins, and both the wine and the wineskins will be ruined. no, he pours new wine into new wineskins." mark 2:22

you're not strong enough to make it on your own. you cannot be the source of your joy and contentment, no matter how hard you try. you can't control things enough to make your life unfailingly perfect. when God pours Me into you- because I am a true free gift from Him, you will become an entirely new creation! the "old" you will be forever gone!

this infusion of power can be imparted directly from Me and through the laying on of hands. ask wise people to pray for you- seek strong friends out for prayer and a touch of grace from Me.

I want to give you so much more than you previously thought was good and perfect about your life. here I am, pronouncing a prophetic blessing over you! it is larger than any natural blessing you may have inherited or worked for. I proclaim health, peace, and complete joy over your life! I am the Umbrella of Eternal Love over your life!

"now joshua son of nun was full of the spirit of wisdom, for moses had laid hands on him." deuteronmy 34:9

"foxes have dens, birds have nests, but the Son of Man has nowhere to lay His Head." luke 9:58

as the holidays approach, try to simplify and focus on family. the world wants you to buy more things, telling you your joy comes from getting more stuff. yet, the essence of thanksgiving is being content with what you already have.

I'm not suggesting you must live the life of an ascetic, but it certainly doesn't hurt to simplify your life somewhat. spend more time instead of more money this year. My original plan was a Garden, close to the earth and close to nature. is that realistic? I sure hope so! love and help each other, love and help animals, appreciate the beauty of this world. give thanks in all that you do!

"in everything give thanks for this is the will of God." 1 thessalonians 5:18

"though the bush was engulfed in flames, it didn't burn up. when the Lord saw moses coming to take a closer look, God called to him from the middle of the bush, moses, moses! and moses replied, here i am! don't come any closer, the Lord replied. take off your shoes, for you are standing on holy ground." exodus 3:2-5

the world has lost the ability to feel the awe of the Presence of God. God, His Presence, and His Reality, are besmirched and made fun of. His very existence is something that needs to be qualified. but see how I still extend My Hand out to anyone who would come near and call out My Name.

moses and joshua were both powerful leaders, willing to go above and beyond all that I asked of them. yet, if you study carefully, their most important character quality is humility. moses was a stutterer. joshua didn't feel he was worthy to lead the people into israel.

I want the real you, not the fake you! I want you to take off your external trappings- fancy clothes, jewelry, makeup- and then come in childlike wonder to Me!

removing the shoes, what can I say? it is a very personal thing between you and I. removing your shoes shows your reverence and surrender. barefoot, you are different, more free- and you participate in My Holiness.

"the commander of the Lord's army replied, take off your sandals, for the place where you are standing is holy. and joshua did so." joshua 5:15

"for He will rescue you from every trap and protect you from deadly disease. He will cover you with His feathers. He will shelter you with His wings. His faithful Promises are your armor and protection (your shield and rampart). you will not fear the terror of night, nor the arrow that flies by day." psalm 91: 3-5

I am surrounding you in the night!

the rampart is a shield, heavy and thick, that encircles all around you. I told you that night was encroaching, and I know you aren't certain or comfortable with what is happening in the world. there are so many charlatans, promoters of truth that actually believe the dangerous theories they propose.

I have given you a discerning mind. even if others are saying things are of Me, you must look and listen carefully to the underlying messages. there's so much information out there, it's almost like swimming in an ocean full of seaweed.

stay close! don't wander off, My child. pray this entire psalm ninety one as a prayer of protection.

"the Lord says, I will rescue those who trust in My Name. when they call Me, I will answer. I will be with them in trouble. I will rescue and honor them. I will reward them with a long life and give them My salvation." psalm 91:14-16 "on hearing this, Jesus said, it is not the healthy who need a doctor, but the sick. go and learn what this means: I desire mercy and not sacrifice. for I have not come to call the righteous, but sinners." matthew 9:12,13

oh, here is the challenge- to be totally loving and compassionate toward others while at the same time not giving the appearance of endorsing ungodly behavior. I know how tough that plumbline is to walk, as I walked it! it is almost more like a fault line, where everything you do is critiqued and torn down. I will elevate your faith for those times when I put you in the front line position.

don't judge- but don't actively participate in wrong practices either. harsh words against certain behaviors may only drive some people further into satan's traps. we are called to be wise. let your silence set you apart and show your standard.

be merciful. say a kind word when there is an opportunity to do so. refrain from back biting and criticism of those who are trapped in false doctrine. if you need to speak to something, have the courage to say it truthfully with love to their face. pray for their eyes to see and their hearts to turn and turn away. return to Me- "teshuvah" in hebrew.

"the Lord has told you what is good, and what He requires of you; to do what is right, to love mercy and to walk humbly with your God." micah 6:8

"may your roots go down deep into the soil of God's marvelous love; and may you be able to feel and understand how long, how wide, how deep, and how high His love really is; and to experience this love for yourselves, though it is so great that you will never see the end of it or fully know or understand it, and so at last you will be filled up with God Himself." ephesians 3:18,19

I hope this thrills your soul! this is one of the most beautiful sentences in all of Scripture, another one of My Masterpiece writings from paul! if ephesians is your favorite letter, then you are truly wise, for it contains very deep truth.

Jesus is My love exhibited in the Flesh and when you hear that gospel truth over and over, hearing and continuing to hear, it forms a tap root that goes down really deep, even into eternity.

when we finally get to see each other (did I say finally?!) the rest of your mind, your mental capacity to understand what you didn't or couldn't access here on earth, will be opened up like a magnificent flower. even so, here and now on earth, you can experience many foretastes of My love. spend a majority of your time worshiping, in the Word, and just being silent. the adversary wants to distract and keep you plugged in all the time.

silence brings awareness of Me, as I am the Radiant One within you.

"try always to be led along by the Holy Spirit, and to be at peace with one another." ephesians 4:3

"men of galilee, why do you stand there looking up into the sky? this same Jesus, Who has been taken from you into Heaven, will come back in the same way you have seen Him go." acts 1:11

I know it seems like such a long time that Jesus has been absent from the earth. one generation to the next expectantly waits and looks up at the sky. I am honored that you have a desire to see Him and to have the earth be perfected in the Millenial Kingdom! I am looking forward to that day as well. lift up your heads! it isn't too far off now, in fact, at any moment it will be firmly established.

now, while there is still time, use this urgency to embolden you to speak of My saving plan. do you have the words to convey the salvation plan to someone? do you know how to gently lead them in acceptance and prayer? if you knew I were coming this very day, how would you live differently? who would you contact and how would you speak with them? how urgent would your perspective become?

the winds of change are blowing. don't miss any opportunity because of embarrassment. be My Voice!

"at that time men will see the Son of Man coming in the clouds with great power and glory. when these things begin to take place, stand up and lift up your heads, for your redemption is drawing near." luke 21:27,28 "the following week almost the entire city turned out to hear them preach the Word of the Lord." acts 13:44

here it is sabbath day and the majority are doing their own thing today. if you understand what I have for you, you will literally run to meet Me on the road!

in the parable of the prodigal son, the young man is caught up in the world- and he is young, so you can understand how that happens. upon his return home, I run to him, welcoming him home. now, imagine if he knew the reception he would receive- wouldn't he run as fast as he could to reunite with his family?

how do you get to the place where <u>you</u> are running toward Me as hard and fast as you can? how do you get to a place where it's not just church ritual anymore, where you feel a thrill each time you come near Me? I'm so glad you asked. I'm not a religion! I am a Person and I inhabit people as you gather together and pray, as you gather regularly and worship, as you gather and love one another, as I love you.

"but his father said to his servants, quick! bring the finest robe in the house and put it on him. get a ring for his finger and sandals for his feet, and kill the fatted calf. we must celebrate with a feast, for this son of mine was dead and has now returned to life. he was lost, but now he is found. and so the party began." luke 15:22-24 "how precious are Your thoughts about me, O God. they cannot be numbered! i can't even count them, they outnumber the grains of sand on the beach!" psalm 139 17,18

I have just cause to wipe out all evil from the face of the earth, and I will one day soon! yet, My anger is always productive, not destructive. when Jesus chased the money changers out of the temple, it was not self-righteous anger, although it is the one time in history when that would have been justified self-righteousness. He was being faithful to His Holy Nature of justice and He was defending those who were being taken advantage of.

do you feel that way today? have you given all you can and feel disrespected or forgotten?

I am here to validate and lift you up- to smash the false pretenses that the world deems worthy. your faith and pure humility is priceless to Me, My child. I am watching you each moment and I am so proud of you. I am brimming with excitement to one day tell you to your face how proud you make Me and how much I love you.

"when they arrived, samuel took one look at eliab and thought, surely this is the Lord's anointed. but the Lord said to samuel, don't judge by his appearance or height, for I have rejected him. the Lord doesn't see things the way you see them. people judge by outward appearance, but the Lord looks at the heart." 1 samuel 16:6,7

"I have told you all these things so that you may have peace in Me. here on earth you will have many trials and sorrows. but take heart, for I have overcome the world." john 16:33

you seem to have a lot of concerns on your mind today. just give it all to Me and let Me take care of it. whatever it is that may seem unjust or frightening, I've seen and dealt with it all before. I love you too much to sit back and let you worry about so many things!

our love Relationship gives you the ability, even the right, to transfer these thoughts over to Me. little by little, as you sit in daily silence and contemplative prayer, the problems of the world and what others are saying and doing will matter less and less to you. you shouldn't be surprised that the world is on the trajectory it is on- the attitude of tolerance for blatant sin is nothing new.

use your time and gifts, but don't waste them. I provide discernment so you don't burn yourself out. relate with individuals I bring to you and stay in fervent prayer for revival within the Body. as you live with My radiant Peace emanating from you, you will touch and minister to many people.

"those who are wise will shine as bright as the sky, and those who lead many to righteousness will shine like the stars forever." daniel 12:3

"he is like a man building a house, who dug deep and laid the foundation on a rock. and when the flood arose, the streams beat vehemently against the house, but could not shake it." luke 6:48

if you know someone who is knowledgeable in construction, someone who is honest, ask them if they would build something on a shoddy, unstable foundation or renovate something by cutting corners to do it with cheaper materials. they will tell you that it must be done to code, be permitted, and be completed to highest standards of quality.

spiritually, the exact same principle is true. your salvation needed to be accomplished by a Perfect Sinless Man Who would take your place. He is the Chief Cornerstone of the whole building of your eternal life. He is the Rock! if you wonder why people make such a big deal over the Messiah, Maschiach, the One Who saves, Jesus- this is why! without Him and His complete obedience, you would be lost and alone forever.

"unless the Lord builds a house, the work of the builders is wasted. unless the Lord protects a city, guarding it with sentries will do no good." psalm 127:1

"be prepared to give an answer to everyone who asks you to give the reason for the hope you have." 1 peter 3:15

there's a reason Jesus became human and I want you to understand. your conversation turns so much to worldly things, and sometimes that is necessary. it's your usual modus operandi to talk about what's going on in your life. well, what's going on? what's going on in your vital Relationship with Me?

be prepared to speak and direct conversations toward what I am doing in your life. when you do, there are some who will turn away, even run away from you. these are fair weather friends. try to be empathetic with where they are.

what can you offer as an alternative? you can't just shout or speak My Name to someone who doesn't understand that power. so, here is where your individual testimony can bear great weight. say "this is what God is doing in my life" or "here is how God is blessing me." that will catch someone's attention and send the conversation in a spiritual direction. try it!

"dear friends, don't be surprised by the fiery trials you are going through, as if a strange thing were happening to you. instead, be very glad- for these trials make you partners with Christ in His suffering, so that you will have the wonderful joy of seeing His glory when it is revealed to all the world. so be happy when you are insulted for being a Christian, for then the glorious Spirit of God rests on you." 1 peter 4:12-14

"Jesus responded, didn't I tell you that you would see God's glory if you believe? so they rolled the stone aside. then Jesus looked up to heaven and said, Father, thank You for hearing Me. You always hear Me, but I said it out loud for the sake of all these people standing here so they will believe You sent Me. then Jesus shouted, lazarus, come out!" john 11: 40-43

miracles aren't to prove anything. I don't need to prove anything to anyone.

miracles are a sign of My Presence and restorative Power, of which Resurrection is the biggest sign. lazarus was a forerunner of Jesus' own Resurrection. focus on this important historical event for a moment here!

I will one day call your name, as I did lazarus'. feel that now! know Me now! your strength doesn't come from what you have or where you are in life- but from who you are- Who you have inside! I move into you- occupying all space and time within you. let ME occupy everywhere! resurrect your dreams and desires and offer them to Me in the here and now.

I created your body and mind to be connected to one another. in this intricate connection, I made it easier for your mind to relax when your body is not moving. yet, you think you always have to Go Go Go. sit down with Me, be still! let Me relax you!

"at the end of ten days, daniel and his three friends looked healthier and better nourished than the young men who had been eating food assigned by the king...God gave these four young men wisdom and to daniel the special ability to interpret the meanings of visions and dreams." daniel 1:15,17 "some men came, bringing to Him a paralytic, carried by four of them. since they could not get him to Jesus because of the crowd, they made an opening in the roof above Jesus and lowered the mat the paralyzed man was lying on. when Jesus saw their faith, He said to the paralytic man, son, your sins are forgiven." mark 2:3-5

I briefly mentioned this story before, but let's examine it closer. these four men here were determined and audacious in their pursuit of healing for their friend. they were relentlessly pursuing Jesus and they didn't care if they had to do something completely unorthodox, crazy even, by coming through the roof!

I know you have that fire and that resolve within you and I want you to press in today like never before, with prayer and also fasting if necessary. I will make it clear if the situation is that dire. do you know someone who needs a miracle? maybe you've been praying for them diligently already- but it's get up on the roof time- I want you to get up on the roof! I want you to push through, press through, fight through for your friend. I want you to not only go down through the roof, tearing it open to seek Me, but also go UP through the roof, literally raising the roof with praise, worship, and power!

I've said, come, let us reason together.

I am also saying now, come, GET UP and let us fight together.

"I looked for a man who would build up the wall and stand before Me in the gap on behalf of the land so I would not have to destroy it." ezekiel 22:30

"there was a judge in a certain city, He said, who neither feared God nor cared about people. a widow of that city came to him repeatedly, saying, give me justice in this dispute with my adversary. the judge ignored her for a while but finally said to himself, i don't fear God or care about people, but this woman is driving me crazy. i'm going to see that she gets justice because she is wearing me out with her constant requests. and the Lord said, will not God bring about justice for His people, who cry out to Him day and night? will He keep putting them off? I tell you, He will see that they get justice, and quickly." luke 18:2-8

I have tried to teach you and explain many of the instructions and intricacies of prayer and persistence. only a mature person can discipline themselves to remain in the eye of the storm as the lightning flashes all around. most will become afraid and want to run. see, I have called you to a higher standard. I search hearts and I know that you can withstand and overcome. I did not desire nor bring this sorrow about. instead, I use it to release a pertinent prophetic blessing over you, imprinting My Very Self on you.

hold firm, keeping not only high standards but high expectations. I'm sorry, there are many reasons that I can't impart the full revelation of everything right now to you. full disclosure doesn't foster deeper faith and I need you to trust Me implicitly.

hold fast, as a sailor lifts and lowers the boom for the sail to billow out in the wind. I am the Dove that flies, carrying Fire in My train and creating plentiful forests and teeming rivers in My Wake.

"perseverance must finish its work so that you may be mature and complete, lacking nothing." james 1:4

"God is Spirit and His worshipers must worship in spirit and in truth." john 4:24

Jesus is talking to the samaritan woman at the well here. in the story, He calls her out for her behavior, yet He does it with a loving spirit. He engages her in an irresistible manner, offering her the Water of Life, which is Himself.

if you read the whole story, which I suggest you do, you will notice that He keeps pursuing her. He directs the conversation in a manner that is intriguing to her, that keeps her attention. this is a Master class in evangelism, literally! Jesus is showing you how to seek out (I will also help set up divine appointments), gently engage (your part), and finally, win people over (I will help with that also).

this retelling of the old, old story is the best type of worship! I love when you sing, that has eternal significance and power, even in the heavenly realms- but this effective engagement with those who are seeking water is so vital.

look each day for the woman at the well, at the grocery store, at the beach, at the gym, in your neighborhood.

"do you not say, four months more and then the harvest? I tell you, open your eyes and look at the fields. they are ripe for harvest. even now, the reaper draws his wages, even now he harvests the crop for eternal life, so that the sower and the reaper may be glad together." john 4:35,36 "in a desert land He found him, in a barren and howling waste. He shielded him and cared for him; He guarded him as the apple of His eye, like an eagle that stirs up its nest and hovers over its young, that spreads its wings to catch them and carries them on its pinions." deuteronomy 32:10,11

sometimes it appears as if living this sanctified life, set apart, brings only ostracism, testing, and attack. realistically, that's part of taking a stand for something, for Someone. your human nature makes you generally not like to surrender control of your life, even if it is certain to promote peace. your ego keeps driving you to push forward. there are too many opinions and not enough focus on My pinions! pinions are the flight feathers at the distal, or outer, edges of the eagle's feathers. when the pinions are cut off, it prevents the bird from flying. pain can make you forget you can even fly at all. see how in this verse above, I am carrying you on My pinions (and Opinions!)

please rest in Me today! I want to keep you safe in My Refuge- the place where you can just come and feel total acceptance and unconditional love.

I understand your pain from past events, your physical pains, your broken relationships. that's why I guard you in the Secret Place. test Me on that. throw down the gauntlet. ask Me for a tangible sign of My Presence, for I love to confirm Myself.

I am Love and I will never let you down.

"taste and see that the Lord is good, blessed is the man who takes refuge in Him." psalm 34:8

"the Hand of the Lord was upon me and He brought me out by the Spirit of the Lord and set me in the middle of a valley. it was full of bones. He led me all around among the bones that covered the valley floor. they were scattered everywhere across the ground and were completely dried out. then He asked me, can these bones become living people again?" ezekiel 37:1-3

I have talked about prophecy and how it is given as a gift to edify the church. in these end times, prophetic blessing is very important since you face severe attacks as believers. I bestow this thunderous blessing individually on you as well and your legacy of faith continues even to each member of your family because of our Covenant agreement! I cut a Covenant with you and will never go back on it.

along with this blessing, there is the Warning Prophetic Word. jeremiah, isaiah, and ezekiel used this gift heavily, as was necessary in their time. your time is growing more contentious. division and violence are overtaking civility. I advise you not to allow yourself to participate in worldly negativity. don't compromise your beliefs. there are spiritual teachers that sound acceptable, but are promoting other gods and self-sufficiency.

breathe only the life-giving Truth of My Word! you must keep a lucid mind and breathe in My Spirit alone.

"so I prophesied as He commanded me and breath entered them. they came to life and stood up on their feet- a vast army." ezekiel 37:10

"we proclaim Him, admonishing and teaching everyone with all wisdom, so that we may present everyone perfect in Christ. to this end i labor, struggling with all His energy, which so powerfully works in me." colossians 1:28,29

perfect.
is there anything perfect on earth? the definition is pure, complete, precise, entirely finished, without fault.

when I created the world and all that is in it, I told you in genesis that I said, "it is good." good is not perfect. perfect Love did not come down until Jesus was born. He exemplified perfection and beauty, gifting you by His sacrifice with eternal life! it is such a simple, perfect gift. I can't understand why people knowingly reject it.

you become perfect IN Him when you acknowledge His love and your dependence on Him as Savior. a perfect day becomes a day when you and I have been together throughout and you are perpetually and continually conscious of My Presence and your Righteousness in Me. then, your striving can cease- and although you still certainly want to please God, your peace and eternal position don't depend on anything you do or don't do. you are free!

"as for God, His Way is perfect." psalm 18:30

"haven't you yet learned that your body is the home of the Holy Spirit God gave you, and that He lives within you? your own body does not belong to you for God has bought you with a great price. so use every part of your body to give glory back to God, because He owns it." 1 corinthians 6:19,20

I know this is a difficult teaching as you have spent your life attached to your body- the way it looks mostly, but also its care. it makes Me feel whimsical to see the way you struggle so hard to clothe, sculpt, and tattoo your body- all the time and money you spend in these pursuits!

truly, the body looks and functions the best when it is lit from within! your internal nature yields so much strength and confidence to your appearance. I'm suggesting you turn from external concern just a bit and continue to spend time growing in faith, as you have been. spiritual growth has eternal benefit to you and others, so the majority of your time should be there. this is what will reflect from you and give you that glow- My reflection! once you are aware of the poetry of My Presence inside you, you will have the secret to eternal youth and vitality!

does anyone write poetry anymore?

"I will provide peace in this place." haggai 2:9

"blessed are the pure in heart, for they shall see God…you are the salt of the earth. but if the salt loses its flavoring, what will happen to the world? you are the light of the world- like a city on a hilltop that cannot be hidden. no one light a lamp and puts it under a basket. instead, a lamp is placed on a stand, where it gives light to everyone in the house. in the same way, let your good deeds shine out for all to see, so that everyone will praise God." matthew 5: 8, 13-16

the beatitudes stand as Jesus' ultimate teaching and blessing over you. He speaks tenderly and with such grace to those who are poor, humble, grieving, and persecuted. afterward, He validates you, immediately calling you the salt and light of the world.

salt preserves and also gives richness and flavor to food. light permeates and brings a sense of safety and hope- illumination.

as I am teaching you, I am also throwing you suddenly into the trial by fire, as a mother bird ejects her young forcefully from the nest. I need you to learn how to stand on your feet, how to FLY! open out those pinions of yours!

be salty!

shine out for the world to see!

can you do this for Me?

"come away, my beloved! be like a gazelle or a young stag on the mountains of spices." song of solomon 8:14

"if we have trouble, or hunger, or are persecuted, or threatened with death, does it mean He no longer loves us? no, despite all these things, we are more than conquerors through Jesus Who loves us. for I am convinced that nothing can ever separate us from God's love. neither death nor life, neither angels nor demons, neither our fears for today nor our worries about tomorrow- not even the powers of hell itself can separate us from God's love. no power in the sky above or in the earth below- indeed, nothing in all creation will ever be able to separate us from the love of God that is revealed in Christ Jesus our Lord." romans 8:38,39

I have saved this verse for the end of the year. it stands alone as an exultant testimony of victory! you are not just a conqueror, you are more than a conqueror, more than an overcomer! say that out loud and notice how your faith arises. through Jesus' annihilation of sin and death, you no longer have to worry about anything. I hate to see you get caught up in trivial worries that displace your focus and attention. concentrate only on Me! life is so brief! live it with all the energy you can, each day waking up ready to move with excitement into your activities.

I understand there are aspects of your life physically, mentally, or emotionally that are very hard. adam necessitated the concept of work through his disobedience (yes, and eve also). just as the pain of childbirth brings the blessing of children, try to appreciate the dignity of your work. one of these days, just like thomas, you will see the Hands that took the nails for you.

"whatever you do, work willingly at it, with all your heart, as though you were working for the Lord and not for people, since you know that you will receive an inheritance as a reward. it is the Lord Jesus Christ you are serving." colossians 3:23,24 "a week later, His disciples were in the house again, and thomas was with them. though the doors were locked, Jesus came and stood among them saying, peace be with you! then He said to thomas, put your finger here; see My Hands. reach out your hand and put it into My side. stop doubting and start believing. thomas said to Him, my Lord and my God! then Jesus told him, because you have seen Me, you have believed. blessed are those who have not seen and yet have believed." john 20:26-29

even at the closest proximity to Jesus, with credible witnesses to His Resurrection, thomas still doubted. yet, Jesus didn't rebuke him here, so how much more do I understand your questions from a distance of over two thousand years. I'm not surprised by any of your thoughts, fears, or doubts. just when everything seems to be going along fine and you're in a strong season of grace, the wind gets knocked out of your sails. sometimes the mast is even broken, sometimes the rain is a deluge, descending out of nowhere, a dark curtain, and you drown. or someone you love drowns.

I'm not going to pretend everything is okay- it's not. there are, though, specific purposes why the time has not yet been fulfilled. have you heard the word "tarry"? I tarry for a perfect reason.

"the Lord is not really being slow in keeping His Promise, as some people understand slowness. He is being patient with you, not wanting anyone to perish, but wanting everyone to repent. but the day of the Lord will come like a thief. the heavens will disappear with a roar, the elements will be destroyed by fire, and the earth and everything in it will be laid bare." 2 peter 3:9,10 "then He breathed on them and said, receive the Holy Spirit." john 20:22

here are seven important Promises. look at them and hear them over and over, for by repeated hearing and speaking of the Word comes increased faith!

I love you! 1 john 4:19
I will strengthen you. ephesians 3:16
I will provide for you. 1 timothy 6:17
I will answer you. 2 chronicles 2:14
I am for you, not against you. romans 8:31
I will give you rest. matthew 11:28
I will be with you. matthew 28:20

there are a great number of Biblical references for each of these Promises. go to your concordance, look up strength, rest, healing, peace. read about mephibosheth. each of these is an indication of the Eternal Covenant I have with you. it has been notarized by Me- I, Who am the Deposit, the Seal, and the Guarantor of your Contract with Me.

"one day david asked, is anyone in saul's family still alive, anyone to whom I can show kindness for jonathan's sake? ziba replied, yes, one of jonathan's sons is still alive, he is crippled in both feet. so david sent for him and brought him from makir's home. his name was mephibosheth." 2 samuel 9:1,3-5

"behold, I have placed before you an open door."
revelation 3:8

"after this I looked and there was a door standing open
before me in heaven." revelation 4:1

sometimes it seems there are many closed doors in your
life. there may be people who won't see, or even speak, with
you. there seems like there are many missed opportunities,
many broken relationships.

I want to assure you that although there was a door placed
between you and I because of rebellion and sin, it has been
removed. now, you have the free will choice to walk through
that open door or not; to allow Me to come through the open
door into your life. I am still knocking on the door even though
it is open- I will not barge in. I am still asking you to accept
My love.

more than even an open door, there are open heavens
above you!

"test Me in this, says the Lord Almighty, and see if I will
not throw open the floodgates of Heaven and pour out so much
blessing that you will not have enough room for it." malachi
3:10

"anyone who has ears to hear must listen to the Spirit and understand what He is saying. to everyone who is victorious I will give fruit from the Tree of life in the paradise of God." revelation 2:7

I see you when you feel the most vulnerable and alone. even the person who is closest to you- your spouse, child, trusted friend- can't be there all the time, turns away, or betrays you. but I will never leave you. there's no daylight between our togetherness.

as you are facing your fear of an uncertain future, worries about that bill you can't pay, attack in the form of physical pain or doubt, or the silence of night when you feel utterly alone- please know that I am there with you in all that and more. My Promises are for the present moment's unbearable heaviness and the future's remarkable lightness. My Promise of Heaven is for NOW but also for a seamless eternity.

the sheer bliss you feel as you read the above Promise out loud is real, overwhelmingly so, and eternal!

"let anyone who is thirsty come. let anyone who desires drink freely from the Water of Life." revelation 22:17

"I am praying not only for these disciples but for all who will ever believe in Me through their testimony. I pray that they will all be one- just as You and I are one- as You are in Me Father and I am in You." john 17:20,21

here is Jesus' final earthly intercession for you- His great High Priestly prayer. as usual, time collapses in His Presence and He pours out His heart here, sweating drops of blood. this is a prophetic blessing from Jesus directly to you- read it in entirety to receive that!

can you feel the depth of His concern and love for you?

no one and nothing can take you out of His Hand. you could never run far or fast enough to get away from Me! I am the essential part of you, the eternal part.

you <u>can</u> and WILL come home again!

"and the angel said to me, write this: blessed are those who are invited to the wedding feast of the Lamb." revelation 19:9

"Jesus answered, My Kingdom is not an earthly kingdom. if it were, My followers would fight to keep Me from being handed over. but My Kingdom is not of this world. pilate replied, so you are a king? Jesus responded, you say I am a king. actually, I was born and came into this world to testify to the Truth." john 19:36,37

allow Me to come in and sit on the throne of your heart as King. once I do, that Throne will become the place you can take refuge, where you can run to, day or night. I am always available to you! I lovingly and patiently wait for that time we can have together uninterrupted.

I have been called "the Great Interrupter" by c.s. lewis because I pursue you passionately, always seeking to reunite our lives and purposes. Heaven is in your heart, as intertwined as your breath and heartbeat when they work together. Heaven is right here, right now, where I am within you!

"Jesus replied, the Kingdom of Heaven can't be detected by visible signs. you wont be able to say here it is or it's over there, for the Kingdom of God is within you." luke 17:20,21 "but you, dear friends, must build each other up in your most holy faith. pray in the power of the Holy Spirit and await the mercy of our Lord Jesus Christ. in this way, you will keep yourselves safe in God's love." jude 1:20,21

there's no need at the end of the year to make weak resolutions or false commitments. the best of your intentions pale in comparison to allowing Me to pray through you. I want to baptize and fill you so that these living waters will flow through you. it's not an emotional thing. it's a choice to follow what I say and to believe that I am able to speak and take action through you. I know exactly how I can use you and exactly what you need to be happy because I formed you, I created you! I am willing and able to bless you and your families. you are being held safely in My love.

look forward to the new year with hope and wonderful expectation! look forward to good days. use the fancy dishes and the fine candles, wear the white clothing! being alive is the special occasion!

"God blesses the one who reads the words of this prophecy to the Church, and He blesses all who listen to its message and obey what it says, for the time is near." revelation 1:3

"for I am about to do something new. see, I have already begun, do you not see it? I will make a Highway through the wilderness. I will create streams in the desert." isaiah 43:19

I have My part in the creation of the Highway and you have your part as well! it is now a finished, dedicated Road, yet it is still in the process of being cleared in the natural. obstacles abound. the Road is somewhat obscured, although it has been pointed to since the beginning. mark the path with a flag, as when you climb the heights of mount everest. My Holy Highway is broadening! My Red Sea is parting! I don't want anyone to miss the signs.

I have heard your humble pleas! I have completed all the Plans, the Permits, and the Purchase orders!

"go through the gates! prepare the highway for My people to return! smooth out the road, pull out the boulders. raise a flag for all the nations to see." isaiah 62:10

"in that day, the wolf and the lamb will live together; the leopard will lie down with the baby goat. the calf and the yearling will be safe with the lion, and a little child will lead them all." isaiah 11:5,6

for all time forward from the Lord's Day, there will be complete peace. even the animals will turn from their natural predatory instincts. there will be no desire to kill, or steal, or tear down anyone because there will be divine abundance for all. this is the original paradigm for earth and My desire for you.

even though I knew this peace wouldn't last in eden, I still continued the grace anyway. now, there is no more need for guilt. it has been removed- the debt has been paid!

what an overwhelming day it will be when all evil is finally removed. this prophecy will be totally fulfilled for all mankind. I can't wait to see the recognition of that holy moment in your eyes, the joy of our reunification!

"nothing will hurt or destroy in all My holy mountain, for as the waters fill the sea, so the earth will be filled with people who know the Lord." isaiah 11:9

"but the angel reassured them. don't be afraid! he said. i bring good news that will bring great joy to all people. for unto you is born this day, in the city of david, a Savior, Who is Christ the Lord and this shall be a sign unto you: you shall find the babe wrapped in swaddling clothes and lying in a manger." luke 2:10-12

there are many beautiful, magical moments during Christmastime. the world lights up with gladness, homes are twinkling and shining, and everything seems brighter and more hopeful. express feelings of love and admiration freely- it doesn't cost anything! everyone loves to receive handwritten letters or cards, with loving thoughts written from the heart. I will give you the gift of encouragement to write just the right thing to them, a word in season to uplift them.

some people are very lonely during the holidays and isolation is a desert that can quickly lead to despair. can you call someone today? I know you are very busy with all the preparations- reach out to family and friends anyway! it only takes a moment to say hello. be extravagant with your love, as I am!

"i have written this to you who believe so you may know that you have eternal life. we are confident that if we ask anything according to His will, He hears us. and since we know He hears us when we make requests, we also know that He gives us what we ask for." 1 john 5:13-15 "and there was the baby, lying in the manger. after seeing Him, the shepherds told everyone what had happened and what the angel had said to them about this Child. all who heard were astonished, but mary kept all these things in her heart and thought about them often." luke 2: 17-19

imagine how it felt to be born, out in a chilly night, in a stable filled with hay, animals all around, and stars glimmering overhead. there was plenty of wonder and awe, lots of silent radiance, but also a healthy dose of reality.

as you sit or lie quietly where you are, contemplate My humility. I submitted to having only the most meager possessions, probably a scratchy blanket, laid in a dirty feeding trough, completely helpless.

close your eyes and sit with Me as mary did, thinking and marveling in the still of the moment. think of Me lying there, willing to come to earth just to touch you, little fingers wrapped around another's hand, giving My best to reach you with all My love. try to experience the awe of that first Christmas, as well as the first time you heard of My birth in bethlehem. sing "silent night" to Me now, quietly. worship and sitting at the feet of Jesus is the secret place. prayer, Bible study, ministry- they are all important to your growth, but worship is the key to our closer Relationship.

enjoy a beautiful day today with your family, the family you are blessed with. yet, if you are alone, I am here. I laid in the manger. I hung on the Cross alone. I understand.

"remember your First Love!" revelation 2:4

"when Jesus' parents had fulfilled all the requirements of the law of the Lord, they returned home to nazareth in galilee. there the child grew up healthy and strong. He was filled with wisdom, and God's favor was on Him." luke 2: 39,40

after any celebratory time, there's a bit of a let down. you had so much to look forward to that after the holiday, wedding, birth of a child, or vacation, life seems mundane and colorless.

come to Me and tell Me of your feelings and disappointments. I prepare wonderful surprises for you each day, if you will only notice, so that your life will have that spontaneous joy!

slow down! work smarter, not harder. see who is most open and available to spend your time with because, as the year comes to a close, you somehow start to realize and see more clearly that your time is precious and your resources of energy are limited.

make it a priority to let Me renew you so that you will be able to pour out from a servant heart properly and not feel drained.

"and the Spirit, Who is truth, confirms it with His testimony. so we have these three witnesses- the Spirit, the water, and the Blood- and all three agree. since we believe human testimony, surely we can believe the greater testimony that comes from God." 1 john 5:6-8 "how can they call on Him to save if they have not believed in Him? and how can they believe if they have not heard about Him? and how can they hear about Him unless someone tells them? and how will anyone go and tell them without being sent? this is why the Scriptures say, how beautiful are the feet of those who bring good news!" romans 10: 14,15

I am going to be succinct here. these verses are actually self explanatory questions. I want you to hear The Call.

I am calling you!

I am calling you not just for your own edification or blessing, as much as I want to do that and as much as I AM blessing you! I want you to go and tell others! how can they know of My love if you don't tell them?

please tell them! this is a heartfelt imperative I give you.

"Jesus came and told His disciples, I have been given all authority in heaven and on earth. therefore, go and make disciples of all nations, baptizing them in the name of the Father, and the Son, and the Holy Spirit." matthew 28:18,19

"I saw Heaven standing open and there before me was a white horse whose Rider is Faithful and True, for He judges fairly and wages a righteous war. His eyes were like flames of fire and on His Head were many crowns. a Name was written on Him that no one understood except Himself. He wore a robe dipped in blood, and His Title was the Word of God." revelation 19:11-13

here is the most dynamic and accurate description of the Lord Jesus Christ, the Messiah, King of Kings, the Lord of Lords, ever given. He is coming in glorious splendor, such as you have never seen. it will be beyond the dimension of anything created on earth. My enthusiasm for this conclusion is because I saw Him at His most humble and vulnerable times on earth and to Me those were the most beautiful and perfect moments. we've talked about perfection. we've talked about faith and submission. can you see it all exemplified in Him? oh, that day when I return will be so glorious and I can't withhold the blessing much longer.

today, go out and look up into the vastness of the clouds and sky. let your heart cry out in an appeal. come, Lord Jesus! the Spirit and the Bride participate together to enthusiastically summon Messiah.

this time He will return as the Lion to bring justice and recompense. justice will be paid for all the torment that has been inflicted. that's My concern. you wont have to worry about that, for you will be safe and secure under My wings, under My armor, under My banner of love.

"and be sure of this: I am with you always, even to the end of the age." matthew 28:20

"then Jesus got into the boat and started across the lake with His disciples. suddenly, a fierce storm arose, with waves breaking into the boat. the disciples woke Him up shouting, Lord save us! we're going to drown! Jesus responded, why are you so afraid? you have so little faith! then He got up, rebuked the wind and the waves, and it was completely calm. the men were amazed. Who is this Man? they asked. even the winds and waves obey Him!" matthew 8:23-27

I purposely saved this story as one of the last of the year so you would pay attention and complete the year full of faith. notice, Jesus doesn't say "you don't pray enough" or "you don't read your Bible enough". no, He says "oh ye of little faith." strengthen your faith by remaining in Me.

resting is the highest honor you can give Me- resting in My directed activity that I have shown you individually. don't overdo yourself. don't worry or rush about. I am in the boat with you and I will take care of every circumstance and person you care about, if you surrender them to Me.

I am Faithful! once you cast that care to Me, once you put that person in My capable Hands, don't take them back! trust and go about the Kingdom's business today. you have much more important things to focus on. this is My Heart. speak about Me to whom I present before you today. tell them this story of the storm on the lake, share your testimony, speak from a heart of love.

"Jesus called out to them, come, follow Me, and I will make you fishers of men! and they left their nets at once and followed Him." mark 1:17,18

"faith comes by hearing and hearing by the Word of God."
romans 10:17

when you accept and believe what Jesus accomplished for
you- you have been saved in your spirit from all sin.

you are being saved in your soul each moment, each day.

you will be saved, your body glorified for eternity one
day.

the Word of God is the hinge that opens the door of faith
and I am the Key! if you understand what full and complete
salvation is through Jesus' death and Resurrection, you will
have peace in the present and hope for the future.

you don't have to achieve anything. you don't have to earn
this! salvation is not a goal to achieve- it is a free gift from
God to receive because of His indescribable love for you!

"we beg you to accept this gift of God's marvelous love.
for God says, at just the right time, I heard you. on the day of
salvation, I helped you. indeed, the right time is now. today is
the day of salvation." 2 corinthians 6:1,2

"Holy Holy Holy is the Lord God Almighty, Who Was and Is and Is to Come!" revelation 11:16

the twenty second and final chapter of revelation is the most potent and life-changing writing in history.

there are so many important images and revealed glories in it that I'd like you to take the time on this last day of the year to read all of chapter twenty two out loud. when I say it will shift your perspective, your life focus, and completely transform your life, I am very sincere and serious.

the world tonight is planning and expending all its energy on worldly, carnal celebrations. that is their ultimate focus.

I want you to take Communion in holy remembrance of Me sometime this evening. through the Bread and any liquid representation of My Blood, I will pour favor over the beginning of your new year. thank you for growing in relationship with Me this year, beloved. I offer a blessed, healthy, empowered new year to you, for I love you!

"behold, I am coming soon!" revelation 22: 7

"the Spirit and the Bride say come!" revelation 22:17

"amen! come, Lord Jesus! may the grace of the Lord Jesus be with you all." revelation 22:21

acknowledgements

i acknowledge You, Jesus, as my Lord and my Savior. all glory belongs to You. thank You Abba God for creating this world and Your plan for our rescue. thank You Holy Spirit for Your ministry to all mankind. amen.

this devotional came out of Holy Spirit's hearts desire to reach people in a meaningful way. although it will be most appreciated by Christians, there is much wisdom for people of any faith. Father God's desire is for everyone to know of His great love and mercy. He prepared The Plan before He even created the world, and it is expounded upon throughout the Bible. keep an open heart as you meditate on these devotions. it was written with supernatural, prophetic urgency and prayers for blessing and elevated faith to you. may you know the grace and shalom peace of God exhibited in Jesus and then imparted to you through the Holy Spirit. selah.

thank you to those who help me- my loving mom and dad, viola jean and bill, for your legacy of faith, my namesake and maternal grandmother rea, a woman of strong faith and servanthood, our church family, especially kelley and mike, my barefoot friends, our patient puppy shanti, my earthly family, especially our wonderful children steve, chelsea rea, and daniel who make me proud everyday, our inspiring and joyful grandchildren olivia rea and jaxson, true blessings from God, and second only to Jesus, my faithful husband joe, a worship warrior with a servant's heart. your strength behind me keeps me going.

Made in the USA
Columbia, SC
24 February 2020